Sarah,
Thank you for being part of the first SCOPE Group
Blessings,
MD

Personal Growth
Conscious Community

King of Trees
Publications

Breaking Open the Stone:
Unfolding the Soul of Youth

Copyright 2012 by Joe DiLeo

ISBN-13   978-0615536552
ISBN-10   0615536557
BISAC – Education/Counseling/General

Also Available from King of Trees Publications:

Books

Student Journal and Workbook for **Breaking Open the Stone**
Group Leader's Manual for **Breaking Open the Stone**

Audio CD's

Spoken Stories from **Breaking Open the Stone Vol. 1**

Spoken Stories from **Breaking Open the Stone Vol. 2**

I would like to thank the following people for all of their support:

Everything I know about working with teens I learned in the muddy trench of daily living known as the high school classroom. I wish I could personally thank every teen I have taught for the past 35 years.

To my colleagues at Wolcott High School, I express my admiration for your dedicated professionalism and my appreciation for your support and friendship.

The Wolcott, CT Board of Education and the administrators of the Wolcott Public School System are thanked for allowing me to unfold my own ideas, in my own way, on my own time. Walt Drewry is personally thanked for his friendship, support, and thoughtful reflection and criticism in the weeks before this book was released.

I thank the parents of Waterbury, Wolcott and Prospect, CT for trusting me with the precious lives of your children.

Thanks to my family and the people in the streets and neighborhoods of my beloved city of Waterbury, CT for providing me with a hungry soul and the wealth of stories that power this book.

Thanks to John Bale Book Store in Waterbury for providing me with a launching pad. And thanks to Chrissy and Heather at Sir Speedy in Thomaston, CT for expert marketing advice and skills.

And most of all, I thank my wife Penny for her love, her patience, and her forgiveness in supporting me in my quest to learn and to practice the very things I try to teach.

**I Dedicate This Book to the Memory of
My Mom and Dad
The Two Best Storytellers Ever**

And

**To Robert Bly
For Opening My Eyes Wide Again**

Table of Contents

African Women Story
Heroes and Bums
The Story of Delaware Bay

Challenge # 3-Expand Vision with a Mature Relationship to Power

Your Personal Relationship to Power
The 12 Steps of Growth
Accepting Powerlessness
The Butterfly Story
The Squirrel Story
Letting Go – A Leap of Faith
The Great Mystery of Life
Shepherds on a Hillside
The Story of the Universe
Black Holes and Quasars
Particles and Waves
Your Life as a Story
The Tree of Sorrows
Letting Go in Community – Grief Ritual

Challenge # 4 -Locate and Respect the Source of Happiness

The Wound and the Separation
Light and Air and Attention
The Mask and the Long Journey
Attachments– Reaching For a Special Friend
Cures Become Consequences
Finding the Courage of the Empty Cup
The Long Journey Back Home

Challenge # 5-Realize Potential through the Portal of Forgiveness

The Baby with Big Bright Eyes
What is Forgiveness?
The Story of the King of Trees
The Burden Basket – A Tool of Forgiveness
Understanding the Box of Perception
What is Your Sacred Space?

Preface

The Road Less Travelled to Effective School Reform

This book is a proposal for a new way to provide for the emotional growth needs of our teenagers. After 26 years as a group counselor working with at risk students in a program designed to address their emotional as well as behavioral issues, I have come to understand that we need a new approach in our public schools. We need to create a broad emotional and personal growth course for all students which would be embedded into their school day. The purpose of this course would be to recover the passion in our students by making their lives more meaningful.

The course I am going to propose in this book would result in a restructuring of the high school schedule of each student. It would require a course to be added to each child's schedule that would provide a chance to explore the journey of a personal life in the context of a heroic mythological journey.

The entire school reform movement is based on raising scores through improved teaching techniques. Could it be that a missing link to raising the scores of our kids might be to impassion them through a grueling and dignifying initiation to adulthood?

I have something to offer to school reform, to teachers, to parents, and to the teens of the 21st century. The process advocated in this book recovers a discarded, long lost art that was once at the very heart of education. You might call this book "The Road Less Travelled to Effective School Reform".

Who Should Read this Book?

Teenagers should experience *Breaking Open the Stone* in a group under the supervision of a counselor, mentor, or teacher. It is not meant to be read from cover to cover by a teenager in his room. The themes are too complex to be understood by the average teen. The book is meant to be experienced in a group process that brings personal stories and challenges to life in an interactive way under the guidance of a trained 'elder'.

Parents will find that *Breaking Open the Stone* will resonate in a way that gives them a fresh look at ways to understand and to deal effectively with teens. Medication and diagnosis will always be a part of educating and facilitating growth in our youth, but they should be the last intervention tried, not the first. Our children are starving for a course which impassions them by making life sacred again, by teaching them reverence, and by giving life meaning and purpose. The main issue in school is not poor teachers. It is a profound sense of meaninglessness in youth.

Counselors, mentors, and teachers should read *Breaking Open the Stone* because it exposes and tackles an unrecognized reason why our test scores are low – a lack of level of concern in too many teens that has been enabled by the educational establishment for the past fifty years. Teachers experience a student deficiency in the vital ingredient needed to achieve excellence in school – passion! *Breaking Open the Stone* provides hope that student passion can yet be unlocked and set free again in the educational milieu.

Politicians, Professors, Bureaucrats, and School Reformers need to read this book because it is essential that the entrenched oligarchy understands that it is their laws, philosophy, and policies that bypassed the little red school house and replaced it with our current diagnostic medical model atmosphere where law rewards and even encourages mediocrity in students. Law, policy, practice, and trend have strangled the sacred relationship between elders and teens. That sacred relationship is the essential ingredient of *Breaking Open the Stone*.

Why is this Book Needed?

Lack of meaning and purpose along with the absence of a 'soul education' in our schools and public organizations is an unrecognized cause of low test scores and failing schools. The related problems of student apathy and lack of level of concern and passion are caused by our failure to lead youth in transition to adulthood through a challenging, intense growing down into the roots of soul and human being.

We have discarded sacred methods that were once at the heart of education for a brave new world that has clearly not worked.

A revolution needs to occur at the grassroots level which diminishes the overuse of diagnosis and treatment and the constant tweaking of methods of delivery in favor of a new paradigm. Education of the soul has been eliminated by modern educators in favor of a lopsided effort to educate the brain only. The resulting imbalance is the cause of many educational and mental disabilities. It is the major issue facing public schools.

Initiation is a growing down into the muddy truth. Modern youth are ungrounded with no sense of soul or center, and so, the pervasive diagnoses of bipolarity and attention deficit go on unabated

We need a new consciousness at school where teachers are once again respected elders instead of clinicians, diagnosticians, entertainers, buddies, and technical experts trying to manipulate more favorable data outcomes.

This book is a radical attempt to address real problems from the vantage point of the trench where I work – the American public school classroom where most teachers surely realize that things have to change and that we have to change too.

It is my strong contention that a core counseling curriculum that alters education at its philosophical roots must be established in our local public schools, embedded into the school day, and that the focus of that philosophy needs to be rooted in a journey of initiation. We must create a new generation of fierce, young warriors who understand that school is a big challenge, that the challenge is to grow up, and that failure is a very distinct possibility.

School needs to be a place where the young understand that they have a gift to bring in the form of their life purpose, that we desperately want them to bring that gift, and that the journey is going to be grueling and difficult. Some of it won't be interesting. And a lot of it is not going to be fun.

We must face students with the simple fact that if they want to be warriors and to succeed in the world, they are going to have to adapt themselves to the realities of school life and they are going to have to solve their own educational problems.

We must stop excessive diagnosis and treatment at school which leads to enabling and entitlement. We must encourage students to recognize their weaknesses and strengths and work with them to strive to adapt to the reality of the world around them. That's the way it is going to be in the real world they face after school, and that is the way to help them in school. No one is going to have a meeting with these kids after graduation to make a plan how the world can adapt to them and their problems. If we want these kids to grow up, they have to be the adaptors. The law that stated that it was a school's job to adapt itself to each child has been stretched way beyond its original intent. Schools cannot adapt themselves to each of the one thousand or more students in a building. First, it is not educationally sound practice. Second, as we have seen in modern public education, it is impossible.

While our current emphasis on reform through improved teacher techniques and data analysis is helpful in some ways, it does not address the central issue. We have lost the hearts and souls of the kids at school. We are not going to recover hearts and souls in the context of our current paradigm because our current paradigm addresses the education of the brain only.

This book makes an impact at the deeper level where we once again address the education of the heart and soul. We need a revolutionary approach. Politicians, professors, and bureaucrats must acknowledge this. So far, they have not been able to get past their data and their hawk-like focus on teacher deficiency.

Grassroots teachers and local school boards and administrators must make the entrenched oligarchy of politicians, bureaucrats, and professors see realities they have ignored for fifty years. We must stop being afraid to speak truth to power! The appropriate education and mental health of youth depend on it.

This book is my humble contribution to that noble cause.

How to Teach This Course

Teaching this course will surely be a major personal challenge to many public school counselors, social workers, and mentors. Most school counseling programs offer only one or two courses in effective group process application. The first challenge in this book instructs students in the art of group process. However, it is expected that the teacher or mentor will have an educator's understanding of group process. Group process is the vehicle for unfolding the soul.

Second, this course is going to require more self disclosure than many counselors tend to share. Since the purpose of this course is to explore the personal story as a mythical heroic journey of self growth, the counselor running this course is going to be willing to explore her own story in the same mythical context.

Therefore, the teacher who wants to run this type of group must show willingness to share, and must also have a mature sense of herself as an elder so that the exploration and sharing will always be appropriate.

Self disclosure surely does not mean sharing minute details of one's own personal life. It means finding a way to put your own life experience into each challenge presented so that you are demonstrating what it means to tell your story in the context of the bigger story of the universe. Telling your story as it is presented in this book is not a laundry list of details, nor is it a personal confession. It is an examination of choices, conclusions, consequences, and most importantly, 'turning points' and 'twists of fate' as they fit into the heroic journey of your life. The story does own mistakes and periods of your life when you were 'off track', but the telling is done in the context of a mythical narration that is unfolded sequentially through each challenge.

There are no lesson plans presented in this book. Teachers need to be creative storytellers. Teachers should create their own stories but may also use my stories if they seem to have relevance. Thus, the teaching of this proposed course is a personal journey for each counselor and child. The book is a map more than it is a curriculum.

How to Read the Book

Although this book is written as if it is being spoken directly to teens, it is not meant to be read by teens. It is written the way it is in order to stress to the counselor/teacher that in this course, she will need to present herself as an elder rather than as a clinician.

A suggested name for this course would be *The Seven Challenges of Passionate Engagement* (SCOPE). The title ultimately is up to the individual and the school that incorporate the course. Name it what you will.

As the counselor reads through this book, he will notice that each of the challenges revolves around a theme. It should be further noted that each theme is connected into a progression that will end with a meaningful, cohesive personal story that allows teens to see their lives in a new context. During the process of the journey, a teen has a chance to revision himself as a young warrior approaching adulthood while mastering and completing each step of the journey. It is up to the counselor to construct meaningful lesson plans from the journey that is mapped out here. Be creative. This book is your blueprint.

I have included personal stories to demonstrate my own journey through the process. While I do not mind if a counselor uses my personal stories, it is really not what I am proposing in this book. Each teacher should construct personal stories and lessons from his own life during this process. Use my stories as a guideline. This is not a static curriculum.

Using my examples, counselors may construct their own unique journey. This is what makes the course mythological and heroic. My stories are personal to my own geographic location, my ethnic background, and my own unique experience. It is very challenging but I am asking that counselors attempt to use my stories as examples of how to create unique stories to you and to your geographic, ethnic, and unique situation. Students will do the same as they relate their own heroic journeys.

Skills Suggested For Leading a Group

Counselors, mentors, and teachers doing this curriculum need the following skills:

- Knowledge of Group Process and Stages of Group Functioning
- An ability to tell stories skillfully in an animated way
- An ability to convey the concepts and metaphors in the stories and themes in each challenge.
- A willingness to coordinate a cohesive group experience where students and participants may be dealing with complex daily issues in their lives. The group leader must show an ability to teach the themes; tell the stories; find ways for the students to integrate the stories and themes into the happenings of their daily lives; and keep the passion of group consciousness and self responsibility alive, while also acknowledging and honoring time for students to discuss daily crises that may come up.

Group Leader Procedures

In each challenge, the group leader will:

- Present the material found in the sequential challenge.
- Tell a story that serves as a metaphor for the theme
- Use the 'talking stick' to allow participants to put themselves inside the stories and themes through sharing of personal experiences.
- Allow students to write in a journal as a way to self reflect and as a way to gather notes for what will become their written and spoken personal story at the end of the course. The journal may be utilized either before group discussion or after group discussion.
- Put closure to each challenge on the journey and find a way to recognize passage to the next challenge. This keeps the whole process alive for students as the course progresses.
- Allow at least one day per week for daily concerns of students. Integrate discussion of concerns into the curriculum

Benefits of This Group to Participants

Participants can benefit from the group on multiple levels. The Group Leader can assess the success of students and participants by using the following progressive rubric as a common form of assessment. Students should also assess themselves at various intervals throughout the course. Individual success in the group can be assessed as students master each deepening level on the rubric.

1. Rise above the Life of Consequences
   - Students are able to master the art of daily living by doing well in school and staying out of trouble
   - Students are able to be respectful in all situations with elders

2. Understand the Stories and Themes
   - Students are able to understand the meanings and metaphors of the stories and themes
   - Students are able to add to the discussion or add meanings of their own to the stories and themes

3. Apply the Stories and Themes in Personal Ways
   - Students take the talking stick and express how a story or theme applies to their personal lives
   - Students have insight into a how a story can help them in the future

4. Apply the themes to Daily Living
   - Students are able to walk out of the group experience into the experience of daily living and remember the themes and stories
   - Students are able to apply the stories and themes in the laboratory of the present moments of their lives

The Seven Challenges

Of

Passionate Engagement

SCOPE

Navigating the Passageway

Toward a

Meaningful Adult Life

The Seven Challenges of Passionate Engagement (SCOPE)

A Proposed High School Curriculum

The Seven Challenges is a personal growth, counseling course for high school students. It incorporates a meaningful group experience which guides students through an intense self exploration of personal story in the context of the bigger story of the universe.

The result of successful completion of the seven challenges is mastery of a deeper understanding for life where meaning, urgency, and purpose are inspired by successful passage through a mythological birth canal that delivers adolescent potential toward a responsible, productive adulthood.

The course provides a group experience where advanced communication skills, self reflective writing skills, widened life perception, and deepened self knowledge are developed in a peer based community where empathy, support, and confrontation require a reverent practice of daily living.

Students who successfully navigate these seven challenges will know what it means to be a mature, self responsible young adult in a society that cherishes them as individuals fully prepared to contribute their unique gifts of life purpose to a world in need.

.

SCOPE

The Seven Challenges
Of
Passionate Engagement

1. Practice Respectful and Direct Communication

2. Maintain a Fierce Desire to Fulfill My Life Purpose

3. Expand My Vision through a Mature Relationship with Power

4. Locate and Cherish the Source of Happiness

5. Realize My Potential through the Portal of Forgiveness

6. Recognize, Accept, and Navigate My Emotions

7. Unfold My Soul through the Story of My Life

The Seven Challenges of Passionate Engagement (SCOPE)

Student Course Summary

A Train, a Stone, and a Story to Tell

This course is a train. The train carries a group of students, one elder, and a very large stone. At times, the train moves fast and furious. Other times, it plods slowly and barely moves. It is, however, a non-stop train that is committed to the completion of its journey.

The stone is an ordinary looking stone that time has slowly created since the day you were born. It has a core or a center which is surrounded by layers and layers of hardened sediment that has made it a stone. Within the center of the stone is the secret of your life purpose. Slowly breaking open the stone is the purpose of the journey. Within is the key to happiness that unlocks the treasure of your authentic self, shorn of the hardened sediment of its masks, mirrors, and excuses. It is very powerful.

We will break open the stone on this train through the telling of the stories. As we ride the train, each of us has a story to tell. The story is a mythic narration whose form and landmarks will be unfolded to you along the ride. A myth is a partly factual and partly fictitious story that somehow points to a truth that otherwise is impossible to define or to explain. It unlocks your true essence and it illuminates your potential.

This course raises the quality of your life from the boredom of its meaningless everyday existence into a meaningful and purposeful journey, an adventure that has been patiently waiting for your attention and commitment. It is a hero's quest. A hero is an individual who confronts a seemingly insurmountable task, yet chooses to press forward anyway. In the process, the hero sees his own life in the context of the larger community which is in desperate need of heroes. The hero has the option of turning away, but he does not.

On the journey of this course, we are all the heroes and the heroines as well as the villains and the irresponsible ones in our own personal stories, each embarking into unknown territory in a daily process in which each of us will give and receive gifts that multiply the purpose, meaning and the quality of the community.

An individual life with no community is an isolated, lonely life. At worst, this life becomes derailed on the obstacles of personal madness or mental illness. At best, the isolated life becomes a boredom inducing, unfulfilled wish for some elusive happiness through the daily selfish quest for power and possessions.

But on the hero's journey, the perceived safety of isolation is courageously abandoned. The dedication to community rekindles a sense of the sacred. There are some important values that become inviolable. There are some needy and selfish lines we refuse to cross in our dedication to community. We develop reverence for process and self discipline.

Community consciousness shines the light of day on the place where before we blindly searched in the darkness for some 'thing' or some 'one' special that might soothe our neediness and our lonely desperation.

None of your goals in life can be accomplished until this journey is undertaken. Under the direction of elders who have made the journey before, we will learn to value the ordinary in a way that will transform every day earth life into a sacred place of purpose.

When the journey is completed, we will be engaged in life at a whole new level. We will not just be children anymore waiting for the world to serve us. We will be adults prepared to bring our gifts to a world that needs these gifts. We will be opened to receive gifts too.

This will not be an easy journey. If you have come to this course looking to be coddled, entertained, enabled, entitled, diagnosed, or cured, you have bought the wrong ticket and you are on the wrong train. This train will travel through some dark terrain marked by moral struggle, confrontation, failure, and even some direct in-your-face challenges to grow and to strive to be a better human being.

The path will be unfolded by the elders and will be clearly laid out before you. We embark on this journey as a group and we will complete the journey as a group.

Along the route, we will learn to tell the truth as it emerges from our own opened hearts while we look into each other's eyes for affirmation and encouragement. At times, we will feel like quitting and getting off the train. But we will stay the course to reach our final destination. We are heroes!

This course is not about cold facts and data. It is about meaning. It is not about hallway drama and cafeteria politics. It is about ordinary miracles. It is not about opinions. It is about the willingness and courage to feel deep emotion and to learn to transform that emotion from paralyzing inaction into a force for life.

It is not about finding the light and getting high chemically or spiritually. It is about the courage to plunge into the depth of the very darkness where you have gotten lost. It is not about information and answers. It is about truth and mystery.

We will arrive at the truth as each of us tells his story along the trail of the journey. The stories we tell will resonate so truly that they will crack open the stone. The stone, broken open, unlocks an endless flow of desire and passion and commitment that began long ago with the ancestors. This flow, restored and unblocked, frees the trapped energy that opens each of us to the potential of who we were meant to be as human beings. We will shed the old skin of childish neediness and self absorption. We will embrace the life of the adult ready to bring our gifts to a hungry community that needs our nourishment and creativity and our healthy boldness.

This is the mythical journey that has come to be called *Breaking Open the Stone*. It is a BIG commitment. Whether or not to risk this journey is up to you. This is a very demanding course with very high expectations. And in this course, it is up to YOU to make the adjustments needed to succeed in this group; in school; in your family, and in life after this group. The train is on the track and the train leaves the station today. All aboard who's coming aboard!!!

What is a Village?

Why Would You Want to Join One?

First of all, a village is a big commitment. You must make a clear choice. Choose to get in - or else get out. If you are in, there are several aspects to the village experience that we will briefly describe in this short introduction.

A village is a community. A community is a group of people who band together to face all of life together. All of life means happiness and joy. It also means suffering, sadness, confusion, and frustration and sometimes even intense anger with one another. If you are in, the village does not have any cure for you. You are choosing to experience joy, happiness, frustration, sadness and grief, anger and confusion with a group of individuals who also chose to make this commitment.

In a village, adolescence is a time of initiation. Your initiation is your second birth. Every teenager must pass the tests of initiation to become a full adult. Turning 18 years old does not mean you are an adult in a village. Only passage through the tests of initiation makes you an adult.

As the elder of this village, your teacher will take you through this initiation. Your life is a story. Initiation puts you in the driver's seat so that you can write the rest of your life story. You have a purpose, a gift to bring to the village, and we need for you to bring it. No one else can bring your gift.

As the elder, your teacher is not here to make school fun, to entertain you, to baby sit for you. He is not here to increase your self esteem or to make you feel special. You are nobody special. The teacher is here to break you and your will. Your stubborn will has caused you more problems than you have realized. The elder is here to pull you through a second birth canal. But he cannot do it unless you push yourself through as well.

If you feel you have gotten lost in your life as a teenager, you are not alone. Every teenager that has ever existed has gotten lost out on the great red highway sometimes called, "I thought I knew everything but now I am lost" road. No problem. You have the skills you need to come through your initiation already encoded right into your bones. But you are going to have to get real and pay attention to your bones first.

How will you do this? PAY ATTENTION. To your own heartbeat, to the space you are holding on the rim of the circle, to your daily choices and behaviors, to the stories you will be told in group, to the truth of your own story with its own triumphs and tragedies, to the path that will be laid out for you by the elders.

The time for coddling you is over. It is time to grow up. If you meet these challenges, we will celebrate our gratefulness at a beautiful village banquet at the end of the course. It is the mark of your return to the greater village after your initiation. It is a ritual celebration of deep feeling because you know you kept your commitment to yourself and to your village.

Departing the Station

It is time to begin a new group. It is time to take your life into your own two hands and make something happen. You have a gift to bring to this group, and a gift to bring to the world in the form of your life purpose. You are not a baby anymore. BRING IT

Heroic Departure

Gather Around the Stone

Message to Group Leader:

Opening the circle introduces participants to the concepts of the village experience. It presents all the prerequisites required so that the journey of the group might unfold in a grounded, focused, and balanced way that is pointed toward a meaningful experience and a productive completion.

Group Leader's Outline

- ## Joining the Group

  - Gathering around the Stone
  - Significance of the Stone
  - Grounded around the Stone
  - Committed around the Stone
  - Understanding the Electricity of the Beating Heart

- ## The Relationship of Gratefulness and Happiness

  - What are you Grateful for?
  - Understanding Happiness
  - Locating the Key to Happiness
  - Sitting in a Chair – A Warrior's Challenge

- ## The Prerequisites of a Successful Group

  - Understanding the 'Life of Consequences'
  - Rising Above the 'Life of Consequences'
  - Understanding the Victim Stance
  - Abandoning the Victim Stance
  - Understanding My Relationship to Power

    - The Bullfighter Metaphor
    - The 'Book' on the Teacher

- ## Living in a Village

  - What is a Village?
  - Loneliness and 'Mother Theresa's Story
  - The Value of Sitting with the Empty Cup
  - Habib's Grocery Store – Life in a Village
  - What is Initiation?
  - The Birthplace of 'Real Heroes'

Introduction

This is the orientation to the group. It is called 'Opening the Circle'. When the opening is completed, you will be fully utilizing the group process, and the community concept of the village to set yourself on a course for the celebratory banquet. Hopefully, you will also be setting yourself on a course to complete your transition to adulthood so that you may realize the purpose you were sent to accomplish on earth. This opening of the circle is a map pointing the way through a passageway to full adult status. Let us Begin.

Gathering around the Stone

Is there anyone in this group who is not here of his own free will? Anyone who is not fully committed to take part in all the aspects of this journey is invited to leave. No one should be here because a parent or a teacher or an administrator, or even a friend has told them they should be in this group. If you are in a group, it must only be because you want to be in a group. Does anyone want to leave at this time?

Look around you. See these people in this circle. You are now a part of a village. Everyone in this group has a unique gift to bring to the village. Everyone in this group has gifts to receive. Everyone here has a story. Everyone has a personal shortcoming to be faced. Everyone here has a future in front of him. You can make the future unfold in a way that is more fulfilling.

This group is going to complete its journey and it will come to an end. But, before this group can even begin to think about completing itself, it first needs to be born. This is not a group yet. It is a gathering of 12 individuals sitting in a circle. In order to be born, this group must pass through a tunnel, a birth canal. If each of us does his part and takes some risk and gets real, the passage will be completed in a few weeks and a group will be born.

If no one takes the risk to get real in this circle, the group will not be born. So today, you will have your first chance as a member to get real in a circle. Do you have the courage?

Once this group is born, we will have a long journey in front of us. It will be a journey where we will have fun, where we will face fears, where we will deal with frustration, where we will confront and get confronted about how we are doing on our journey. This group will also walk into the heart of sadness too. All of these conditions are real and all are part of life, so all will be part of this village too.

This group will close at our celebratory banquet. What you have to celebrate at the banquet will only be what you begin to create for yourself and for your village today. How hard are you willing to work? How much are you willing to contribute? Enough talk!!! Let's begin! Let's see what you've got!

PUT YOUR FEET FLAT ON THE FLOOR
SPEND A MINUTE IN QUIET TIME
GET IN TOUCH WITH YOUR OWN BEATING HEART

Today I am holding up a stone. Does anyone here know what the elders in the village used to say about the center of the stone?

They said that the center of the stone held the knowledge of the entire universe. The tiniest chip at the center of the stone held the truth. Now that was a long time ago and the idea may seem silly to you in our modern age. But I, for one, find it quite interesting that our wonderful invention, the computer, is now revered by us for its ability to hold huge amounts of knowledge for us. We might say in the 21st century that the computer holds the knowledge of the whole universe. What is interesting about this is that the center of our computer, the core that actually is able to hold all this knowledge, is nothing more than a tiny chip of silicon. IT IS THE TINIEST chip of stone!

The elders in the village had an additional understanding of the center of the stone. They understood what made the stone. TIME MADE THE STONE. At the center was a tiny chip, an original truth, that time managed to surround with millions more of hardened tiny chips to make the stone.

So with us as humans, the elders understood that there was a tiny chip, a truth at the core of our being, and, just like the stone, time managed to hide the truth at the core of our hearts by all the millions of chips of life happenings that occurred. The elders understood that by the time a human reached the age of a teenager, the truth at the heart of being had gotten lost by all the accumulated experiences and losses and hurts of life.

Our silence at the beginning of every school day is our way to try to get back in touch with the truth at the core of the stone that is our heart. It is our way to come back into the truth of who we are and what purpose we have come here to accomplish.

"I need to know who I am in order to proceed. I am me!"

We put our feet flat on the floor each day so that we might be grounded. Our lives are a swirl of electric energy. Electricity pulses from the heart at the core of the stone. Electricity that is not properly grounded is very dangerous and is unable to flow or channel itself toward its intended purpose. You also need to be grounded to the stone you are standing on, on the stone where you will live out your human life - the Earth - the so called third rock from the sun.

Putting your feet flat on the floor connects you to something solid. It is hard to accomplish anything in life or in school unless you can start from a solid, grounded place.

"I need to know where I am in order to proceed. I am here!"

The beating heart is the energy, the electricity of your life. The heart is not just a muscle, a piece of material. The heart is a mysterious and wonderful pulse of life energy. Every time your heart beats you are reminded that you are alive and that you have something to accomplish while you are alive here on this planet. You were sent here with a job to complete. The potential, or power, to complete your purpose is encoded right into your heart beat -if you can let yourself get in touch with it.

So then, you get in touch with your beating heart because its pulse is the pulse of your potential. Every choice and action that you make in this life will only be possible because of the beating heart. If you are grounded and in touch with your beating heart today, then you are in touch with your potential.

Potential is unrealized energy. Getting in touch with your potential allows you to be in charge of your energy, where it goes, and how it gets spent. If you never realize your potential today, your heart will go on beating, but your potential will be leaked away.

So now, let's get back to the stone. I am going to place it in the center of the circle. We will gather around the stone each day. Our goal is to break open the stone so that we can find the truth or the soul at the core of this group. To do that, we each have to break open the stone of the self. That is the way to find the truth of yourself and of this group.

You get in touch with your beating heart in order to proceed. It is time to be an adult and to start realizing your potential.

Each day we will gather around the stone and get real with the beating heart.

Initial Group Exercise

Who Am I?

Why did I choose to be in a group?

What is my goal this year?

      In School -

      In my personal life -

What am I grateful for?

Using the Talking Stick, let's each answer these questions one at a time as a way to begin the year, as a way for you to make your first contribution to this group.

What was it like for you the first time you shared in a group? Some students can't wait to get started. They take the talking stick for the first time like they have been waiting their whole lives for the opportunity to be in a group like this. Other students are nervous and even fearful as they begin the group. The fear and uncertainty are normal, for you are embarking on a long journey that is going to make many demands of your courage and your willingness to grow as a person.

Now that we have completed this task I know who you are and why you are here. I also know the things for which you are grateful; and for me, it is a way to start to know what makes you tick - like a beating heart.

Most of us gave some different answers to the gratefulness question. Some gave similar answers. A few have no idea for what or to whom they are grateful. It's all good for now. This is where we start our journey together.

If I could pick one common thread out of everyone's answers, it would be this. Each of you would like to be happy. Most humans want to be happy. If you came to this group to do better in school, what you were really saying to me is that doing better in school would make you happier. People in this circle would like to be happy.

So then, what is happiness? Where is it found? How is it found?

We will finish today's group with a little story. The story is called the "Key to Happiness". I have heard a few versions of this story. I do not know who to credit for this story.

The Key to Happiness

This is a story about happiness. Happiness seems to be what everyone is looking for. Yet, it often doesn't seem that many people are very happy most of the time.

Well, what is happiness anyway? Is it a temporary thrill? Is it a goal of getting what you want or desire? Is it a 'state of mind' where an individual is content and satisfied? I can't answer that question for you. But I have made some observations I would like to share with you.

It seems people who seek thrills are seldom happy people except when they are in the state of being thrilled which is not possible on a prolonged basis. The rest of the time thrill seekers are not very happy.

People who need to get what they want or desire can't be very happy for very long either. Human life does not allow us to get what we want or desire most of the time. And life has also shown that many things we want or desire are not very good for us or for our daily happiness. In fact, some people become 'slaves' to their own desires and wants in a very self destructive and unhappy way.

Happiness can be very confusing. There are people who are suffering, yet they seem to be happy. And there are people who have everything who can't enjoy themselves. Other people wake up in the morning and promise themselves to be happy for the day only to fall into a deep depression as soon as the day's realities begin to present themselves.

It seems happiness, then, is more accurately described as a 'state of mind' which we could define as a daily personal contentment. I have met people who are content and at peace no matter what problems the world may be presenting to them.

How do you find this 'state of mind'?

There is an old story about finding the 'key' to happiness. Happiness then is elusive. It requires a key which opens up the door to happiness.

It was said that all beings originally had full happiness in the garden of happiness. In this garden, all beings did what was needed to be in complete harmony with the laws of nature. In return, each being received a daily share of contentment and happiness. Being was satisfied in the garden of happiness.

At some point, humanity attained the status of consciousness. In the state of consciousness, choice was born. Humans were given the gift of choice. Choice was the most important gift ever given by nature. It freed humans to say and do as they please. This seemed a wonderful gift. However, history showed it had a profound effect on happiness. Yes, humans no longer needed to follow the laws of nature where they once were so happy and content. Now they could try to do things against the laws of nature. In this simple act, which the bible portrays as eating an apple, humans chose to walk out of the garden of happiness as soon as they decided to challenge the laws of nature. Evil was activated with choice. Opposites were born with choice. And so happiness needed an opposite as well. And its opposite was separation and loneliness. This was the fate of Adam and Eve when they left that Garden of Happiness. Every human alive encounters this state of separation and loneliness. Happiness is earned by those who walk in and confront their sense of separation and alone-ness.

Since then, humans have had to know suffering, sadness, and death. And happiness has become elusive. We were asked to leave the garden of happiness by the great mystery of life. This was not so much a punishment on the great mystery's part as much as it was the great mystery's way of respecting our choices.

However, once the choice was made, there was no turning back. The door to the garden of happiness was closed. And humans now had to earn their happiness. The only way back to happiness was through exploration and seeking. Happiness is a door. And the key was hidden by the great mystery of life. It is up to each human to seek and find the key.

At first the great mystery hid the key behind a tree. But humans found the key very easily. This was not good for the great mystery. The great mystery wanted humans to earn their happiness. So the mystery sought a better hiding place.

This time, the mystery found a spot for the key that was at the top of one of the highest mountains. It seemed a good place. But humans were very smart and they soon found the mountain hiding place. Again, the great mystery tried to find a more difficult spot. This was not supposed to be so easy.

In one of the deepest lakes in the world, the great mystery next hid the key to happiness. Once again, humans found the key much too easily. These humans were very smart indeed. They had used their consciousness and ability to make choices to their advantage. They were still not 'earning' their happiness to the satisfaction of the great mystery.

So the great mystery sat in stillness and pondered how to hide the key in a place that would be truly challenging to each man and woman on earth. After a lengthy silence, the mystery smiled for the perfect place to hide the key was found. The great mystery hid the key. And this time, humans were baffled and could not find the key so easily. It was only the humans who became true, fierce seekers who now found the key.

Some humans got quite desperate seeking the key. They looked to substances. And so addiction was born. Addiction did not open the door to happiness. They looked to money. And so greed was born. Greed did not open the door to happiness. Men and woman scoured the world for happiness. But it was not to be found anywhere they looked. It was not in possessions. It was not in anything that could be reached for anywhere on earth. Many humans fell into despair and began to reach out for things in blind hope that happiness could be found. But it was not out there no matter where they searched. There was no special substance, no special person, and no special possession that could produce the key to happiness.

To this day, the key remains hidden in the same place. Some people find the key. But, sadly, many don't ever find it. The great mystery hid the key in the most obvious place. Yet, it has remained the last place that humans look. The great mystery hid the key to happiness in the heart of each human on the face of the earth. It is right there inside the heart. Seekers who want happiness sincerely enough eventually find the key.

The door to happiness is opened on the day that humans rest within their own hearts inside their own skin. In the moment of surrender to the deep heart, the key unlocks the door. When the door swings open, humans are permitted back into the garden of happiness.

This story will become the underlying theme for the entire year. We gather around the stone at the center of our circle as a way to unlock the truth and happiness at the center of the stone, at the center of our group, and at the center of our individual hearts.

Learning How to Sit in a Chair

"If I can't be happy sitting in a chair, then I can't be happy"

As far as I know, I am the originator of the above quotation. It is certainly not the most profound statement an educated man has ever made. But let me explain what it means to me.

If I want to be happy, I have to be able to be content just to sit in a chair. When I learn how to be happy and content sitting in a chair, then I will stop searching and reaching for things I think will make me happy. If you don't think this is a serious problem for youth, think about how many of you have been diagnosed with either bi-polar disorder, or with ADD and ADHD. What are these diseases in their simplest form? They are your inability to be able to be okay just sitting in a chair.

The best example I know to demonstrate this common American malady is to talk about the long list of rock, movie, and hip hop stars that have overdosed on drugs or committed suicide. We are talking then about extremely talented people who have every reason in the world to be happy. They have wealth, adoration, and appreciation. They have supremely recognized talent and their self esteem is boosted every day. But there is one talent they have never attained.

After the show is over and the cheering is gone, they have to go back to the hotel and they have to sit in a chair. And many of them can't do it!!! They don't know how to be alone with themselves in a chair content and comfortable in their own skin. As a result, all they do with all that money and fame is to buy better drugs with which to self destruct faster.

I will date myself now by going back to the two most desired people of the 1950's. I will call Marilyn Monroe the most desired woman of that era. And I will call Elvis Presley the most desired man from that era. I mean neither of these two souls any malice when I say this and I hope they would approve of me using their sad stories to help others. The truth is that the most desired woman that every man wanted to be with, Marilyn Monroe, died all alone in a motel room, apparently a victim of suicide. The most desired woman in America who had more than any of us have ever dreamed of having in wealth and attention, died totally isolated and lonely. She couldn't sit alone in a chair and be content.

Elvis Presley, the most desired man that all women of that era wished they could be with, died all by himself, apparently of a drug overdose. The most desired man in America died totally isolated and lonely. He was unable to be happy and content by himself sitting in a chair. USCD (Unable to sit in a Chair Disease) is a common malady in our country. Do you have this dis-ease?

So now, the journey upon which we have embarked is a community journey where you will learn to be happy sitting in a chair. By breaking open the stone of your story, the loneliness is swept away by a wave of personal honesty. You learn to be yourself with others, and most importantly, alone with yourself – in your room – sitting in a chair.

The ravages and accumulations of time have not killed the truth at the core of the stone. Just like time made the stone, time has made you and has acted upon you until you got lost from the core of your being. As you approach adulthood, it is very important to reconnect with your core because your core holds the essence of your purpose and what you came to earth to do, to accomplish for your people. The key to happiness is found through the courage to walk back into your heart through the portal of your life's story. Telling your story, straightening out your relationship to power, and forgiving others and yourself to the truth of the present moment is peeling back the layers of the stone until you are living from the truth at the center of your being once again. There is the key to happiness. Have courage young warriors. We are boarding the train to the heart together. So gather around the stone and let us begin the journey.

The first step of our journey is to clear away some debris from the track. I am talking about the debris of consequences. The consequences of choices that you have been making in your life may be blocking your passage.

So in order to proceed, let us stop for a second and examine the debris on the tracks. What behaviors need to be cleared away so you can proceed on your journey?

This examination of debris must be brutally honest. If you try to ignore the blockages on the track, your journey is over before it even gathers steam.

Rising Above 'The Life of Consequences'

Before you have any chance of becoming a warrior, you are going to need to make some changes in the way you think, in the way you act, and in the way you perceive and relate to the world around you.

Do you find yourself choosing behaviors that constantly lead you into more trouble than they are worth? Do you find yourself at the end of a marking period faced with one or more failed classes? Do you find yourself in the discipline office often, missing class time and picking up detentions? Have you ever been arrested?

Have you ever gotten up in the morning and felt disappointed in yourself for things you chose to say or do the night before? Does depression ever paralyze you? How about anxiety? Do you find yourself constantly being prodded by others to take anger management classes? Does your anger cause you to say or do things that you later deeply regret but cannot take back?

If you answer yes to any of these questions, you are like the rest of us humans here on earth. You have found yourself caught up in the life of consequences. The life of consequences is a life where you are constantly paying for your behavior by choosing repetitive behaviors that are just not helping you. The more time you leak your beating heart energy to these behaviors, the more off track your life gets, and the more difficult it is to rise above the muck that has you stuck. The life of consequences is a life that can't progress because it is a life caught up in the quicksand of consequences day in and day out.

How to Rise Out of the Quicksand

Once upon a time, an alcoholic went to a psychiatrist. He said, "Doctor, you have to help me please. I am an alcoholic." The psychiatrist saw how desperate the man was and he wanted to help him. The psychiatrist responded with the following comment. He said, "I can help you. But first you have to stop drinking."

I am your teacher. I am not a psychiatrist. And hopefully, you are not an alcoholic. But there is an important lesson for you here as we open the year and the circle of your group.

I can help you. But first you have to start doing your homework, coming to school, going to classes on time, and caring enough to study for tests, and staying out of the discipline office.

Once you rise above the life of consequences, I will actually have a chance to make you a warrior and teach you what you need to learn. If you continue to be stuck in the life of consequences, I will not be able to help you because you will be too angry and caught up in the consequences of your behavior and your hallway politics and drama.

Victim Stance

You will not be able to come to this group every day to complain or to blame everyone else for being unfair to poor you. Life is unfair at times. That is still not an excuse for you to fall into the victim stance on a daily basis.

What is the victim stance? You can always tell a person in the victim stance in life because this is a person who is always super-sensitive to any little thing that seems to be unfair. The person in the victim stance will spoil his whole day fighting for justice. He is sensitive to even the tiniest of perceived unfairness. It causes him to pay many consequences.

The person in the victim stance, however, never seems to acknowledge or see all the dirt he slings out at other people all day. Everything the 'victim stance' person does is justified in his own mind because, of course, he has a right to act this way because he is a victim. This person will go about his day disrupting classes, talking out loud during lectures, making demands to go here or there, making comments that he knows will upset others around him. His behavior is absolutely hurtful to the village that needs him. Yet, he just doesn't see it. His sense of victimization is soothed by the jolt of power he gets from upsetting others. And all of it is totally justified by him. After all, he is the victim.

The victim sees himself in battle against life. There is no community, no village, and no purpose in life to respect and care for. There is only the victim and his attitude that life owes him something because he has been treated unfairly. Get yourself out of the victim stance now. This is the first step on your warrior's journey. Without this step, none of the other steps can be taken because you will be blocked – by the debris of the life of consequences.

Power and the Victim Stance

The power struggle is the activity upon which all victims thrive. You might want to examine how you personally recreate your 'victim' situation with teachers and others in authority. Some students do this defiantly. Others do it passively by failing quietly but purposely to get back at parents or others in authority that may have victimized them. What is your story?

In Greek mythology, a battle was once fought between two armies. As the story unfolds, one of the armies expended so much energy in one single battle that they won the battle but had no energy or resources left, thus, they lost the war. This kind of ill-advised victory where you win the battle but lose the war was called a Pyrrhic victory. Think about how you may have been acting out this scenario in your own life. A person in the victim stance tends to spend so much time and energy fighting each little battle of perceived injustice that he also tends to lose the war. Thus, a student may spend every day fighting and even winning power struggles with teachers but, in the end, he loses the war when he fails and does not graduate. How do you relate to this? What Pyrrhic victories in battle have turned into lost wars for you?

The Bull Fighter Metaphor

A good example of how to win the war, and perhaps forego some battles, is found in the techniques of bullfighting. The bull fighter stands in the stadium and is very aware that the bull is very powerful. He understands that if he fights the battle with the bull head to head, he is going to lose his life.

If the bull were to charge and the bullfighter's response was to lower his head and charge back toward the attacking bull, the result would be very messy. The bullfighter understands that to win the war, he has to get himself 'out of the way'. So, he raises the red cape in front of him and as the bull is about to gore him, he steps aside and says "Ole". The bull rushes by and the bullfighter lives. How have you been a charging bullfighter in your relationships with authority? How might you learn the "Ole" technique and get yourself out of the way?

If you want to rise above the life of consequences, you must learn to fight the right battles with the right opponents in the right way at the right time. If you are in school, you must win the 'war' of graduation and forego the daily 'battles' against every tiny perceived injustice. Get yourself out of the victim stance. It is not helping you.

'The Book' On Your Teacher

If you are in school and having trouble mastering the charging bull of a difficult teacher, here is a simple way to get you started on your mastery of getting yourself out of the way. It is an exercise called "The Book on the Teacher". This exercise should help you focus on what you need to do in order to succeed in any class, and hopefully, help you to succeed with every teacher and boss that you may encounter for the rest of your life.

The exercise follows:

Step One:

As we pass around the talking stick today, each of you will pick out two classes on your schedule. Tell the group what you perceive as your easiest class for the school year that has just begun. Who is the teacher? Why do you find this class easy? What do you have to do in order to pass? The group leader will write down your response as a way to keep track of what needs to be done to pass in this teacher's class.

Step Two:

Next, state the class that you find to be the most difficult as you begin this school year. Who is the teacher? What makes you think this is going to be a hard class for you to pass? Let's explore what needs to be done to pass that class. Group members who have had that teacher and passed will share their observations.

Adrian's Story

Let me give you one example of a real life response to step two by a student named Adrian. Adrian stated that his hardest class would definitely be English. His English teacher was a man named Mr. Swanson. When asked why he thought this would be his hardest class, Adrian said, "I think Swanson is one of those teachers who makes you read books 'n stuff." Adrian then said, "I never do homework. And I don't read the books we are given to read. It's just not my thing"

For anyone reading this story that has not been in education for the last 50 years, this may sound like a joke. Adrian is real. He comes to school every single day and he goes to classes with no homework done, no pen, and no book. If the teacher will provide him with a book, he will do some reading in class. If a neighbor will give him a pen, he will do some written work. The novel that the teacher assigns for the marking period is left on a desk in a classroom before the day is over, or it goes into a locker and is left unread until the assignment is past due. The book sometimes doesn't get returned until the teacher threatens to charge him for it if it is not returned. Adrian is not defiant about this whole business. He just couldn't care less. He does get very angry at the teacher and the school, however, when he fails the class at the end of the year; he says things like, "This school is stupid" and "Mr. Swanson is a ^*&$#(!".

For now, let us leave Adrian's Story for just a second, and move to Step Three of our exercise for today

Step Three:

In Major League Baseball, it used to be the practice that the previous day's starting pitcher would sit in the dugout the day after he pitched. Since starting pitchers only pitch every fifth day, he had little to do during a game. In the old days, this pitcher was asked to sit in the dugout with a little notebook and to 'chart' each pitch that the opposing team's pitcher threw that day. The idea behind this was to learn what pitch the pitcher threw in different situations against different batters in hopes of finding a 'pattern' that might help his teammates to hit the pitcher more successfully.

The hitter would have a great advantage if he knew what pitch was coming and in what situation it would come. He could be prepared for the pitch and adjust his response accordingly.

This practice of writing down the 'pattern' of a certain pitcher became known as 'getting the book' on a pitcher. Once you had the 'book' on a pitcher you knew exactly what he was going to come at you with and you knew what you had to do in response in order to have success. Success wasn't guaranteed by this procedure, but the chances for success were greatly improved.

Getting the 'book' on the teacher is very similar. A student, who has had that teacher before, writes down what that teacher does in different situations, and you can then figure out how to adjust yourself in order to be successful. If you know what the teacher is going to pitch at you, you can be prepared and respond accordingly.

So now, let's go around the room and do the exercise with each person completing steps one, two, and three. When we are done, each person should know what needs to be done if he wants to pass that 'hardest' class.

Here was the 'book' on Mr. Swanson that was shared by group members with Adrian. "Mr. Swanson is not hard to pass but he will fail you if you do not hand in his assignments. He does however, make it very clear to you from the beginning exactly what you have to do and how it is to be done.

He takes you through each step of the assignment and if you do each part as he presents it, you will have a completed project when it is due. He will have you read one short novel each marking period. There will be a test on the book. But Mr. Swanson counts your daily discussion on the book to be just as important as the test. If you have something to contribute to discussion and he knows you are reading the book, he is pleased.

The test is very easy to pass if you read the book, take down the notes he gives the day before the test, and study a little the night before the test. If you are not doing the reading, Mr. Swanson will know by your complete lack of knowledge during discussions, if you do not hand in an assignment, he will know you were not following along as he nursed you through the assignment. Your assignment will be complete if you do the daily class work. Mr. Swanson is going to fail you if you don't read the books and hand in the assignments. No make-up. And no second chance."

Okay, Adrian has all the information he needs now to make an adjustment in order to succeed with Swanson. Will he use this information to make the necessary adjustment? That was up to him. We will discuss this technique later in the year during an exercise called "Learning How to Hit the Curveball". For now, put yourself in Adrian's shoes. Understand that you have a choice. Use the 'book' you get this week about your hardest class. Make the adjustments you need to make for success. And success will happen. If you don't bother to make the adjustments, it is back to the muck of the life of consequences for you one more time.

Whether you are taking this course in a school or some other group venue, you have certainly been caught up in the life of consequences at some point in your life. If that is where you are now, this train cannot proceed until you first begin to clear the tracks of the debris of poor choices and paralyzing consequences.

Living in a Village

Schools in the 21st century are institutions. This is especially true of the schools for the kids age 12 and beyond. Our middle schools and high schools often have populations of a thousand or more students. As institutions, schools have come to model themselves on a philosophy called the 'medical model'. With the medical model, it becomes the job of an 'expert' to find the individual 'cure' to solve the riddle of each child's education. If there are a thousand students in a school, it takes 1000 individualized plans to educate each child. School has thus become an institution whose job it is to adapt itself to each student individually. When we attend a PPT meeting for you, this is the purpose of the meeting: "What does our school have to do to adapt itself to your particular situation." Now this is not all bad. If you are in a wheel chair, we should not assign all your classes to the third floor in a building with no elevator.

What has been bad about it is that it has fostered an attitude among students that it is the school's job to educate them and that they do not have to strive. Are you aware of ways that you sit back and expect education to be served to you? Do you come to school each day with a commitment to strive for personal excellence and to adapt yourself to the needs of your school community? Do you understand that you are part of a community that needs you to bring your gift? I must make it clear that this is your initiation. You are about to become an adult. And you are expected to bring passion and a high level of concern to everything you do in this group and in this school.

Thriving in a Village

You are going to be part of a village experience. In a village, In this course, it is your job to adapt yourself to this village. This community needs your gift in order to thrive. You are aware that belonging to the community of your village gives your life meaning again. Without a village, people forget who they really are and why they are alive. And they lose all sense that they have a purpose to accomplish in life and an important contribution to make to the well being of others.

First, we have to recover your passion and deep striving for learning. Why don't students seem to strive anymore? Passion disappeared from school on the day the medical model took over and the village atmosphere of the little red school house disappeared. Our job here is to rekindle passion and to re-establish community.

A purposeless life with no village to confirm its usefulness is a lonely, self centered life. A lonely self centered life needs to be filled up with constant praise and material things, and constant activity, and sometimes drugs or other unhealthy habits. Purpose and meaning are replaced by boredom and self centeredness. In a school culture utilizing the medical model, educators unwittingly try to analyze each student into a private, individualized parcel. They try to parse each student's problem(s) from the student while isolating and treating each problem individually and confidentially. What starts out as an attempt to help students devolves quickly in this atmosphere.

Unwittingly, schools create isolation and loneliness instead of community. School becomes a hospital like atmosphere where students are diagnosed and then sit back and wait for a 'cure'. True community disappeared 50 years ago at school. Student self responsibility is absent or mortally blunted in schools. If a student does not learn, a meeting is held to figure out what the teacher is doing wrong. Each child's education is private, confidential, and individualized. What a price we have paid for this devolution in public schools. An isolated, lonely, diagnosed student body where each student has been led to believe he is 'special' is a passionless student body that is enabled, entitled, and passively waiting for a 'cure'. That student body has no hope to ever measure up on the 'test'.

In this group, you are faced each day with the truth of each other; with the truth of each other's sorrows; the truth of each other's personality flaws; and the truth of the way it really is. Get to work. It is your responsibility to your village and to yourself to strive for excellence. I will work with you on your shortcomings – but you better be ready to 'bust your butt' if you want to be a part of this group.

When you walk through that doorway into the group each day, make sure you consciously understand that you are in a village that needs your contribution. Make sure that you understand that if you are not striving and contributing, your village suffers for lack of your important place and accomplishments in its community dynamics.

Make sure that you understand that your teacher is an elder who demands respect and in return will guide you on the challenging journey through adolescence to adulthood. He is not a diagnostician trying to figure you out so he can adapt himself to you and your problems. Your problems will only help you to become a better person once you learn that it is you that must accept them and work through them.

The Empty Cup

Without a village, you are left with just yourself and your empty cup. Your whole life becomes an attempt to fill that cup to keep yourself happy. Imagine your cup now. Imagine pouring the water of all the things you reach for that you hope can make you happy. Imagine the water of these possessions overflowing the cup and spilling all over yourself. You are still not happy and you are still filling your now full and overflowing cup. Do you begin to see what is wrong?

Walk into the group and empty out your cup. Just sit there with your empty cup. Be part of a village and see what it is you need to contribute to help others, and thus yourself. Realize you need these people and feel honored that they need you. School is not the mall. Nothing out there will make you happy. And school is not a hospital. I have no cure for you. School is a village. Bring your self. And bring your gift. And bring your Empty Cup to the group each day. And let's see what happens when we get real. You will find your place and your purpose in this group. Your cup will fill up with what it needs quite naturally on its own if you show up and do your part every day.

Here are two stories that demonstrate why we will try to create and then respect and cherish a village:

Mother Theresa's Story

Mother Theresa spent her whole life in the poorest countries of the world helping the poor in very simple ways. Yet, anyone who met Mother Theresa was struck, not only by her kindness, but by her honesty, her integrity, and her happiness and contentment. She was a tiny woman who was in awe of the poor.

Yet, as tiny as she was, she was not at all in awe, nor was she intimidated by wealth, by TV cameras, by all the political figures, royalty, or movie stars who liked to take their pictures with her.

One time, Mother Theresa came to the United States to New York City where she was to speak to a group of people. As she walked from her hotel in Manhattan to the place where she would speak, it was impossible not to note the strength of this tiny woman among the skyscrapers and opulence of New York.

Reporters swarmed her as she approached her destination. She stopped briefly to answer a few questions. One reporter said," How does it feel to be here in America, a country so rich and so wealthy with so much opulence, after spending so much time in countries where people have nothing?"

Mother Theresa paused briefly. Then she replied, "I have just walked down this street here in America. As I did, I noticed the people walking by me. In America, you have a different poverty from that in the rest of the world. In America, people are so lonely, they wish they were dead."

That story is quite blunt. But it is a story that you might relate to in some way. How did you feel listening to that story? What reaction do you have to it?

Mother Theresa noticed that the people in the street seemed to have no sense of connection as they hurried about their day. Their eyes told a story of meaninglessness and loneliness. They had a lot of possessions but they had no sense of how they fit into the bigger picture.

Even those of them who had families found themselves cut off as each family member was rarely home at the same time. Each family member had his own car, his own TV in his own room with his own computer. Many didn't even have families to go to at the end of the day. The village had disappeared and with it had disappeared so much that made life meaningful and worth living.

Habib's Grocery Store

We had a grocer in my neighborhood. He ran a small store that sat on a corner on one of the main streets nearby. There were no super duper grocery stores back in those days. This was a small store called a 'mom and pop' store. It was called this because the grocer and his family lived in a house above the store. The grocer's name was Peter. He had a butcher named Danny who knew exactly how to cut the meats my Mom purchased. As soon as she approached the counter, Danny would greet her by name and tell her what he had that she might be interested in since he was familiar with her order each week. He also knew each child in the family and greeted us all by name.

The store owner's wife was named Amelia. She would let my little sister sit on the counter and hand her the groceries that she was ringing up on an old cash register. There was no rush and there was no scripted, empty repetitive phrase like "Thank you for shopping with us. Have a nice day."

Amelia gave my sister an apple and thanked her for helping her ring up the groceries as we headed out the door. My Mom said, "Rose, What do you say to Amelia?" My little sister looked up at Amelia and said, "I have a brother too, you know!"

One time, my father went into the hospital for an operation. The owner, Peter, told my Mom to call the store each Saturday. He had his son take my mother's order down. An hour later, the teen arrived with my Mom's groceries.

My mother tried to pay for the groceries but Peter told her to wait until my father went back to work. Peter sent the groceries faithfully every Saturday until my Dad went back to work and never accepted any money until he returned to work.

One time, my parents told Peter that they were taking us to New York City for two days. Peter took a $100 dollar bill out of his wallet and he told my father to hold it until the following week in case of an emergency in New York.

One weekend each summer, after Peter had rung up my parent's groceries on the register, He would dangle a set of keys in front of Mom. They were the keys to his summer cottage on Lake Harwinton. He would tell my parents to take the kids to the cottage and enjoy the weekend. He would sincerely thank us for our business.

This is not a fantasy. This really happened in my life. We used to live in a village - a real village. Multiply our relationship with our grocer times our relationship with our mechanic etc. etc... I even remember our family doctor, Dr. Ryan, who used to make house visits with his black physician's bag. I remember him sitting on my grandfather's front porch and crying when my grandfather died at home in 1962.

Now, how many group members in this room can relate to this story as told. Let's discuss it in group. We did not have big mega grocery stores back then. Today, if your parents spend $150 dollars every week at a grocery store for ten years, the manager of the grocery store would still have no idea who you even were. He would not know your name, he would not know your Dad was in the hospital, and he certainly would not ask you to hold $100 of the grocery store's money because he knew you were going on a trip and might need it in an emergency.

It is not that he is not a nice guy. It is just that the community where Habib's Grocery store used to exist has been replaced. Our new stores bless us with choices and goods that were not available back at Habib's Family Market.

It is awesome how huge our grocery stores are now. The price we have paid for this affluence is our sense of community with one another. My grocer may be a really nice guy but he doesn't know who I am even though I am a faithful customer spending a lot of money in his store every week for ten years

This book and process is my way to bring my village, my neighborhood, to life again in the lives of all of my students in our village. So, children, find a place on the rim of the circle and hang on. We are going to build a village.

Having a Sense of Place

Being a part of a village is rewarding and meaningful in a different kind of a way from the way many of us have tried to find reward and meaning in materials and possessions. In a village, you are conscious you have purpose. You have a gift you need to bring to your fellow villagers. There is something you have to do while you are here; something has to be accomplished while you are here. That alone is what will bring you happiness. You have to find your place in the village and make your contribution to its well being. You already have all the skills and abilities, and qualities you will need to do your purpose right inside of you. All you have to do now is to start to grow into adulthood and consciously nurture those skills and qualities and abilities. Gather around the stone and get back to the heart of what you have come here into this life to accomplish for your fellow villagers. They need you. And you need them to let you know how you seem to be doing.

The other way of living was not making you happy. Your cup was filling and overflowing with things that were not making you happy and that were only leading you to overfill your cup in desperation.

It is important that you find a way to do well in school now. Your village needs you. Respect your village. Understand your own happiness and well being depends on others' bringing their gifts as well. Encourage them. Confront them when you see them going off course. GO FOR IT! You have a purpose to fulfill here.

The Warrior and the Wound

As we work ourselves toward the end of the first challenge, we have one concept left to touch upon before we proceed to what it means to become a group member. Today, I am passing out small red stickers to you.

I would like to ask each of you to place a sticker on any part of you where you have been injured or wounded. Place a sticker any place that you were badly cut open, or bruised or wounded, or where you incurred any broken bones or sprains.

Let's go around the room now. For the sake of brevity, let's limit each person to discussion about one of her wounds only. As the talking stick passes to you, talk about one of the places where you placed a sticker. What was the wound? How did you get it? What were any other details of the story of that particular wound?

Well, our village group is not a hospital. So why would I ask you to show a place where you were wounded? Let me explain.

Let me ask you a few questions about this physical wound. Did you ignore it when you got it? Did you refuse treatment even though you were bleeding badly? How did the wound heal itself?

The wound needed three things:

- Light
- Air
- Proper Attention

Once the wound was treated to those three ingredients, the wound healed itself! Any successful physician who hopes to remain mentally healthy knows that he is NOT the healer. As a physician he has the knowledge and the skill to set up the conditions for healing. That done, the patient actually heals himself.

The doctor needs a cooperative patient with a positive attitude. The sickness must be acknowledged (given light); it must be given the proper treatment (attention).

The final ingredient might be called the humility and faith to allow the life force (air) to do what it knows how to do.

Now let us relate this healed 'wound' exercise to your psychological life. In the village they believed that every child incurs a wound during his childhood. The wound is a loss of faith, a betrayal, a place where the innocence of childhood dies because time has had its way. The wound happens to every child whether rich or poor. Wounds are a natural occurrence in the realm of time where we live.

Once a child gets the wound, he is not the same. The wound actually hurts so bad in his heart that his head severs its connection to the heart so that it will not feel the pain of the wound.

Now let me ask you again about the wound on your body. If your skin was cut open and you ignored the wound, what would happen? The wound would not just go away. Without attention paid to it, it would fester and become infected. Without treatment, the infection would spread throughout your being. Without the oxygen of the life force, the wound would fester and deteriorate in its own dead matter. One unattended wound on your body could cause you grave consequences in your future. Luckily, you did not ignore it.

But what about your childhood psychological wound?

Many times, this wound is ignored. It is swept underneath the rug of the psyche and denied. It is not exposed to light and air where it can be healed. It festers in the very same way as a physical wound and it changes your life and your ability to live and function as a human being. By the time you are a teenager, the wound is infecting every part of your life. It will NOT heal until it is given light, air, and attention. That is what our group is for.

Many times the psychological wound is cut very close to the heart. So, ignoring it causes you to cut yourself off from your own heart. You try to live on your brain alone. Your brain has been busy anyway accumulating knowledge and separating your life into various parts so it is easy for the brain to figure out a way to separate you from your heart.

Once done, the brain keeps itself occupied through all the activities and strivings that keep a brain occupied. The result is a grown person who is disconnected from his own heart with a serious disability caused by the massive infection of an unattended wound. Becoming a warrior is to delve back into your story and to embrace your wound. Give it light. Give it air. Begin the healing process so you can reconnect your brain to your heart and be whole again.

The village understood that you needed a veteran elder who had made the journey back to the heart already. Without an elder's guidance, your brain would probably choose not to go back to the heart ever. Brains have good memories and they don't like pain.

But our journey is a warrior's journey that each person must accomplish to become an adult. Without the journey back to the heart, a man or a woman remains in a state of adolescent longing and continues to drift away from center for the rest of his life. This is the isolation that Mother Theresa noticed on the streets of New York-People with fancy clothes and cars and cell phones drifting hopelessly and aimlessly away from center - forever.

Initiation

In the village, this process was called initiation. Adolescents were taken out into the countryside and were put through a grueling mental, physical, emotional, and spiritual test to earn their adulthood. It was the journey back to the heart that adolescents no longer are required to accomplish in modern society and in modern education.

In fact, our educational system has unwittingly sent students out to the haystack of information on the internet without first providing the needle of wisdom. Our students are only getting more lost. Initiation will give you the needle of wisdom BEFORE we send you out to the haystack of information looking for the heart and soul that you have no hope of ever finding out there. And that is what is wrong with how we have been educating you. And it is why teachers struggle daily with students who don't seem to care.

In this group, we are going to make the journey and put you through the test. In order to pass the test, you are going to have to take the chance to get real and tell your story in a group. Everyone has the same basic story. Only the details are different. We will explore how to get real in the next challenge.

For now, let us say there is a birth in your story. There is an innocence and childlike joy. There is a wound. There is a separation from the heart and the whole. There is a reaching out for happiness in things of the world which is carried out by your brain.

There is a day when you feel lost and alone and life has no meaning. There is a jolt that occurs in your life either as the result of a formal initiation by elders, or by the form of some catastrophic occurrence that tears your life apart when you least expect it.

There is a chance for healing and a return to the heart if this is experienced like a warrior. But first you must understand the 'test' and what it is for. And then you must understand you will never be a man or woman until you pass the test. That should raise your level of concern and your passion for striving.

We will end this section on the warrior, the wound, and initiation in the village with a short story called "Real Heroes of the Candy Land" I wrote this story one day when I was amazed at the depth of caring and passion that was evolving in all four of my groups. It is a story that is my tribute to those students and all students that have ridden this train since then.

Real Heroes of the Candy Land

Once upon a time, there was a wonderful country called the Candy Land. The country was born of wanderers and seekers. It was born of displaced people looking for a new life.

The heart of the country was gold - made of honesty and a willingness to be real. And so, the heart of the Candy Land was given to simple joy. The people lived in simple, honest community and they knew joy.

In addition to the heart, the country also had a brain. The brain of the country was given to economic prosperity and progress, to material accumulation. The years passed and the country grew.

The brain of the country worked very hard and so economic prosperity began to grow by leaps and bounds. It expanded from one ocean to the other. Its markets then expanded to the entire world. The country was a marvel to behold.

All would have been just fine in the Candy Land. The early fathers were very wise and humble. They warned that the brain and the heart of the country should grow equally. They placed a saying on all of their money to remind themselves of the need for heart growth together with brain growth. The saying was, "In God We Trust".

In the beginning the brain and the heart did grow in balance, and so, simple joy and economic prosperity grew side by side. But soon, the economic prosperity expanded and grew while the heart became forgotten. And so, the children of the country were more and more given to reach out for the material benefits the Candy Land had to offer, without the also receiving the 'heart' benefits. Candy Land had every stimulation and material comfort that life had to offer. People soon began to give their whole lives to the purpose of accumulating these things. It was a heaven on earth.

But more and more, it was noticed that the children were seldom very happy. There seemed to always be this gnawing emptiness within. And so, the children seldom went within. The children were very young and had no way of knowing any other way of life.

And so, in the Candy Land, the heart was eventually forgotten and lost in the sea of material things.

There was a pill or a quick fix to soothe the gnawing emptiness. But the emptiness always returned. Simple joy, born of simple honesty, became unknown, buried under the weight of things and images.

Thus, the Candy Land became a country of impressive appearances that had lost its heart. Everything was phony. Everyone had their own personal image to spin. No one remembered how to just be real. And so, simple joy disappeared from the land. It became a land filled with rich people who were never very happy for very long.

The elders in the Candy Land noticed that the children were never very happy. And seeing this, they tried to give the children more and more things. Suicide and violence and greed took over the land. Honesty nearly disappeared and was valued by fewer and fewer of the children. What went wrong? They had everything - but it always felt like life sucked.

One day a bolt of lightning struck the country when no one was paying attention. The light flashed and it jolted the brain, refocusing it away from all the material and all the stimulation and wealth. The light revealed what lay beneath all the appearances of wealth. Beneath it all, lay a vast wasteland, a desert where nothing grew anymore. It was horrible to behold.

The children stood together on the wasteland without their 'things' and they were terrified. It felt like all was lost.

Some of the children gathered together in a circle in the desert. They looked into each other's eyes, and with no 'things' to reach for, they began to get real with one another. They just sat in that circle and honestly told how it really was for them in the heart.

In the hopelessness of that moment, a sad funeral occurred in the circle of children. It was the funeral for the useless journey in search of 'things' to make you happy. At the end of this brutally honest funeral, there was a silence in the circle. And in the space of that sad silence appeared the first hint of something long forgotten and left for dead by the children - the heart.

The heart appeared. And now it was cherished and honored again like it was always supposed to be cherished and honored. All the children had to do was to be honest, to be 'real' with one another about how it was for them today. And with the heart appeared the first glimmers of what the children had always wanted from life - simple joy.

And so the children learned to balance the heart of simple joy and the brain of material well being. These children, in this simple circle, found their way home out of the desert.
They were heroes - real heroes.

The Opening Challenge

This opening challenge has asked you to do some very difficult things. Although you may have many problems in your life, this challenge has asked you to identify what you are grateful for in your life. How did you do with that?

Next, it asked you to begin to rise above the life of consequences by examining behavior and choosing what stays and what has to go because it is blocking the train tracks and getting in the way of your successful journey.

You were asked to get honest and to identify the ways you may think of yourself as the 'victim' of your own life story. Have you ever read a book that told you that you were 'no one special'? This one did.

Finally, you were hit with the fact that you are wounded because all humans become wounded; you were hit with the fact that happiness becomes a confusing and difficult-to-attain state of grace. In this course, you are going to try to learn how to be happy while just sitting in a chair. Think you are up to this challenge?

This is truly counter cultural in America. Imagine a TV commercial whose only purpose was to tell you that you already have all you need. The commercial would be very short and it would go like this: "Hi everybody. Tonight you are sitting in a chair and I have good news for you. You don't need to buy a damn thing. So just sit back in that chair and relax. Be grateful. You already have everything you need. And now, we return to our show."

Rest assured, you will never see that commercial in your lifetime on American television. But this course will challenge you to find contentment by simply sitting in a chair.

The Source of Energy

As you completed this challenge, you may have noted that it taught you that you already have all you need within you. It taught you that your job is to get in touch with your center where the key to happiness can be found.

In early 2012, as I write these words, teens and young adults are currently preoccupied with instant energy hits that can be purchased at any convenience store. These mini drinks and inhalants promise that an energy boost is on the way with one big swallow or puff.

So then, we can assume that young people for some reason identify themselves as lacking in energy. Second, young people seem to assume that energy can be ingested. You apparently have never been taught that a center of limitless energy can be accessed from inside the soul.

Why do you think that energy can be infused through a drink or inhalant? Why aren't you in touch with a center, a sense of ground, a soul? You aren't in touch with it because elders and teachers are not directing you inward. We are not opening the pathway that accesses the flow of that inner energy. And so, you gulp and inhale.

Get ready, young warriors, I have nothing for you to gulp or inhale in this course. It will be very intense. And we are going 'in' to find the source of unlimited free energy!!! Are you ready for this?

QUESTIONS FROM HEROIC DEPARTURE

Group Leader: Some questions are school specific questions. Please adapt questions to your particular institution or situation.

1. Why are you in this group?

2. What are your personal goals this year?

3. If you are in school, what are your school goals this year? Or, what are your goals in your current situation?

4. What are you grateful for?

5. What is your most difficult class?

6. What is the 'book on the teacher' in your most difficult class?

7. What adjustment do you need to make to pass the difficult class?

8. How do you relate to the victim stance in life? How do you play the victim role?

9. You are 'nobody special'. What does this mean? Can you accept it?

10. What do you have to contribute to the village of your group?

11. What is the wound and why did you get it? What do you do with it?

12. Are you willing to accept responsibility for your life?

13. What does it mean to be a warrior?

14. Are you committed to your obligation to the group process?

Heroic Journey
Challenge #1

Practice Respectful and Direct Communication

Message to Group Leader:

This challenge lays down the process by which the group is conducted each day. The group must be rooted and grounded in procedures that are very clear. The group leader must establish this atmosphere if the group is to thrive. This group is not a therapy group. It is a community, a village. A true village is a place where respect and reverence for the community of the group is established by a strong elder.

- ## Purpose and Consistency of Our Group

  - o What is a Circle?
  - o What are the Four Consistencies of our Circle?
    - Being Present
    - Being Real
    - Holding My Place on the Rim
    - Trusting the Center of the Circle

- ## Roles and Procedures in Our Group

  - o The Group Leader
  - o The Group Guardian
  - o The Role of the Elder
  - o Using a Logbook
  - o Conducting the Group
  - o When the Circle Wobbles

- ## Rules and Process in Our Group

  - o Group Rules
  - o Group Process
  - o Use of the 'Talking Stick'
  - o Group Counseling Techniques

- ## Trust – The First Stage of a Group

  - o 7 Ways to Establish Trust
  - o Utilizing the 'Trust Exercise'
  - o Message in a Bottle – The Risk of Being Vulnerable
  - o The Birth of a Village
  - o Applying Group Challenges/Themes in the Laboratory of Real Life

Introduction

Stone was the theme of the last challenge. The theme of this challenge is fire. Creating a group is much like building a fire. Fire is energy. It burns bright and hot when it is doing its thing. Once your group is born, it will be the vehicle that will take you through the course of the year and through your initiation to adulthood.

Fire is not something to play with. It is capable of causing terrible destruction if it is not tended to properly. But fire is also the source of warmth and energy and passion - all the things that make life worth living. So as we light this fire of our village group, we need to take care of the fire, pay attention to the fire, and most of all use the fire to generate the energy that will power this group.

Our group is held in a circle. There is a reason for this. One is that we can all see each other and find a place on the rim. But the biggest reason for the circle is its ability to contain things. A circle can keep a fire burning and can contain that fire within the rim of its closed circular line. Our circle, then, is like a fire line. It keeps the fire burning but contains it so it may not become destructive or out of control.

As each of you takes the risk of becoming a member of this group, you will add your own spark to the fire of our group. Once the fire is hot and bright and contained properly, your warrior training can begin. Don't forget the last challenge though! You must also have begun to rise above the mud of your life of consequences. Fire will not burn well in mud.

If everyone here does his part, when we complete this challenge, our fire will be burning and another group will have been born to the noble pack of groups that have been born over the past 20 years. The energy of those groups and those warriors is here with us right now to help you light your fire now.

The Circle and the Four Consistencies

The Four Consistencies

Group process is the consistency that weaves together each of the aspects of our group. Everything happens in the context of something called group process.

The four consistencies that encompass group process are

1) Be Present

2) Be Real

3) Hold My Place on the Rim of the Circle

4) Trust the Power of the Center of the Circle

Being Present

Presence in our group means more than being a body present in a chair. It means total attentiveness to what is happening now in the group as well as attentiveness to what is happening inside me in the group now. Presence is a willingness to listen to others as well as a willingness to listen to my own heart.

The symbol of presence in our group is 'feet flat on the floor'. We begin each session with feet flat on the floor as a way to remind ourselves to be grounded here and now, present to ourselves and others. We begin the school year by each of us tracing a foot onto a poster board. The overlapping feet on the poster which will hang on the wall is a reminder to be present here and now.

Feet Poster Activity

Each student traces one foot onto a large blank white poster. The activity symbolizes presence and grounded-ness each day. When students from all four groups have completed the exercise, students use crayons to color within the lines of all the overlapped feet.

The result is a colorful mosaic which hangs in the group room all year. Place the saying "Put Your Feet Flat On The Floor- Spend A Minute Of Quiet Time- And Bring Yourself To the Presence Of Your Own Beating Heart" at the top of this poster. It becomes the daily reminder to be present and grounded in the presence of the spark of your own beating heart.

Being Real

'Being real' means that you express your authentic feelings. Even if you do not know your feelings, you can be authentic and say that you don't know what you are feeling.

This consistency values 'feelings' rather than 'opinions'. It is a commitment to drop the mask that we may wear to hide our authentic selves in public.

The symbol of being real in here is 'the open hand'. We begin the school year by each of us tracing a hand on a large poster board. The hands all overlap. This board hanging in the group room is a reminder to 'be real'.

Hand Poster Activity

Each student traces one hand onto a large blank white poster. The activity symbolizes being real through the honesty of the 'open hand'. When students from all four groups have completed the exercise, students color within the lines of all the overlapped hands. The result is a colorful mosaic which hangs in the group room all year. Place the saying "Everything Is BS But The Open Hand" at the top of the poster. It becomes the daily reminder to be honest and real in group everyday so that our fire may burn clean and hot and bright. Credit goes to singer-songwriter, Bruce Cockburn, for the quote.

Holding Your Place on the Rim of the Circle

Holding your place on the rim of the circle means that you have made a commitment to this circle and this process. Being in a group will be pleasant as well as unpleasant. There will be fun times. There will be sad times. There will be crises in the group too. You must choose to get in or get out. If you are going to be in, be committed.

The symbol for this commitment is 'sweat'. During the first week, we ask each person to put his finger to his own forehead and to then place the finger on the box of perception in the center of the circle. This fingertip of sweat on the box is a symbol of our joint commitment to realize the full potential of this group and to the 'sweat' that will be required to stay committed to making this group become all that it can be.

Sweat Exercise

Each student in the group acknowledges that a commitment is necessary to see the purpose of the group through to completion. It will take work and commitment and sweat to see this group through and to help each individual member also complete a successful experience and a courageous journey into the unknown land of adulthood.

The box of perception sits in the center of the circle. After a discussion, each student makes a decision. Anyone that wants to leave our group at this point is allowed to leave. Each student then reaches to his forehead with one finger to gather some moisture on his fingertip. The students one at a time touch their fingertips to the box of perception at the center of the circle as a symbol of commitment to purpose, a commitment to self and to the other members of the group. The commitment is to see the journey through no matter what obstacles come before us or frustrate us through the school year.

Trusting the Power of the Center of the Circle

Trusting the center means that you have faith in the spirit of our circle to work all things through. 'Working through' does not mean finding solutions. It is more like faith just to be real until the path opens up and you know what to do or say next.

The value in our group is not to find a solution to a problem. The value is to just dump the truth into the center. The center is a place to empty the self. It has a still point at the very center, like the center of a stone that holds all the wisdom of the universe. If you tell the truth and you dump the truth of how you feel into the center, the center will eventually speak to you.

The power at the center of the circle also holds all the power of all those brave warriors who sat in circles throughout the years. We call on them to be here in spirit today too.

The symbol for the power at the still point at the center of a circle is 'silence'. We begin each group with a minute of silence to try to connect with the sacred space that exists here. We respect this space we have created and we have reverence for what we are about to do today in this group.

In the silence you try to find the silent still point in your heart and connect it to the still point at the center of the circle. In this way, the center will hold the truth and will also radiate the truth outward toward you.

On the rim of the circle, we may go through times when we lose balance, when the rim begins to wobble with tension and issues that are difficult. But at the center, there is no wobble. So placing your trust in the center will correct all wobbles on the rim of the circle. For this reason, anybody in group may call for silence and re-centering when it is perceived that the rim is wobbling.

Silence Exercise

Each day the group begins with feet flat on the floor in a moment of silence. The teacher says, "Put your feet flat on the floor. Spend a minute of quiet time. Bring yourself to the presence of your own beating heart"

Roles and Procedures in our Group

Roles in this Group

GROUP LEADER - Each week a different student should be assigned to take the students through the check in process as well as choosing who should speak and in what order. The group leader co-leads the group with the elder. However, the elder lets students take the helm as much as possible. By the end of the school year, most students in our group have become accomplished group leaders. Teachers from around the building often state that our students often take the lead and are more comfortable than other students in group discussion activities.

GUARDIAN – Christina Baldwin introduced me to the idea of a 'group guardian'. Each week, a group guardian should be assigned. The guardian is different from the leader in that the guardian is assigned to keep an eye on the group energy to see when tensions are arising. The guardian would also notice when an individual group member may be upset when the leader or elder do not notice. The guardian can also suggest a minute of silence as can anyone in the group.

The guardian is the keeper of the fire. He points out the heat of the fire, if someone appears to be getting lost in the fire, if someone needs attention, if some unspoken issue is taking place in the group. His job is not firefighter. His job is fire guardian. He acknowledges hot spots so they may be recognized and burned in a hot yet contained way.

ELDER - Since this intends to be an initiatory group for the purpose of taking students through the doorway of adulthood, the elder is your teacher. In addition to the job of illuminating the process in a group, it is also the job of the elder to keep elder consciousness alive in the group.

Elder consciousness should naturally be present in all school situations. It often is not present, having been replaced by diagnostician consciousness, professional consciousness, buddy consciousness, specialist consciousness and even entertainer consciousness.

Your elder is going to expect respect for elders in all situations. If you think your place in here is equal to that of the elder, you are going to have a problem. The elder has a job to do and he is going to do it. Part of that job is 'expecting respect for the elder'.

The elder is going to be very understanding at all times. There are very few mistakes that students will make that the elder has not made at one time himself. He is not ever going to judge you. But he is going to come right at you and challenge you right in your face. He will never be personally disrespectful to you but he is going to make you angry at times. He is the elder and it is his job to put you through the test until you begin to show the discipline of the adult warrior.

Group Procedures

Logbook

Each group should have a logbook maintained by that week's group leader. The teacher may also add to the logbook each day.

The purpose of the logbook is to provide a place to record each student's bottom line commitments for review each day. In addition, the logbook ensures some kind of continuity. Because most groups are time limited by the schedule of the place where the group is held, the logbook enables you to know which students have spoken on an issue, which students still need to speak, or to record any unfinished business from the preceding meeting.

Circle Procedures

1) Prepare the space - usually a defined center with objects that have meaning

2) Make the circle real - begin by making the circle round and orderly

3) Minute of silence - with feet flat on the floor to bring focus and attention as well as reverence for the 'sacred space' of the circle.

4) Group Process – carry out the body and purpose of your group.

5) Reframing - About five minutes before the group will end, teacher should sum up the group, make connections between all that happened today in group, add any insight that the elder may have for the group.

6) End the group with a minute of silence. This is done to acknowledge that we are leaving the sacred space, returning to normal life out there in the hallways or cafeteria.

When the Circle Wobbles

The purpose of this group is not to create a phony warm and fuzzy place where we are all one big happy family all the time. Being in a group is not always easy.

When tension arises, it is first acknowledged, and then explored through group process. What is the issue? Who is mad, sad, scared? How is each person in group affected by the issue? Encourage 'how it feels to be here now' rather than 'my opinion of this is...'.

Solutions are not what you search for when the rim wobbles. What you search for is truth - the truth of how it is for me here and now in this group. Out of this truth dumped into the center, the circle will eventually balance itself again.

You should consciously remember that the center never wobbles because it is still. Only the rim wobbles. So when there is something going on that causes tension and discomfort (wobbling), it becomes each member's duty to hold his place on the rim, steady himself, get in touch with himself, and to focus himself to the center core energy of the group.

The circle usually wobbles because someone is upset (off center), because someone is seeking attention, because someone is trying to control or manipulate, or because someone is disappearing (isolative) on the rim. Whatever the issue, it must be addressed and given proper attention through the group process.

Experience is not always a comfortable teacher. Don't jump to correct the tension, or to enable someone. Let the discomfort exist and do group process.

Eye Contact Exercise

Today we will do a non verbal exercise. The purpose of the exercise is to demonstrate that not all communication is verbal. Talking can be highly overrated in a group. Listening ends up being the thing that most new students need to learn more than talking.

But even beyond talking and listening, there are other ways that messages are sent. They say that the eyes are the windows of the soul. The eyes express so much more than the mouth can usually communicate.

After we do quiet time today, we will remain silent until everyone in the group makes eye contact with everyone else in the group. Take a minute after quiet time to let your eyes travel around the circle until you make eye contact with everyone else in your group.

We will not discuss this exercise today. We will just let the non verbal communication stand for now.

GROUP RULES

- Arrive on time each day

- Be alive and involved in group each day

- No personal attacks of any kind ever

- Talk about yourself. Focus on how you feel, how the situation affects you, what you will do. Do not spend your time talking about others or in describing every detail of a situation. Tell the truth about how you feel from the deep heart.

- Everything said and done in group is confidential. This includes discussion about the group by group members. As soon as the group ends, it should not be discussed again.

The elder will break confidentiality for the following reasons:

- If a student is talking about hurting himself in a specific way
- If a student is talking about hurting someone else in a specific way
- If the elder becomes aware that you are using heroin, cocaine, ecstasy, meth amphetamine, or massive amounts of cough syrup, confidentiality will be broken.

The common side effects of the drugs named above include brain damage, heart attack, and sudden death. The elder will not hold this information in confidence. Amen.

In all cases, the teacher will tell you to your face when he feels he needs to break confidentiality. An exception to this would be if he cannot locate you in order to inform you he needs to break confidentiality.

TALKING STICK

Each day the group leader will begin by asking if anyone has anything to say. Any member of the group may take the talking stick.

Taking the talking stick means a group member would like to speak about something important to him/her. Time is allowed for this purpose.

Talking Stick is held to help give strength to the speaker. The speaker understands the warriors who took the stick before him/her found courage and strength to speak. The warrior now hopes to gather that same courage.

The Talking Stick will also be utilized in activities during various themes and stories from the curriculum. These activities require courage and the attention of your peers. Use of the talking stick indicates that attention is required.

RULES FOR USE OF TALKING STICK

1. The member holding the talking stick should be honest and should identify feelings. Holding the talking stick means you are going to talk about yourself. What is happening with you now? You never take the talking stick to talk about someone else. Pour what you need to communicate into the center of the circle where the whole group can simply observe and sit with it.

2. Other group members should not interrupt

3. When done, the student holding the stick might request feedback

Follow the group process with your comments. Relate anything in your own life that you may have been reminded of when the sharer spoke. Be honest. Be respectful – even if you need to confront an uncomfortable situation

.

GROUP PROCESS

1. Be aware of your feelings and reactions in your body.

2. Listen to others without judgment.

3. Do not give opinions or advice.

4. Do not interrupt when someone speaks.

5. When you do speak, use I-messages.

6. Do not try to fix anyone or anything.

7. Be honest, present, and real.

8. Respect the silence when it arrives.

9. The process will always work if you do not interfere.

Group Counseling Techniques

1. Active Listening -
You seem… today

2. Reflect Back –
You just said …

3. Clarify
Correct me if I am wrong, but are you saying..

4. Empathize
I felt like you do now when I…

5. Support
How can I help you with this?
I am here for you.

6. Confront
We have to talk. I am upset about…

First Stage of a Group

- Establish Trust – Take Risk

- Express Feelings, Not Opinions

- Balanced Participation – Listen/ Share

- Expect Some Disruption in Your Life

- Expect to Discover Wonderful Things

- Learn How You Affect Others

- Be Present and On-Purpose

Trust Exercise

The trust exercise is completed somewhere within the first month of the group. It is a very difficult exercise for some students, but you must complete the procedure. The group does not proceed without the establishment of trust. Trust does not get established without risk. Risk is scary.

Answer the following questions during group today when the talking stick is passed to you:

- What is it like for you to be part of this group?
- What have you contributed?
- Who is the person in the group that you find the easiest to trust? Tell them about it.
- Who is the person in the group who you find it most difficult to trust? Tell them about it
- What can this person do to help you trust him?
- What do you suppose it is like to be in a group with you? Well, you are about to find out!

At this point each group member lets the student know what it has been like to be in a group with her. Students are not allowed to make personal attacks during this exercise. You are to let the student know what they say and do, and how it affects you. Try to be specific rather than general in your comments. The teacher will help you through it.

This exercise is completed as often as necessary throughout the life of the group. It is necessary whenever the circle is wobbling and the group is ailing.

The goal is to keep the group present and real while also teaching students to become comfortable and courageous in being willing to face difficult situations. Group intimacy requires willingness and courage on a daily basis.

The next story speaks to the isolated place that traps us when we lack the ability to trust, to be real, and to truly connect to others.

Message in a Bottle Exercise

A small piece of paper has been handed out to you in group today. Take a few minutes to think about a time when you felt isolated or alone. It should be a time when you were harboring feelings that were hard for you to express to the point where you were fronting one thing while holding painful 'real' feelings beneath the surface.

In a way, you might think of this time in your life as a time when you were marooned on a distant island with no means of communication to the outside world. Traditional stories tell of a time when a person marooned and alone on an isolated island has lost all ability to contact the outside world. As the story goes, the person finds an empty bottle and scrawls a message describing his location and the need for rescue. The bottle is floated into the water with the hope that someone on a distant shore might find it and bring help.

In our group today, we will recognize the isolated island in ourselves during a time when we too have felt inside as if we are marooned and alone on this island of isolation. Our group is a harbor that has received your message in a bottle. We are here to make isolation go away. We are here to get real; to free you from isolation; and to lead you back home to your heart.

Today, you will place a message in the empty bottle being passed around the circle. I am handing you a small blank piece of paper. We are going to sit quietly and place the 'intention' of something we would like to write or say to someone we love. It should be something that we would like to communicate that we have been unable to communicate to this point in our lives.

When we are finished, we will discuss what we wrote in our 'message in a bottle'. In this way, we will each discuss something that is hard for us to communicate to others – some worry; some sentiment we find it hard to communicate; some hope for the future; or some disappointment we have been unable to discuss. An optional addition to this theme is to play the song "Shores of Stone" by singer Kevin Welch. The song is recommended because it explains the concept well. "This is just a message in a bottle baby. This is just a sad communiqué. These are just some things I'd like to tell you"

This group is designed to end your sense of separation and loneliness. It is designed to infuse you with an intense awareness of the importance of bringing your 'gift' to a village that desperately needs the gifts of all of its villagers.

Much of what has been covered in this challenge will be utilized throughout the school year. It is not something you just learn and forget. The procedures are useless unless they are applied to your daily life

We will close the challenge with a story called Kathy's Story .

Kathy's Story

This is a story about the first person to ever share a personal issue in our group. Her name was Kathy. I had just finished explaining the BS Board and I told students that no excuse will be accepted for not doing well on point slips or in school. I asked students if they understood. After they said that they did understand, I asked students for some examples of BS that they have used in their lives. Students gave very typical responses like "I couldn't help it", like "I didn't realize we had homework" etc.

When the turn came around to Kathy, she said, "I am late for school because my older brother is a drunk and I wait up for him all night because I am afraid he is going to crash the car and get hurt again." Kathy's eyes gazed down at the floor as she finished. But then, she raised her head and looked right into my eyes and the eyes of her fellow group members.

There was silence in the group. For the first time, the silence that sometimes overtakes a group happened. The power of that moment cannot be explained, but the fire of the first group was lit on that day and it has never gone out.

Kathy came to school every day and graduated from high School with honors that year.

QUESTIONS FROM HEROIC JOURNEY CHALLENGE ONE

1. What are the four consistencies that we respect in our group?

2. What are the roles that must be filled in our Group?

3. What do we do when the circle wobbles and the group starts to fall apart?

4. Are you aware of the rules that must be followed each day in Group?

5. What is confidentiality? When will confidentiality be broken by the teacher?

6. What is the Talking Stick and how is it used in Group?

7. What is trust and how is it established in a group?

8. When trust is broken in the group, what do we do?

9. Do you have the guts and courage to keep the fire of this group burning?

10. What was your first contribution to the group? Was it difficult?

11. Have you been confronted in a group? Have you confronted someone?

12. How do you feel about being confronted in a group?

13. How do you feel about confronting others?

14. Do you know what empathy is? Do you know how to empathize in group?

15. How is empathy different from sympathy?

16. How is empathy different from giving advice?

Heroic Journey
Challenge #2

Maintain a Fierce Desire
To Fulfill My Life Purpose

Message to Group Leader:

This challenge connects the growing inner group consciousness that is striving for community among group members to a new consciousness that understands that each individual life has a 'purpose' or 'gift' to bring to the larger communities of family, village, country, world, and universe. In this way, participants begin their initiation to adulthood. The inner potential energy of the initiate must be recognized, nurtured, and released so that the individual gift may be birthed on the path toward a healthy, productive adult life. For many teens, this the first time they have ever been impacted by the fact that they have 'something they have to do' while they are here on planet earth. It is time to marshal and forge their energy and desire into a conscious, responsible striving.

- ## What Does It Mean to Be on Purpose?

  o African Woman Story
    - Welcoming a 'Gift' into the World
    - Developing a Consciousness for "Purpose"
  o The Story of Heroes and Bums
    - Are You On Purpose in Your Life?
    - Purpose- a Choice You Make Each Morning

- ## Destiny and Fatalism – Two Ways to View Life

  o Destiny as a Point of View
  o Fatalism as a Point of View
  o 'Twists of Fate' in the Unfolding of Destiny
  o The 'Ripple' I Make Each Day

- ## The Story of Delaware Bay

  o Choice – A Blessing and a Burden
  o The Synchronicity of Birds and Horseshoe Crabs
  o Ways of Going 'Off Purpose"
  o Why is the World So Messed Up?
  o Putting Your Story into the Story of Delaware Bay

- ## How Do I Know If I Am 'On Purpose'?

  o Listening to the Voice inside the Beating Heart
  o "Mr. Intention' as a Teacher

Introduction

The theme of the opening challenge was stone. The theme of the last challenge was fire. The next challenge takes us to the theme of air. This challenge is about flight.

Once you became grounded, balanced, and conscious to the center of the stone, you were ready to build the fire of your group. Now that the fire is built, the group is like your nest. It is the place to come back to. It is the place that anchors you. But it is time to learn to take flight.

When an airplane takes flight, all the instruments on the control panel keep it balanced and on course in relationship to the ground. The ground is the reference point for all the indicator measurements. If the airplane did not have these instruments and this point of reference to the ground, it might fly out of control off the edge of the atmosphere or it might crash. In any case, it would not be able to get where it is going without reference point and a conscious destination.

Airplanes were created by studying the birds. Birds have their own internal instruments to achieve flight, balance, reference to ground, and destination. They fly on course and on purpose everywhere they go.

Being on purpose in your life is the subject of this challenge. It is one of the shortest challenges in this textbook, but it may well be the most important. So pay attention!

What Does It Mean To Be On Purpose?

The purpose of your life is encoded right into your bones. Just like a tiny acorn knows what it has to do to become a mighty oak tree, you and I have all the tools and abilities to do the thing we were sent here to do. What we have lost, however, is the consciousness that we have to accomplish a purpose here on earth. Nowadays, we just sort of grow up with this vague idea that we need to get a job and make some money. The importance and interconnectedness of what we do and how it will affect others so intimately is lost.

Being on purpose in your life means you are consciously working and accomplishing what you were sent here to do. If you do not believe that you have a job to accomplish while you are here, pay attention to the stories that will be told in this challenge. The elder is not going to waste time trying to convince you that you have a purpose in your life. If you choose to see your life as an independent entity disconnected from the rest of the universe, you may do so without any struggle to your chosen viewpoint from the elder. However, you will pay the price for that point of view and it is a steep one.

African Women Story

A few years ago I met a woman named Sobonfu Some. She told me a story that I would like to relate to you now concerning purpose in life.

In an African village, when a woman becomes pregnant, all the women of the village gather in a circle with the pregnant woman. They begin to discuss the coming child's birth. They begin to say things to each other like this, "There is a baby coming" "What gift is this child coming to bring us?" They then begin to talk to the child inside the woman's belly as they sit there in the circle. They ask the baby why he is coming and what gift he or she is bringing to the village.

As with most indigenous practices, it is so easy for educated, modern people to just write this exercise in the African Village off to superstition or to 'primitive cuteness' which is another way to say 'useless ignorance'. However, please think about these things.

First, please take into consideration the beauty and welcoming peacefulness of this village practice and contrast it to the loneliness of the teenage girl in America who finds out she is pregnant. There is no group of women to celebrate the importance of this pregnancy to the whole village; there is no welcoming to the developing fetus. Maybe the indigenous people remember something we forgot?

More importantly, those women sitting in that circle understood that if a baby was coming, he was bringing something. This birth was not an isolated chance happening. The village was still small enough that the women understood that if a baby was coming to the village, it was bringing something with it. It had a job to do, a gift to bring the village. Now think how cherished the whole village would feel about this one child. He was not just some lady's kid. He was a holy vessel coming to live among us with something to accomplish and contribute to the village. The village needs this child.

By the time some children today get to the point where we need to teach them and give them a test, they are paralyzed and can't move. They have never been properly welcomed and nurtured and honored like the child from the village.

You are in our group. Our group is a village. We desperately want to acknowledge you and encourage you to accomplish your life purpose. You have to open your eyes now and see that you are growing into an adult. No matter what your problems are, or have been, we need you to bring your gift. There is something you have to do while you are here. You were sent here with a mission to accomplish. If you do not complete your mission, your own life will be unsatisfying and unhappy, and worse, the village that needed your gift will have to go without it or compensate in other ways.

Your life is like a ripple of energy on a pond. You are a stone thrown into the pond of life. You are making a ripple by the energy of your daily choices. Your ripple is either moving with the purpose of life and it is enriching your village; or it is moving against the purpose of life and it is negatively affecting everyone who comes into contact with its energetic ripple.

Pay attention to what you are saying and doing? Is it helping you? Is it contributing something worthwhile to us?

Why be On Purpose in Your Life?

This question is partially answered by the last paragraph. Going off purpose does not just affect you. It affects the whole village. Here is another story to try to demonstrate the need for you to do your purpose both for your own happiness and for the survival and enrichment of your village.

Heroes and Bums

Heroes and Bums is another true story from my own life. It happened one morning when I was driving to school from the other side of Waterbury. As I passed under the railroad tracks on West Main Street on my way through town, I noticed a group of drunken bums sitting by the railroad tracks. They were passing a bottle of wine back and forth at 6:30 in the morning. One was lying on the ground, too drunk to stand.

I mean no disrespect to homeless people. People like these guys on the railroad tracks come from all walks of life and all levels of education. And every one of them has a story that has lead them to the point of being on those railroad tracks at 6:30 in the morning with a bottle of wine. And I have been on the railroad tracks of my own life several times.

But I could not help but think that each of these men came to earth with a purpose to accomplish. Each one of them had somewhere he could be this very morning accomplishing something that enriches the life of the village. How do I know they are not doing their purpose by being on the railroad tracks? I don't know. But let me continue with my story.

As I sat in traffic looking at these men, I suddenly had a thought that if I could make a movie about these eight men, it would be a very fascinating movie. I would begin my movie right there on the railroad tracks and then I would pan back to earlier times.

My movie would go back to the birthplaces of each of these men and it would tell their individual stories. Each man's story would then unfold to the final scene of my movie right there on the railroad tracks.

It would be a fascinating movie for sure. Each of these men has reasons for being on those tracks. Their life stories are filled with heartache, wounds, disappointment, and betrayal.

This was a momentary thought. It was a good idea, but now the traffic had cleared and I proceeded up West Main Street. As I approached the Green at the center of town, I had to pull over as two police cars went speeding by with their sirens screaming. Before I could get back into the lane to drive on, I also heard the sound of a helicopter above me flying very low. It felt like I was in Iraq.

As I approached the next traffic light near the police station, here is what I saw:

I glanced down the street and saw that the two police cars were blocking the two ends of South Elm Street on either side of St. Mary's Hospital. The helicopter had just landed in the parking lot across the street from the hospital. With the street free of traffic and the helicopter on the ground, I saw four people pushing a stretcher with a patient on it. They rushed across the street from the emergency room of the hospital to the helicopter.

Before the light had time to change, they loaded the patient on the helicopter and the helicopter was airborne with the patient. The light changed and I began to move on as the policemen went back about their daily routine and the hospital workers walked back into the hospital. This procedure was completed with lightning precision. The next day I timed the traffic light and discovered the whole procedure took place in less than three minutes.

Obviously, that patient was near death and needed some specialized emergency care that St. Mary's could not provide. I do not know what happened to that patient. But I do know this. The police took their positions, the helicopter hit the ground, the medical personnel transported the patient across the street, loaded the patient, and that helicopter was on its way in less than three minutes.

I felt so grateful. Everyone had a job to do. Everyone was well trained. Everyone worked in unison with precision even though they were from different professions, different agencies, and different backgrounds. Each person - two policemen, two helicopter personnel and five hospital workers were all right on the money that morning for that one patient in crisis.

Suddenly, sitting there at that light, I had a thought that this scene could make a great movie. My movie would begin right there outside the emergency room where that helicopter transfer had taken place. Then I would pan back to the birthplaces of each of those workers that morning. My movie would tell the stories of the lives that led them all to be in that place at that time right on purpose for that one person in need.

I realized my movie would depict lives of heartache, sorrow, and disappointment. The life stories of these workers had deep incidences of betrayal. These workers were wounded by life and had a lot of reasons to give up. But there they were on the final scene of my movie: right on the money for that one sick person in need.

I began to think about all I had seen as I completed the journey to school. I felt so glad those workers did not get drunk the night before and call in sick. I felt so grateful they learned their jobs so well. It made me feel like I wanted to do my own job with that kind of care and precision so I might have the same affect that they had on their village that morning. Maybe the patient died on the helicopter. I don't know. But it doesn't matter.

Then, I thought about the bums on the railroad tracks. I wondered what important task in life was left undone today by the ones who just couldn't get off the railroad tracks. God bless the people who help the men who want to get themselves off the railroad tracks. We need them in the village.

Who are you and I? Are we the men on the railroad tracks or are we the heroes at the hospital? Discuss this for a while with your teacher or mentor.

I have my own answer. We are both the heroes and the bums. We choose when we get up in the morning who we will be. If we are the heroes today, may we find the courage to keep doing our life's work by staying on purpose in life. And if we are the bums today, let us find the help or the courage we need to join the village again and to do our purpose in life.

Every morning when you wake up, you are like a stone thrown into a pond. You make a ripple. Is your ripple helping you and your village?

Who are you? Are you the hero? Or are you the bum? Share a story in group when you have accomplished something and been right on purpose in your life like the heroes. It need not be a dramatic rescue story. But you do have a story about a time when you know you came through for someone in a tough situation. Discuss it.

Then relate another story when you know you were far off track in your life like the bums. You may have never been a drunken bum on the railroad tracks, but there is a time when you know you did not come through and do what needed to be done in some situation.

As you think about this, realize that every day you wake up, and you choose who you will be that day. It is very important as we saw in this story that you choose to be on purpose in your life. The village of your school, your town, your family needs your gift very badly. The village needs you to be on purpose. And when you go off purpose, the village needs you to forgive yourself and right yourself.

The point of this story is not to say that heroes are good people and drunken bums are bad people. The point of this story is for us all to be conscious that we live in a village that needs our contribution. We all go off purpose at times. We must forgive ourselves. We will need the forgiveness of others at times. As soon as one of those bums puts down the bottle and rejoins the village, we should forgive him and welcome him.

Destiny and Fatalism

"Heroes and Bums" is a story which deals with the issue of fate as it relates to the words destiny and fatalism.

'Fate' is a word that represents all of the chance circumstances that become the stories of your life. According to ancient books, there are certain "twists of fate" in your story that become important turning points in your life. How you perceive these "twists of fate" in your life will determine what you do with them. For some people, a 'twist of fate" leads them directly to their life purpose – their destiny. Destiny is the root of the word 'destination'. It is a life perception by which an individual life is seen as a thread that plays an intricate part in the bigger story of the universe. As you look at our galaxy, you see a vast expanse of space and matter that is inexplicably connected. Although you cannot perceive the connections at a human level of perception, you know they are there and you see yourself as a vital cog in that pattern since you reside within the galaxy. You have a destination in the form of a life purpose.

A life stance that acknowledges destiny is a life stance that understands that a "twist of fate" that might wound you in the short run may actually lead you directly into the direction where you can complete your life purpose. In a life perception of destiny, the so-called chance occurrence of a "twist of fate" eventually takes on significant meaning in your life. There is something you have to do while you are here. There is a gift you must bring. And each twist of fate in your life story is not seen as a bad thing. As you look back, you will notice that some of the twists of fate that seemed horrible at the time actually led you directly into your destiny.

In this life perception, fate and destiny suggest everything is connected. You have a part to play in the weaving of a majestic tapestry that is the story of life. Your part may seem tiny, but your part fits and it is an intricate part of the story. And only you can choose to do your part. No one can force you, not even God or not God. You are free to choose.

With this perspective on life, even the supposedly 'bad' things that have happened in your life may be part of a fated pattern where you learn something that you will need in order to do your life purpose. Many times, it is the difficulties and sorrows you face that actually build the character that will be required to do life purpose. Have you ever thought about that?

The story of "Heroes and Bums" suggests that we all make a choice in life whether or not we will strive to accomplish our life purpose and to bring the gift.

"Fatalism" is a life perception that chooses to see life as predetermined. Perception in a fatalistic life outlook dismisses choice as illusory. There is no choice. A 'fatalistic' life stance would see the bums in our story as predetermined to act as bums and it would not acknowledge that the bums made the choice to be on those railroad tracks on that day. Instead of seeing "twists of fate" as roadmaps into our destiny, we interpret these "twists of fate" as proof that life is a disconnected mess and there is nothing anyone can do except to follow the 'fatalistic' pattern of life.

There are no connections to a greater story. Fatalism would further believe that it really doesn't matter what you choose to do as a human even if you do have free choice and even if there is a predetermined outcome. The ending is fatal.

This course chooses to see your life as a life where free choice, destiny, and purpose play a part in the story. If you choose to see your life as disconnected or predetermined, you may do so. There is no absolute proof either way. You will see your life as a disconnected journey that ends with you as a 'fatality'.

You are probably going to be a very angry, selfish, and depressed person if you choose to see life this way. I have no proof that you have a destiny to fulfill. But still, even if all we are doing as humans is choosing which dream to live in, why would anyone want to choose a dream that leaves them disconnected, alone, isolated, and desperate?

There seems to be something in the core of a soul that longs for the completion of its destiny. That destiny is arrived at through the portal of fate. If you pay attention and make choices from the still heart where each pulse or ripple from your heartbeat affects the world every day, you can come to realize that even the so-called 'bad' things that happened to you were the twists of fate that built your character and led you directly to your life purpose and destiny.

Staying On Purpose in Your Life

This is the whole game of human life. We got a wonderful blessing when we signed up for the human deal. That blessing came to us side by side with a terrible burden. The blessing and burden of humanity is found in the gift of choice. You are free to choose to do your purpose in life. You can do whatever you choose. What a gift and blessing! But also, you can use your freedom to go way off purpose and to cause yourself and others tremendous heartache and trouble. What a burden! Choice is the blessing and burden of the human deal. You choose to be the hero or the bum every day. What are you choosing in your life right now?

Next, we will explore the subject of life purpose through a story.

Delaware Bay

What does it mean to be 'on purpose' in your life? Why is it important for you to be 'on purpose'? What happens to people when they go off purpose? What are the consequences both to the person who goes off purpose and to the village?

Some things are hard to teach. It's not like you can just give a lecture and have kids take notes. Some things will never be learned unless your students can chew on the material and eat it for breakfast. That is because some things that get taught are not taught to the brain. They are taught to the heart. When you teach the heart stuff, you can't teach it in a lecture. You have to serve it for breakfast. In my experience, the best way for a teacher to serve a new challenge for students was to serve it up as a story.

But still, I could not find a good story to teach the themes of bringing your gift and understanding that you were born with a purpose on this earth. But then, one night, I was flipping through the channels on my TV. And there it was! The perfect story appeared before my eyes. It was the story of Delaware Bay.

The story goes like this.

I got into bed one night. I took my remote control unit and I began to flip through the channels on TV. It was just another boring night on TV. I couldn't find anything I wanted to watch. So, I just kept flipping through those channels around and around the wasteland of night-time TV. Then, as often happens, my remote settled on the Discovery Channel. It was there that my attention remained for the rest of the evening. It was a story about birds, a documentary produced after years of study.

It seems that there are these birds that reside in South America every winter. These same birds then make the same flight every year in the spring time to a location in Canada. They spend the warmer months up in Canada. Now that doesn't seem like a big deal. But you know what? Venezuela to Canada is a heck of a long flight for tiny little birds. Even though they don't have to deal with the traffic on Interstate 95, it is still a very long journey for such tiny beings with such low functioning brain ability. After all, we do call each other 'birdbrain' when we want to insult each other for lack of intelligence.

That is enough evidence for me that something is going on, that everything in life has a purpose and place in creation. It is an incredibly long journey. But the birds seem to know exactly where to go, when they need to go, what route they need to take, and what they need to do along the way to survive the trip. It is like clockwork except that the birds don't have clocks like we do. They seem to be able to listen to this internal clock and this internal voice that tells them where to go and what to do when they get there. Science calls this 'instinct'. You may call it what you will, but the fact remains that it is somewhat of a miracle that these tiny beings can make such a trip.

This story, were it to end here, would be amazing enough, and would be proof to me that there is some great mystery or pattern to life that is beyond my ability to comprehend. But that is not the end of the story.

It seems that this particular bunch of birds make an important stop every year on their way to Canada. They stop at a place called Delaware Bay.

Let us leave the bird story for just a minute and get our geography straight. Delaware Bay is located on the east coast of the United States. Its mouth consists of a New Jersey town called Cape May. The eastern bank of the Bay is New Jersey. The western bank of the Bay is Delaware. The Bay ends by the City of Philadelphia and is fed by the Delaware River.

The Bay is a bit out of the way for the birds. They have to fly east further than would be necessary for their final destination. But this is the route they take very year. As the story proceeded, it now focused on a new subject. Horseshoe crabs crawl out of the water of Delaware Bay every year and crawl up on the shore where they lay their eggs. The crabs then scurry back to the water leaving their eggs to be hatched at a later time.

There are so many crab eggs on that beach that it would be an ecological disaster to the whole New Jersey-Delaware area if they were ever all hatched. Fortunately, the crabs only come ashore and lay their eggs one single day every year. And fortunately, all the eggs do not hatch.

And why don't they all hatch? What saves New Jersey and Delaware from an ecological nightmare? The saviors are those tiny bird brained flyers going to Canada.

Somehow, every year, these same birds always manage to land for a rest at Delaware Bay on their way to Canada. And every year, they arrive on the exact same day that the crabs come out of the water to lay their eggs. The birds land. They feast on crab eggs. They have a rest. And then they proceed on to Canada.

The result is that these birds and crabs, by synchronizing their arrivals perfectly every year, save the entire east coast from a disaster. They do their small part to keep everything in balance so that we can live in peace another season on the east coast of the United States. Don't forget. If all those crabs were born, the story would not end there. The ripple effect to the rest of nature would be devastating and perhaps even fatal to all of us.

It happens like clockwork every year. They never go off purpose and they never let the universe down. This is just one small part of the story of the universe. At a later time, I will add other stories that show the amazing way that things thousands of miles, even thousands of light years, apart are connected to keep everything in balance. Whether you look at Delaware Bay or the pattern of stars in the galaxies spinning around a black hole, or the miracles of birth, death, and rebirth going on all around us, the universe is an amazing place where things fit and do their purpose everyday without ever complaining.

Now, if you believe in God, I guess this story can solidify your faith. And if you don't believe in God, we can just say that there is a great mystery to life and it is beyond our ability to understand or grasp. But, because of stories like Delaware Bay, we know that something is definitely going on in our universe. And it is all connected!!!

Where is the commander of this order? Have you ever thought about that? Who is the commander? How does all this stuff stay connected in such mind boggling mysteries of connection and coordination. We aren't going to answer those questions in this group, nor are we going to argue about the existence of God. There is a great mystery beyond my comprehension and it may be God or it may be not God. Science gets around the God-Not God argument by calling this the implicate order. Let's leave it at that.

THERE IS SOMETHING I NEED TO DO WHILE I AM HERE. AND IT IS JUST AS IMPORTANT TO THE UNIVERSE THAT I DO MY PURPOSE IN LIFE AS IT IS THAT THE BIRDS AT DELAWARE BAY DO THEIR PURPOSE. IF MY PURPOSE IS LEFT UNDONE, THE UNIVERSE IS INCOMPLETE. THE UNIVERSE NEEDS ME. WITHOUT MY PART, THE UNIVERSE WILL NOT END, BUT A NEGATIVE RIPPLE WILL BE CREATED THAT WILL AFFECT PEOPLE FOR YEARS.

That is essentially the story of Delaware Bay as told on the TV program. But I thought about this further. Birds and Crabs do their purposes automatically. They just listen to that inner voice that is built into them and they do what they should do and they go where they need to go without question.

But you and I are human. A long time ago our brains developed to the point where we could make choices. Not just choices about what shirt to wear today, but choices about whether or not we complete our purpose on earth just like the heroes and bums in our last story.

In a famous story called Genesis from a book called The Bible, the first two humans bit an apple from the TREE OF KNOWLEDGE. When we became conscious of ourselves, the history of human choice began. As we discussed earlier, the choice to eat the apple and to go off purpose put us out of that garden of happiness. We now had to live in a world of opposites where things like evil and death became part of our consciousness.

On that fateful day is when we were given the blessing and the burden of our human condition. Whether we came from apes, or whether Adam and Eve were created by God doesn't matter. You may believe either story. What is important is that you understand that a day arose when we as humans could make the choice to go off purpose. And then we did make the choice. And when it was done, the reality of human existence was born and we had to leave the garden of happiness for a life where we had to make choices every day. Choice is our most cherished gift from life as well as our most terrible burden. We can choose to go off purpose. And we do go off purpose - all of us. We are the heroes and the bums.

I need to be on purpose in my life if I want to be happy. And I need others around me to be on purpose because my life is directly affected by them.

The next morning I picked up the newspaper. I sipped some coffee and I gazed at the morning headlines that showed me just how far off purpose some people have gotten. There were stories of crime, of greed, of corruption and worse. I began to think about this and about the story of Delaware Bay. It dawned on me that if ten birds left Venezuela for Delaware Bay, they would all start flying directly to Delaware Bay and they would arrive on the right day at the right time. They might get blown off course by a storm or one of them might be eaten by a predator, but the bottom line is that they would all be doing their purpose to the best of their ability. Maybe that is why birds seem to be able to sing so happily every morning. They do have a hard life but they don't suffer from guilt or greed and they don't feel guilty or ashamed and feel a need to get so drunk that they become a functional mess.

What would happen, I thought, if ten humans made this trip? Would they all make the choice to arrive at Delaware Bay? How would such a human flight proceed? What would go wrong? What would be the consequences?

Here is what I came up with.

Ten human birds leave from South America for Delaware Bay. It is very important that they all arrive. The universe is counting on these birds to do their part. NO ONE ELSE WILL BRING THEIR INDIVIDUAL CONTRIBUTION AND GIFT.

The flight starts off just fine. They leave right on time, all flying together over the Caribbean. As the birds reach the southern tip of Florida, the first signs that something might go wrong appear. Two birds named Oscar and Wilbur are having a conversation as they fly. It seems innocent enough at first and no threat to the mission. But then, Oscar notices something down below. He looks over at Wilbur and he says, "Hey Wilbur, isn't that the Bird Drop Inn Bar and Grill down there?? Wilbur looks down below and he replies, "It is!"

Oscar thinks for a moment and then says, "I don't suppose it would be a big deal if we stopped in to have a quick shot and a beer, do you?" At first, Wilbur hesitates and thinks about the mission to Delaware Bay. But then the thought of a nice, cold pop to get them through the night sounds quite appealing so he says, "Yes, we can stop in for a quick one. We will still get to Delaware Bay. No harm done to anyone." The two birds start down and leave the pack of ten. As they descend, the other birds call out to them, but Wilbur and Oscar pay no attention to their calls. Down to the Bird Drop Inn they go.

Once inside, Oscar buys Wilbur a shot and a beer. And then, Wilbur buys Oscar a shot and a beer. While they are drinking this second round, they meet a really nice guy named Spike and his girlfriend, Esmeralda. Spike is so nice. He decides to buy a round for everyone. And then, Esmeralda is having such a good time that she buys one for Oscar, Wilbur, and Spike. This goes around all night until the bartender finally says, "I have to close the bar now, folks" Wilbur and Oscar are both quite drunk when they hit the night air. They both immediately pass out in a Palm Tree that is sitting close by.

In the morning, they wake up hung over and they realize they missed Delaware Bay. They are off purpose. At first, they feel sad. Then they feel a bit guilty. Then they wonder what they should do. They realize now that they are sober that it is too late to get to Delaware Bay on the right day. Finally, they just say, "Oh well" and they decide to head back to the bar. Delaware Bay is going to be short two birds. And the Bird Drop Inn suddenly has two steady customers who are seriously off purpose. But at least there are still eight birds on purpose toward Delaware Bay.

Next, two more birds named Topsy and Turvy start to have a conversation. Well Topsy doesn't like Turvy's style or personality. She also hates the way she dresses and does her hair. She starts to call Turvy names. Then she starts giving Turvy dirty looks. Oh my God! Dirty looks!!!

Turvy speaks out in a loud voice. "What are you looking at and what is your &*%#$ problem you $^&$#*." And Topsy then replies, " I don't have a %^&# problem, you ^&%#$." Before anyone in the flock can say a word to stop them, Topsy and Turvy were punching and kicking each other. Turvy ripped out some of Topsy's feathers. Topsy punched Turvy until she bled. They fell right out of the sky toward the ground below. The other birds called out to them that they needed to be in Delaware Bay, but Topsy and Turvy couldn't get beyond their own selfish egos. They both wanted to win this one. They both wanted to be right. To hell with Delaware Bay! They wanted to teach each other a lesson.

And friends, that is exactly what they did. They woke up in the morning all bloodied and tired from fighting all night. The flock was way ahead almost in Delaware Bay. But Topsy and Turvy were not there. They missed it. They were off purpose. They both got so angry when they realized it that they began to fight again. Once again, they exhausted each other as they wrestled and punched. And that is the frustrating story of Topsy and Turvy, two human birds who lived out their lives as miserable, angry beings, both way off purpose.

Well, now we have only six of the ten birds still on course for Delaware Bay. It is beginning to look like the universe is in trouble. These birds are not getting their purpose accomplished. We have two substance abusers and two birds so blinded by their anger that they cannot function to do their purpose.

Well, the other six keep on flying. But now two more birds named Hapless and Hopeless are getting tired of the grind. They are both pretty nice birds but they have had hard lives. And they are feeling a bit depressed about it all. Well, actually they are very depressed about it all. So Hopeless and Hapless decide to drop out of the flight. The other birds call out but Hopeless and Hapless pay them no mind. They land on a branch in the Prozac Tree and they just keep reinforcing each other with statements like, "I hate Flying" and "Who cares about anything". They are not going to be at Delaware Bay. They are off purpose.

The universe is in trouble. An ecological disaster is about to occur at Delaware Bay. There are consequences when we go off purpose. They are not pleasant and they last for years. And they affect a lot of people.

Well, at least there are still four birds heading to Delaware Bay. I mean someone human has to do their part on this earth. We are falling apart.

Two more birds named Slick and Cool are flying along on their way to Delaware Bay. And now, yet another conversation begins to take place. Slick says to Cool, "Hey Cool, I was on the internet the other day. I got some great information. Do you know what, Cool? We don't have to go to Delaware Bay at all. I found a short cut to Canada, Cool, follow me." Cool looks at Slick and he says, "But Cool, weren't we supposed to be in Delaware Bay for some reason?" And Slick replies, "Let these last two fools fly to Delaware Bay. I can get us to Canada in half the time." And Cool finally replies, "Great, let's take your short cut."

There are only two birds left flying to Delaware Bay. They call out to Slick and Cool as they fly off to the northwest. But it is no use. Slick and Cool just laugh at the last two Delaware Bay voyagers. Cool calls out, "See ya, suckas!"

There is just one slight problem that Slick and Cool were unable to foresee. They were both so slick and cool that they forgot to notice that they were flying right over the center of North Dakota in early March. They were almost in Canada. But on the day that would have been in Delaware Bay, Slick and Cool were hungry so they started to look for a place to stop to eat. But all they saw below in all the farmers' fields was about two feet of snow. So Cool, who was now cold, said to Slick, "Hey Slick one! What are we going to eat?" Slick looked down and had a sinking feeling inside of him. He looked over at his friend the cold, Mr. Cool and he said, "I don't know". Cool was shivering and hungry and he yelled out to slick, "You #%^&$%#. We are going to starve out here."

Well, this is a family story so we won't go into the details. But about six weeks later, when a North Dakota farmer was plowing his field, he came upon two dead birds in the middle of his wheat field. They were Slick and Cool. Both had frozen to death. They chose not to go to Delaware Bay and they never made it to Canada either, victims of their own egotistical slickness and coolness.

We are nearing the end of our story. Just two birds landed at Delaware Bay on Delaware Bay Day. Their names were Humble and Grateful. Humble and Grateful ate some of the crab eggs but not nearly enough to save New Jersey. They flew to Canada and they were happy to see their relatives. They told the sad story of the ten birds that had set out for Delaware Bay. They told about all the birds that had chosen to go off purpose. They described the misery and disaster being experienced by the poor people of New Jersey and Delaware who were inundated with crabs which set off a chain reaction of other ecological consequences.

And so now, here I am in Waterbury, CT. I am reading the morning newspaper. The world looks like an evil place. It looks like a messed up place. It looks like an unhappy place.

It doesn't look like anything fits or makes sense most days. It seems to suck no matter what you try to do. Should I even bother to try to do my purpose today? It feels like it will be no use.

I can't speak for you. But I know what I am going to do. I am going to try to stay on purpose in my life. And I am going to forgive myself when I do slip off purpose. I will surround myself with other people who are trying to stay on purpose and we will cheer each other on. And we will forgive one another when someone does go off purpose because someday I am going to need forgiveness for my own faults.

I am responsible to keep myself on purpose, but it means a lot to have you watching out for me. And I am here watching out for you too. It helps.

There is a silent inner voice that speaks to me when I am still enough to listen. There is also an inner clock that is congruent with the clock of all creation. The voice and the clock tell me what to do, what to say, and when to say it. Time will grant me my precise measure of happiness and sadness and joy and desire if I will listen and flow along with the rhythm of my purpose.

So keep an eye out for me and give me a yell when you see me drifting off course. That is what the village is for. You need me to do my life purpose and I need you to do yours. Forgive me when I make mistakes. I am only human. And I will do the same for you.

You can't change me when I go off purpose. But you can reflect back to me what you see. And maybe when you do, you are giving me a chance to right myself and get back on purpose if I have the humility to listen. Your observation and even your confrontation are a gift to me when I am drifting away from my center too far. It doesn't have to be a lonely life even though it does have to be a hard and a sad life at times.

It can be a meaningful and good life if you manage to do your purpose like Humble and Grateful managed to do.

The world is not such a horrible place because evil rules. It is not in horrible shape because life sucks or because nothing fits or has any meaning. It is not life that is messed up.

The world appears to be messed up for one reason and for one reason only -

TOO MANY PEOPLE ARE TOO FAR OFF PURPOSE TOO MUCH OF THE TIME

TOO MANY PEOPLE ARE TOO FAR OFF PURPOSE TOO MUCH OF THE TIME

TOO MANY PEOPLE ARE TOO FAR OFF PURPOSE TOO MUCH OF THE TIME

And that is the story of Delaware Bay.

Character Recognition Exercise

In this exercise, each student in the group is asked to identify with any character they want in the story of Delaware Bay. Review the story briefly and then I will pass the Talking Stick around the circle. If you choose to speak, identify a time in your life when you were one of the birds in the story. Which bird were you? Did you go off purpose? How did you go off purpose? Did you stay on purpose and have to watch someone else who chose to go off purpose? What was that like? There is space to write about this in your journal before we have a discussion.

In your exploration of the times you went off purpose, choose a time when you are like each pair of birds as they flew off purpose in anger, or in a search for substance or escape, or in trying to take some short cut that was ill advised. Let this discussion be lively and animated.

We have all been off purpose. And none of us gets back on purpose until we can own our mistakes. This discussion should not be a somber discussion but a discussion where we all laugh at ourselves for our human propensity to go off purpose.

Finally, see if you can identify character traits that developed in you as a result of times when you were off purpose. People who remain off purpose forever tend to develop very negative, or at least non functional character traits that hold them back. But people who own their mistakes often find that the best character traits that have made them a strong person have actually had their roots in their journey off purpose. Try to relate at least one time when something unpleasant happened which knocked you off purpose at first. Can you identify a strong characteristic in yourself today that was born from your need to face up to something from your past? If you can, then you are identifying a time when a "twist of fate" became a turning point that made you a better person.

Now, try to identify at least one time when you know you were right on purpose in your life. No one in this group has been on purpose or off purpose 100% of his life. We will end our discussion with a warrior's encouragement to stay on purpose and to confront each other in this group when any of us goes off purpose.

Conclusion

If you have begun to rise above the life of consequences by now, and if you have become honest and real in group, and if you are conscious that you came to this earth with a purpose to accomplish for your village, you are now ready to fly to Delaware Bay.

The best way to know whether your life is on purpose or not is to 'listen' to the beating heart. Your purpose is encoded right into your bones. Another way to know whether you are 'on purpose' in your life is to listen to the teacher known as 'Mr. Intention'. If your intentions are open and unselfish, and if you are not trying to force your will on a situation, you are probably on purpose.

We conclude this challenge with encouragement to be conscious of your choices. As group members, it is our job to notice if we see another member off purpose. We care enough to mention what we see. But we have no power over whether our friend actually gets back on purpose. Power is the subject of our next challenge.

QUESTIONS FROM HEROIC JOURNEY CHALLENGE TWO

1. What does it mean to be on Purpose in your life?

2. Describe the activity of African women when they knew someone was pregnant?

3. Why did the African women talk to a fetus?

4. How were you welcomed into the world?

5. Can you describe a time when you felt like the bums on the railroad tracks in the story about Heroes and Bums?

6. Write about a time when you did your purpose perfectly just like the heroes.

7. What gift from the Story of Delaware Bay makes you totally unique as a human being?

8. Why is choice both a blessing and a burden?

9. Which character in the Delaware Bay story do you identify with most? Why?

10. Write about a time when someone you cared for went off purpose?

11. What did it feel like? Did you try to call them back on purpose?

12. Are you doing your purpose in school this year so far?

13. What still needs to get done?

Bridge to Challenge Three

As we move to the next three challenges, we are moving into your formal warrior training.

They will challenge you to do some difficult things, to face life in an honest way with an adult viewpoint. Your relationship to power will be examined. Your relationship to mystery will be examined. You will begin to recognize that the universe has a story. You will begin to explore how your own story is woven right into the bigger story of the universe.

Once your relationship to power and mystery is explored and adjusted, you will be ready to take hold of your story and begin to write it from your own deepest heart. As we examine your relationship to power, you may find that you have not been writing your story. Your story has been writing you. This is another way to say that your relationship to power is not yet mature.

A point of reference for the next three challenges is something called the 12 Steps of Growth. On the following pages the 12 Steps of Growth are presented in their entirety. As we proceed through the themes of the next three challenges, you will come back to study and practice specific steps of these 12 Steps of Growth.

A Warrior's Journey for Teenagers

The Village Is Where I Find

Purpose

Place

Meaning

12 STEPS OF GROWTH

Student Text

Purpose of 12 Steps of Growth

The 12 Steps of Growth are designed to help a student begin the process of experiencing a genuine soulful connection to life in community with others.

This group is committed to helping students find a center or core being. The idea of these 12 steps is to change perception to the point where the search for meaning and happiness is reoriented in the student from an external, material search for happiness to an internal, soulful search for happiness.

The 12 steps also explore the student's relationship to 'power'. As with the search for happiness, the 12 steps seek to change the student's perception of the source of power. This change of perception exposes the external search for power in substances, material, and possession of people or things as illusory. The 12 steps identify the source of power to be at the core or center of one's being.

Finally, the 12 steps identify a door or boundary that protects the center of my being. This door has only a single doorknob with which the door to my central being can be opened. In most students, that single doorknob has been placed on the outside of the door where the external world may open the door and enter at will. This affects my choices and the wellness of my inner being.

During the course of the 12 steps, the doorknob is changed. It is removed from the outside of the door and it is placed on the inside of the door. It reestablishes my boundaries. It also firmly establishes my life as one that is lived from my inner core outward, rather than allowing the external world to dictate control over the person that I am, how I think, and how I feel. Thus, I am alive here and now writing my story, instead of allowing my past story to write me into the useless ruts of my habits of thinking or substance.

These steps are meant to be explored in a group where trust has been established and where each group member finds the courage to explore her own life.

While the 12 Steps of Growth were inspired by the 12 Steps of AA, they are not an adaptation. Rather, they were created specifically to be used with the current program and should not be construed otherwise. A.A., which is a program concerned with recovery from alcoholism, is not in any way affiliated with the program that is the subject of this book

TEACHERS/MENTORS: Specific themes exploring the 12 Steps of Growth are found in the next three challenges. It is suggested that you introduce students to the 12 Steps of Growth on the next page, and then, proceed to Challenge three. You will refer back to each of the individual 12 Steps as you proceed through the next three Challenges.

12 STEPS OF GROWTH

1. I WILL ACCEPT MY POWERLESSNESS OVER ... TODAY.

2. I CAN LET GO OF CONTROL AND I CAN ALLOW THE GREAT MYSTERY TO LEAD ME TODAY.

3. I CAN "GET REAL" AND I CAN "TELL MY STORY" WHEN I AM READY

4. I WILL RECOGNIZE THE ATTACHMENTS I HAVE USED TO TRY TO CONTROL THE WORLD.

5. I CAN BE FREE OF MY ATTACHMENTS WHEN I LET GO AND I TRUST GREAT MYSTERY.

6. ALL I WILL EVER NEED FOR HAPPINESS, I HAVE RIGHT WITHIN ME. I CAN REACH WITHIN TO GET IT.

7. I FORGIVE THE WORLD. I FORGIVE MYSELF.

8. I CAN USE MY BURDEN BASKET WHEN I NEED IT.

9. I WILL BE TRUE TO MY DEEPEST HEART TODAY.

10. I WALK A SACRED PATH. I WALK IN SACRED SPACE.

11. I CAN TOUCH THE WORLD WITH MY LOVE.

12. AS I LEARN TO LIVE IN HAPPINESS, I MAKE A COMMITMENT TO HELP OTHERS IN MY GROUP, IN MY FAMILY, AND IN MY COMMUNITY.

1

I WILL ACCEPT MY POWERLESSNESS OVER ... TODAY.

What do I truly have control over? Am I ready to admit my powerlessness over people, circumstances, and things? What is the price I have paid for not being able to admit my powerlessness? Am I ready to explore this in my group?

It does not take too long to learn that the world abounds with many overwhelming problems. I may have family problems I cannot control. I may have some things that have happened to me that never should have happened to a kid my age.

I am powerless over ...

Worse than this powerlessness is the way it seems so unfair that these things are happening to me. It is not fair. I feel like a victim because all these problems were not my fault.

Today I surrender to my powerlessness over ... I cannot control my family or my friends. I cannot change the past.

This insane attempt to control what I know I can never control has caused me too much pain.

Just being able to admit this powerlessness takes such a load off my back. I wanted to be able to change my father, my mother, my friends, all the things that have happened. But it isn't going to be that way.

2

I CAN LET GO OF CONTROL AND I CAN ALLOW THE GREAT MYSTERY TO LEAD ME TODAY

Admitting my powerlessness means I admit all the things I do not control. It is not easy to do.

But I am not hopeless because now I see that there is a great mystery that I cannot see with my eyes or figure out with my brain. The great mystery has a law. It lives in all the oceans and streams, in all the animals, in every tree in the forest. The great mystery lives in me. It is the voice that gets the birds to Delaware Bay. I trust the great mystery though I cannot explain it. I have felt the great mystery stirring in my group when everyone is listening, when someone is sharing his heart, when we all feel so close.

Great mystery holds all creation in balance. Great mystery holds my life in its infinite wisdom.

If I let go of control and if I trust in the great mystery, I will be in balance with the laws of the universe. I will live within love. I will give love.

I let go of control over ... and I trust the rhythm of the great mystery today.

3

I CAN "GET REAL" AND I CAN "TELL MY STORY" WHEN I AM READY.

Trusting the great mystery and beginning to trust the great mystery that lives in my group frees me to tell my story whenever I am ready. Telling my story gives me a chance to get honest and to free myself of the terrible load I have carried all this way. It can free me from the past and allow me to get on with my life now in the present.

I must first "get real" with myself before I can tell my story. What has happened in my life? When did I get the wound? When did I first feel cut off or alone as a human being? How has it affected me? What mistakes can I own? What's going on with me? What is really bugging me? What does it feel like to be me? If I am brave enough to answer these questions honestly, I am ready to tell my story.

How does my story fit into the bigger story of the universe? Why am I here? What am I supposed to be doing? Where have I been? Where am I going? How am I doing on my life purpose? What is my life purpose?

I will choose the time to tell my story. When I do, it will be from my deepest heart. I will not just tell 'war stories' to impress everyone. I will get real about myself.

I will no longer allow the past and all my feelings to control me. I will get honest with myself. I will also respect others in the group by 'listening' to their stories and letting them know that I understand.

I will get real. I will tell my story. I will set myself free.

4

I WILL RECOGNIZE THE ATTACHMENTS I HAVE USED TO TRY TO CONTROL THE WORLD.

An attachment is something I use to try to avoid just being me. It is something I 'reach out' for to make me feel good for a while because I have forgotten how to feel good by just being me.

All human beings have developed attachments. Today I want to begin to recognize my attachments. Some of the most common attachments according to Wayne Dyer are:

attachments to stuff and to shopping for stuff
attachment to a lover or 'special' person
attachment to the past
attachment to my appearance
attachment to always being right
attachment to money
attachment to winning
attachment to drugs and alcohol
attachment to gambling
attachment to perfection
attachment to failure

There are as many attachments as there are things. They help me avoid my pain. But they also prevent me from just being me.

An attachment always starts out as a way for me to control things and as a way to feel better for a little while. Attachments seem to work so well at first until the day I wake up and find myself stuck in the rut of my attachment. In the end, an attachment always ends up controlling me.

Attachments are very hard to get honest about because it is scary to think about life without them. In fact, I have started to think about my attachment all the time.

5

I CAN BE FREE OF MY ATTACHMENTS WHEN I LET GO AND I TRUST THE GREAT MYSTERY.

My attachments helped me for a while. But now I can feel how they are controlling my life. I want to let them go. What started out as a successful escape from my wound has turned into a form of slavery.

If I learn to trust the great mystery and life's simple law, I will find the strength to let go of my attachments. The great mystery will keep me safe. I have forgotten about the power of the wave my life rides on. I was too busy trying to control the whole world as I thought it should be. I have a purpose and a reason for being alive. I cannot fulfill my purpose and be happy while I am enslaved to my attachments.

Today I turn my attachment to....over to the great mystery. I will allow the great mystery to fill the empty space with truth and love.

6

ALL I WILL EVER NEED FOR HAPPINESS I HAVE RIGHT WITHIN ME. I CAN REACH WITHIN TO GET IT.

My true happiness can only be found within me in my own heart. Here is the key to happiness. It is never selfish to stay true to my deepest heart as long as I know I am not seeking power that is not mine by manipulating people and things.

I have allowed my past to control my present. I am tired of being disappointed that things and other people never make me happy for very long. I want to find my own happiness in my own heart that is mine to keep forever.

Anger, drugs, sex, food, shopping, abusive relationships, perfect relationships gambling, etc. etc. etc. all eventually get out of hand when I make them "attachments" in my life. They come to own me.

I commit myself to my own happiness. I promise to get real, to stay true to my deepest heart, and to listen to the truth of the great mystery in my own heart. My happiness will grow out of this commitment if I am faithful to it one day at a time.

There are many people who will help me if I let them.

7

I FORGIVE THE WORLD. I FORGIVE MYSELF.

The past is gone. Yet, the past will always control me unless I can forgive. Forgiveness does not mean that what another did was okay. It does not mean that I will allow another to continue to hurt me over and over.

Forgiveness is an honest acceptance of the present moment without the baggage of the past or the anxiety of the future. Forgiveness empties the heavy bag of the past I carry on my back every day. Forgiveness trusts the future to the great mystery of life.

The result is awesome potential at my disposal today. I will take care to use that power for the good of my own heart and the good of my village that needs me so much.

Forgiveness simply means that I accept what happened in the past. Even though it hurt me, I let it go so that it can no longer control all my emotions and my actions today. Therefore, forgiveness is freedom. Forgiveness is standing on my spot in this moment in time with the power of the great mystery of life alive in my heart.

I am here now. I am alive. I am safe within the law of great mystery. I am free to get on with my life.

I forgive you...for hurting me and I get on with my life today. If I cannot forgive even one other human on the face of the earth, I will also never be able to forgive myself.

I forgive myself for...and I get on with my life today. I am only human. I have gone off purpose. The sooner I forgive myself, the sooner I can get back on purpose in my life and the sooner I can go back home to my heart where my happiness is.

Forgiveness is the hinge to the door that the key to happiness unlocks.

8

I CAN USE MY BURDEN BASKET WHEN I NEED IT.

The burden basket may be a tiny straw basket. Yet, it is strong enough to hold any problem that gets too big for me. I can put my pain and my trouble in the burden basket and let the great mystery hold it in powerful wisdom.

The Burden Basket adjusts my relationship to power by taking away the unbearable and putting me back in the driver's seat of my present energy and power. Burden basket is the grease that oils the hinge of forgiveness so I am not paralyzed by life and the way I wish it could be.

I will then be free to wait in silence until the great mystery tells me what to do. The message I hear will always tell me to be true to my own heart no matter what the problem. - And to stop trying to control what I cannot control.

If I let go and trust, in the end, all will work out for the best even if it doesn't seem that way to me.

I am grateful for this simple burden basket. I am free.

9

I WILL STAY TRUE TO MY DEEPEST HEART TODAY

My deepest heart is the sacred place within me that is one with the Great Mystery of life. I know my deepest heart when I admit my habitual excuses, when I let go of my attachments, and when I drop my mask and just 'get real' with myself and others.

When I am aware of this very moment right 'now', I know what is going on with me. I can bring my body to stillness and my brain to quiet. I can just feel my feelings and then let them pass. I can then know the real me.

Happiness happens forever every time I stay true to what I know is right in my deepest heart without trying to demand that this world go the way I want it to go.

I can stay true to my deepest heart today. I will. I will ask for help when I feel like I am getting lost. I will listen and wait for the great mystery to show me what to do and what to say.

10

I WALK A SACRED PATH.
I WALK IN SACRED SPACE.

Staying true to my deepest heart is walking my sacred path. Every time I stray off of my sacred path, I go down a pathway that always seems great at first, but ends up being just another 'trail of tears'.

What you have to do today is right in front of you. Pay attention. Don't ask too many questions. Don't stop. Don't try to turn back. Just keep going.

I can only walk my sacred path when I am awake, here and now. I cannot walk my sacred path when I am asleep in the trance of my excuses and my attachments.

I will walk my sacred path today. There are many people who can help me if I ask.

My sacred space was given to me by great mystery. It is my respect for my own heart and my body. It is also my respect for the heart and the body of everyone I meet.

I choose who I will allow to enter my sacred space. I choose what actions of others will be acceptable in my space. I will exclude anyone from my sacred space if they cannot accept me as I am. Anyone who cannot accept the sacredness of my boundaries and respect me for how my heart feels today will only be poison for me in the long run.

11

I CAN TOUCH THE WORLD WITH MY LOVE.

I love when I listen without judgment. I love when I drop my habitual excuses and my masks and I just give my 'real self' to another.

Love is getting involved in life. Love is getting beyond my own little selfish ego. Love is creating a myth my heart can live with. Love is making that myth become real. Today I will find a way to get involved in the mystery of life by finding a place to give my real self, my love, to the world.

Great mystery has a plan for me to accomplish in this life. I will fulfill my simple part in the plan when I am no longer preoccupied with my own little self and my own problems. I will be happier. I will be creating a better world from the one that I grew up in.

I may not see it with my eyes. But my love will touch the world. It is a law.

12

AS I LEARN TO LIVE IN LOVE AND HAPPINESS, I MAKE A COMMITMENT TO HELP OTHERS IN MY GROUP.

As my own life comes together in happiness, I will lead by my example. This is the village way. It is my turn to be the leader. It is my turn to show the new kids that you can own up to your excuses and be responsible for yourself. I will confront others with respect, and I will take the responsibility of being a leader.

I will listen, I will support, I will confront, I will get honest. I will be grateful for my group, for the Great Mystery, and for Life.

Heroic Journey
Challenge #3

Expand My Vision
With a Mature Relationship
To Power

Message to Group Leader:

The next step in the unfolding of a young adult entails the exploration of power and mystery. Each teen has a relationship to power. It is the group leader's job to begin to explore this with each group member. "What do you have control over?" "What must you admit that you have no control over?" This exploration leads into a discussion about faith and its relationship to 'letting go'. The process of letting go requires an acceptance of faith because it also requires an acceptance and willingness to experience deep grief. We are proceeding into very challenging territory for the average teenager. Participants will become very conscious of the fact that this initiation is not a child's game or a warm fuzzy. It requires willingness and courage.

- **Introduction – Welcome to the World of Choices**

  - o The Role of Consciousness in Being Human
  - o The Role of Choice in Being Human
  - o Issues of Power – The Confusion of Opposites

- **Accepting Powerlessness**

  - o Why do I Teach that you are Powerless?
  - o Why do I Teach that you are 'Nobody Special'?
  - o The Butterfly Story
  - o The Squirrel Story
  - o Putting Yourself into the Stories

- **Letting Go: A Leap of Faith**

  - o Clinging to a "Dock of Dysfunction"
  - o Brad's Story
  - o What is "Turning It Over?"
  - o Explaining the Metaphor of the Train
  - o Ways of Relating to Trains
  - o To Ride or not to Ride (the Train)

- **Great Mystery**

  - o The Other "F" Word
  - o The Ocean as a Great Mystery
  - o Shepherds on a Hillside
  - o Black Holes and Quasars
  - o Quantum Mysteries

- **Your Life as a Story**

  - o Elements of Your Story
  - o The Tree of Sorrows – An Acceptance of Loss
  - o Grief Ritual – A Willing Sadness

Introduction

The last challenge asked you to consider that you were sent to earth with a mission to accomplish. Your approaching adulthood is more than just a passage of time. It is a passage in consciousness from a life where your part was to be secure and to be served and to play every day with your friends. Play time is not over, nor will it ever be, but it is time to consider that your life is interconnected with the lives of everyone else around you just like the birds that fly to Delaware Bay. It is time to get more personal in your exploration of how you fit into the bigger story of the universe so that you might begin to bring the gifts you were meant to give to your village. The theme of this challenge is 'earth'. The best way to get in touch with the great mystery of the infinite universe is to make sure you are standing firmly on the ground.

The human reality, whether it is the story of evolution or the story of creationism, is the story of consciousness. Whether human consciousness, which is our ability to be aware of ourselves being ourselves, was created in one fell swoop by God as the creationists believe, or whether it was created over time as the evolutionists believe, really doesn't matter in the grand scheme of your leap to adulthood. You may accept either story-evolution or creation.

The point of this challenge is not to argue about whose story is the correct one, nor is it to praise either religion or science. The purpose of this challenge is to understand that there came a time when humans became conscious. We had the ability to be aware in a way that no other beings could be aware. We could process and control things to certain outcome, and study things in order to attain mastery over them. We had memory and we were able to be very aware of not only the present moment, but the past and the future as well. We could make CHOICES. This is the central issue of human creation or evolution. Arguing about it is silly. There is danger here at this point of human development where choices could be made as we saw in the story of Delaware Bay. When we try to take our personal power trip too far, we get into personal trouble and we go off purpose and hurt the village that needs us so badly.

Well, what does all this have to do with you? The outcome of 'consciousness' has had a tremendous impact on you and me. Once choice was given to us, some humans eventually thought that they knew everything there was to know. Before choice, beings never struggled with issues of 'power'. But your relationship with power needs to be examined now. Passing through the age of consent to adult responsibilities without a clear sense of your relationship to power can be very dangerous.

The story of Adam and Eve is simply the story of the first time that humans used their consciousness and their power of choice to go 'off purpose'. They didn't think they had to follow or pay attention to the laws of nature anymore. They thought they could BE the laws of nature. Once the choice was made to go off purpose in life, a Pandora's Box of opposites was unleashed. It is this tension of the opposites that you and I struggle with everyday of our lives. Choices! Choices! Choices! And every one of them is either on purpose or off purpose.

This human capacity for consciousness and choice is a daily human struggle with power and mystery. Once you are aware of your relationship to power and mystery, you will be aware that you have a story. I have a story too. The universe has a story as well. My story and your story are woven right into the story of the universe. And that is the purpose of this challenge.

In order to create the life story that fulfills your life purpose and makes you happy, you are going to have to examine, and quite possibly adjust, your relationship to power and to mystery.

Whether it was God, or it was not God, who released us to a life of choice, here we are! Your relationship to power and mystery has crucial implications to both your personal happiness and to your survival. Why would you want to waste your days arguing about creation or evolution when both stories take us to the exact same place in human history - the day we had the ability to make a conscious choice about life purpose. We have so much work to do.

Let us begin!

Accepting Powerlessness

Step 1
12 Steps of Growth

Today we are going to explore the first step of the 12 Steps of Growth. Go back and read the step with your teacher. It is about accepting powerlessness in your life.

Why would your teacher want you to accept powerlessness? Isn't it adults' job to build your self esteem? Shouldn't your teacher be trying to make you feel all powerful?

Well, powerlessness is not that exciting to accept but it is the truth. You have power over very little. You can't control the people you love or the ones you hate either. You can't control the things that happen as part of life. You have control of almost nothing besides your own life choices. I am teaching you this because it is the truth. Do you want me to build your self esteem with a snow job or do you want the truth?

Your own personal self esteem is useless if you have no sense about the journey you are on and no sense of purpose and meaning in life. Self esteem cannot be created or manufactured by constant praise. Your teacher is not going to tell you over and over again how special you are. Feeling special is not the solution to your problem. IT IS THE PROBLEM!

After 15 years of being taught that you are special by adults, you now think you are so special that bad things should never happen to you, that you should never be bored, that parents and teachers should serve you, and that you really don't need to work your butt off because you are so special.

Learn this:

YOU ARE NOBODY SPECIAL

If you can't accept this, you are setting yourself up for a lot of disappointment. You are also looking at life as if it owes you happiness. If you cannot begin to accept your powerlessness now, then your warrior training will have to wait for a later time.

Feeling you are someone special has only made you angry every day. How can life ever throw you a curveball? You are special. How can things go wrong in your life? You are special. How can teachers have such big expectations of you? They should be here to serve you. You are special. How can you accept any unfairness in this life? You are special.

If you came to this group and you want to be told you are special every day, you bought the wrong ticket.

Maybe life is not all about you, Screech! Have you ever thought about that? Maybe you are here to just to do your small part and be your humble self so the village can be blessed another day.

Here is a story about what happens when you cannot accept your powerlessness. It is called The Butterfly Story

The Butterfly Story

Recently, I viewed a sporting event at a stadium in Vermont in the late summer. The front of the grandstand was open air. But there was also a roof on the stadium and the sides were enclosed in Plexiglas.

All along the sides of the Plexiglas inside the grandstand were thousands of beautiful monarch butterflies. These butterflies were frantic in their attempts to get free of the grandstand. As a result they were battering themselves into the Plexiglas again and again.

Many lay dead on the ground. In fact, the front of the grandstand was wide open. There was nothing obstructing the butterflies in that direction. But the butterflies were not looking in that direction, so they just went on slamming themselves into the Plexiglas.

They could not understand that freedom lay just a few feet away in another direction. They were stuck in a repetitive action that was causing themselves harm and death. They could not figure out the 'illusion' of the Plexiglas. They could not see that they would never be free as long as they continued to be so frantic and panicked.

Still, the butterflies were frantically involved with the 'universe' of the Plexiglas which was all they could experience while they looked in that direction. As I watched this go on, I first thought to myself how silly and stupid the butterflies were for killing themselves slowly all because they did not know any better. But then, suddenly, something dawned on me. Maybe I was like those butterflies.

I began to relate the actions of the butterflies to my own life. I began to see myself as one of those butterflies banging my own head against the glass to the point of exhaustion and death. I remembered times in my life when I was so unhappy and frantic just like the butterflies. Just like the butterflies, I could not see in the direction where freedom lay - only a short distance away. Like the butterflies, I just went on day after day trying to force my will on the illusion in front of me.

Because of the experience of watching the butterflies, I came to a new understanding of the need to calm down and accept life as it came my way. Accept powerlessness over that which is not mine to control. Open myself to other directions and perspectives that I have been blinded to in my allegiance to my illusion and my dedication to my panic.

This calming down would not only save me from the futility of banging against the glass, it might also afford me the broader vision to see that I could fly free of my nightmare by going in another direction. In some cases, the open area of grandstand was only a few feet away from these frantic butterflies. Slow down. Relax. Look around. Be here. Stop struggling. The truth is right near you, a new vision that will show you the way clear.

I try to remember those butterflies to this very day. When my life gets crazy, when I am trying to force my will on a situation that is not mine to control, I remember to be still, to calm down, and look around. There is another way to look at any situation. There is another way - if I pay attention- freedom and happiness are closer than I may know.

Powerlessness Activity #1

Today we will pass the Talking Stick around the circle. When it is your turn, you will be asked to respond to the following questions:

How has your life been like the butterflies in this story? The butterflies were unaware of the reality of the Plexiglas in front of them. They didn't see it. But it was there and so they literally beat themselves to death trying to go through the illusion that they could fly in the direction that was blocked.

How have you pinged and pinged against the Plexiglas of some issue in your own life? You obviously didn't suffer physical death. However, many people get so frustrated trying force their own will on situations that won't budge that they become like 'dead men walking'.

What must you admit you are powerless over that you have been unwilling to admit powerlessness over thus far in your life? Pick one person you can't change, pick one life circumstance that you can't change, and one thing about life or nature that you can't change.

If the butterflies could have consciously accepted their powerlessness over flying through the Plexiglas, how might things have been better for them?

How could things be better for you if you could begin to accept your powerlessness over some situation in your life?

Now here is another story about powerlessness. Please remember that there is no test on these stories. They are not useful for a test score and they are not written to entertain you. They are only useful if you apply them to your own daily life.

The Squirrel Story

It is a very cold March morning at 6:00 AM. I am sitting down for my quiet time before leaving for school. The portable heater is running in my Plexiglas enclosed deck while I am getting ready for school. When I am ready for school, I go out onto the deck and sit quietly. The March wind is blowing and it is freezing outside. Spring may be around the corner, but that is not evident today at all. I notice a squirrel in the highest branch of an oak tree in my yard. He is sitting with his head buried in his furry tail which is wrapped around his tiny body. I am struck by this vision. All I can think is how cold it is outside. I cannot help but wonder how the squirrel survives in such frigid conditions.

I close my eyes and sink into the peacefulness of the silence. This is the way I begin each day before going to school. After about 20 minutes, my eyes open. It is time to leave for school. Before I get up, my eyes look back to the branch where I saw the squirrel. He is still there. But something has changed. I notice that the sun has risen just above the horizon since I closed my eyes. I also notice immediately that the first place in my yard that the sun has cast its warming light is right there on the very branch where the squirrel is sitting. Now his tail is unraveled. His face is held up pointing toward the sun. It is still very cold. but it feels like he is grateful for the sun.

Next, I realized that the squirrel knew where to wait for the sun. Even though his IQ was far inferior to mine, he knew where to sit to wait for the sun. I further realized that I would not have had the presence and wisdom to wait on that branch like the squirrel. I know where I would have been on that frigid morning - running in circles on the ground angry and cursing the life of a poor squirrel.

The squirrel story was just like the butterfly story except in this case the squirrel was in his natural surroundings without a human illusion blocking his perception. The squirrel knew just what to do, where to go, and how long to wait.

It was cold. He accepted the cold in his limited squirrel wisdom. He found the branch and he understood the patience that was required. He did not struggle or demand the situation be anything other than what it was. Sometimes, you and I need this squirrel wisdom.

Powerlessness Activity #2

As we pass the Talking Stick during today's group, answer the following questions:

Can you remember a time when you needed to find the branch and patiently wait for the sun like the squirrel? What was the situation? Did you handle it as well as the squirrel?

What does acceptance of powerlessness have to do with patience? Do you lose your patience often? Talk about it in group.

What does acceptance of powerlessness have to do with freedom and happiness?

Make up a story about what the squirrel's day would have been like if he didn't have the patience to wait on the branch.

Conclusion

Step 1 of the 12 steps is now completed. It is a crucial step for you not only to understand, but to apply to your daily life.

If you choose to live your life frantic like the butterfly, you will never slow down enough to see that you are beating yourself against a wall of glass that will not be moved no matter how panicky or frantic or violent you may get.

If you can find the patience of the squirrel during hard times, the sun will rise and shine on you in due time. Slowing down, accepting your situation, and having patience before you act are skills that are hard to learn without the next ingredient. Next, we are going to explore your relationship to faith. That relationship becomes crucial to your successful acceptance of your powerlessness.

Letting Go: A Leap of Faith
Step 2
12 Steps of Growth

You may have noticed as we studied and practiced Step 1 of the 12 Steps of Growth that your task was not to do anything about the fact of your powerlessness. The task of Step 1 was simply to "accept" the fact of your powerlessness. If you were able to do that and apply the lesson to your own life, you have taken a huge step on the road to becoming an adult in the community. "Accepting" powerlessness is a very formidable task. Why? It is a difficult task because you are admitting that you are vulnerable.

Vulnerability is a very difficult fact to live with once you have the wound. After all, you get this wound because you left yourself open to vulnerability. As children then move from childhood to adulthood, an inability to live with powerlessness and vulnerability leads to disabilities be they learning problems; emotional issues; or behavioral flaws.

Inability to live with powerlessness leads directly to bullying behavior for some. For others, it leads to denial which opens us to a whole array of symptoms. Even a compulsion to perfection comes from not being able to accept powerlessness. Maybe the student in our school who gets an 'A' in every class every time and who never has a single discipline infraction for four years of high school is not as healthy as we think she is.

The first step challenged you to accept life exactly as it is, even if the truth is not all that pleasant to view from the branch where you are sitting.

As difficult as it is to accept powerlessness, it is not nearly as difficult as the next step which asks you to 'let go' of the things and people you cannot control. Go back to the page where Step Two is located and read it with your teacher in group. If you have an initial response or reaction after reading this step, please share it with your group. Your teacher will spend time working on this step with you.

Letting go: The Relaxed Fist

What makes it so hard for people to let go? Once it becomes obvious to you that you are powerless over all these people and things, shouldn't it also be obvious that you should let go since you can't control things and people you are powerless over?

Unfortunately, letting go is neither obvious nor easy to master for the average human being.

First, let's see why it is not obvious. Letting go is like untying your boat from the dock and trusting that the boat will be okay. Maybe your life really sucks where you have it docked right now, but at least you are familiar with your surroundings here and at least you feel safe in this predictable situation.

Second, letting go is like trusting that the ocean is your friend. The ocean is beautiful and powerful, but it is also dark and deep and even destructive at times.

This is why some of us remain tied to the dock of our misery and dysfunction year after year. We do long for happiness and freedom - but on the other hand - the mystery of the unknown beyond the horizon of our dock of dysfunction is just too frightening to chance.

So, while it should be obvious to untie our boat from this decaying and rickety dock, quite often we find ourselves frozen in place. Some people stay moored to this dock even when it falls into such disrepair that they stop functioning as human beings. Some people die clinging to the dock rather than ever taking the chance to let go and become vulnerable again.

Brad's Story

Brad is a guy I met at a 12 step meeting. I met him at a time when I was very skeptical about 12 step meetings and what they could possibly have to do with my life.

I was not a person who wanted to deal with, much less accept, the first step which is to admit my powerlessness over what I cannot control. I had always thought that, just because my intentions were good, I should also have the power to control situations for the good. This led my 'control' centered mind down some addictive roadways. This story was the beginning of my healing and my return to a happier life.

I had been to 12 step meetings before in my life but I rarely returned for more than a single meeting. I saw these meetings as indicators of weakness. I felt I didn't need what was offered. But this time, my life was in a place where I knew I needed to stay and see this through, or I was going to die. So I stayed. I wanted to leave – but I did not. I was a reluctant squirrel and life had finally cornered me into a place where I had to sit on the branch. And there, quite unexpectedly, I met a man named Brad who changed my life forever.

I remember the first time I heard Brad talking. He had a chronic eye disease. The doctor had told him that there was one more thing to try in combating the disease. After that, Brad would go blind within a short time. Brad told this story in a meeting very calmly stating, "I have no control over this so I just 'turned it over."

I thought he must be telling a lie. All I could think about was how unfair it was for something to be happening to this guy. He had quit drinking. He was a productive human being. IT IS NOT FAIR. IT IS NOT RIGHT. That was my mentality. How could this guy be so calm and 'turn it over'. To me, it seemed he must be just snowing us over with this calm 'ok' appearance. It was all just a false show.

My skepticism was now at an all time high. But Brad was sitting directly across from me so I kept looking at him. I could not help but see and feel that he really was at peace. And then it dawned on me. "Oh my God, He turned it over". There was no doubt about it. Brad was not angry. He was not upset in any way. He was going with the flow of life as it was dealt to him. He turned it over!!!

After the meeting, I walked up to him and asked him how he "turned it over." He looked at me and he said, "I didn't do it out of any great nobility. It's just that there's a f#**# train coming through. And I have to get out of the way."

That one simple statement changed my whole life. It was as if Brad had walked up to me and slapped me so hard in the face that he woke me up from 15 years of sleep. It was as if I was so educated out of books that I had forgotten the simple fact that I shouldn't be standing on these train tracks night after night..

One evening as I sat in silence, I had a vision of myself. I was a good man. But each evening, I would jump on the train tracks. I always saw the train coming. I was not a stupid man. Yet, foolishly, I would put my hand up and I would demand that the train stop as it came hurtling down the track. Each night the train would come through and run me down. In the morning I would be devastated. I was so angry that life seemed so unfair. I was a good man and if the train would only stop for me, I could be a happy man too. I couldn't accept that this kind of train does not stop for anyone. The next night I would get on the tracks again. Again, I would stand on the tracks and raise my hand to stop the train. Again, the train would come through and run me down.

No wonder, I have been so angry and depressed my whole adult life!

Finally, after my conversation with Brad, one evening as I sat by the railroad tracks, I tried to listen in silence for the wisdom in my heart. I just couldn't take it anymore. Something had to give. I heard a small inner voice speak to me very clearly through the silence. The voice was not a real voice but just an inner knowing that came to me and spoke to me softly just like the voice that helps the squirrel find the right branch in my backyard.

That voice said very clearly but gently, "Don't get on the tracks. Don't get on the tracks. Don't get on the tracks."

And that has made all the difference in the world.

What is this "Turning it Over"?

Brad used a metaphor in his story. He used the metaphor of the train to represent all those things in his life he was powerless over including his impending blindness. When Brad was wise enough to get out of the way of the train, it was his way of saying, "There is nothing I can do about this so I may as well let go and trust where my life is taking me right now because I can't do anything to change this. Brad trusted that a higher power knew what was best, even though he did not like it.

To try to deny or rage against his present reality would be to stand in front of a train that would not be stopped. Why accept it? He accepts it because the train is going to rumble through whether he likes it or not. If he did not get off the train tracks, he would be knocked down. If he got knocked down, he would be very angry or very depressed.

The rage and violence and abusiveness or the addiction or the paralysis and inability to go on would soon follow. If you can't let go on your own as an adult, you will have to find an addiction to help you let go for a while.

The train will not stop for you. When you are grown up enough to see it coming, you should get off the tracks like Brad. And learn to live with the truth even when it is not too pleasant.

The alternative is even less pleasant. You get hit by a train and you find yourself in the victim stance feeling so sorry for yourself and wondering why someone as special as you should have to deal with reality like an adult.

So the point of all this is simple. Can you find the courage it takes to 'let go'? Brad 'turned it over' to the great mystery of life. He trusted enough to accept the truth and just let it be.

Many people ask me what happened to Brad. And the truth is that I do not know. All I know is that he was at peace with himself and at peace with the world whatever happened. Brad decided to move to Ohio where his daughter lived so he would have her support.

So then, Brad is a man who walked into my life for a one time meeting. He said something at that meeting and helped me see something that I had been blinded to my whole life. He was a 'twist of fate' in my life. Brad gave me the gift of vision, even as he himself was going blind, and then he disappeared.

Although I know he was a real flesh and bone human being, it often feels like he was an angel that appeared in my life. He helped me see I should not be standing in front of the train. And then, he was gone as quickly as he had appeared. He changed my life.

Ways of Relating to the Train

- Stand in front of the train and demand it stop for you
- Get out of the way of the train when you see it coming through
- Try to be the train as if you think you are god
- Learn to ride the train and be grateful for what you've got
- Ignore the train and just stand on those tracks
- Avoid the train and the tracks altogether. Become an observer rather than a doer

To Ride or Not to Ride (the Train)

I have good news and bad news about learning to ride the train. The bad news is that some people refuse to board the train for a lifetime. The good news is that you can never miss the train. You can never miss this train because this train never ends. It is always rolling through. You choose to ignore it, to stand in front of it, to stay away from it, or to ride it. All you have to do if you want to ride the train is choose to get on board.

Do the written entries about relating to the train in your workbook. If you are not using the workbook, refer to the questions at the end of this challenge before using the talking stick to discuss how you relate to the train in your daily life. Your teacher will help you get started.

Great Mystery

What is this great mystery stuff in the second step of the 12 steps of growth? Is this about God? Why not just say 'let go' and let it go at that?

First, let me explain why the great mystery has been inserted into this step. Later, we will try to explain the great mystery by explaining why we can't explain the great mystery. As for God, we will just have to leave him out of this whole mystery discussion all together since this curriculum might be used at a public institution.

The great mystery has been inserted into this step because letting go is the most courageous thing you will ever do in your adult life. In fact, on the final day of your life on earth, you will be finding the courage to let go of your earth mooring in order to sail across the border to the ocean of death. Sorry, I didn't mean to scare you - but I said I was going to tell the truth in this curriculum.

Death is just another day when that old train will come barreling through - and you will find the courage to get out of the way at the right time for you.

So it is also true with all the other times the train will come through during your life. Each time you let go and get out of the way, you are inviting and accepting a little death - something you must let go of - some loss that must be accepted. It takes a lot of adult skills to know when to get out of the way of the train. But it also takes more than skills. Skills and information and knowledge are not enough when you have to move off the tracks and let go.

First, you realize there is a train. Next you become conscious about how you relate to it. Finally, you become mature when you learn to 'ride' the train of life no matter what it might present you with in life.

The Other "F" Word

You all know that you should not use the "F" word at school. It is not acceptable. There is another "F" word that has come to be barely ever uttered at school. The other "F" word is 'faith'.

It is now time to present this word to you. This is the "F" word we are going to bring back to school right now. Since we have stopped exploring and encouraging faith both in school and in everyday life, we have found an explosion of problems, especially in youth.

The truth is that very few human beings could ever find a way to do the second step of warrior training without faith. This is the reason few people know how to 'let go'. Nor do they find the courage to let go anymore. It is just too scary without faith. Why?

In order to let go at one level of life, you need to see that it is safe to do so. Human needs begin with security. Security comes even before food. When the birds land at my birdfeeder, before they take even a single grain of food, they twist their necks back and forth to make sure that no predator is close by. Once they feel secure, then they take a bite of food. So it is with us. We need to feel secure before we will take an action as bold as letting go of what we cannot control.

In order to finish the education of becoming an adult, you need to work out your relationship to power. You need to accept what you are powerless over. In order to straighten out this relationship with power, you need to let go. And finally, in order to find the courage to let go, you need security. Faith is another word for security.

Faith is having a secure sense of center and a secure sense of ground that is firm beneath your feet. If you don't have a center and a ground, you can't let go. In order to let go, you need balance. Balance requires a relationship both to ground and to center. This relationship to ground and to center is faith.

Faithless schools have become failing schools full of ungrounded, unbalanced, and unfocused students labeled with all the currently popular adolescent diagnoses.

Teachers try every new technique known to man, but the attention deficit goes unabated because the deeper problem in education has never been teacher technique. Schools have become soulless and faithless. There is a poverty of community. Student apathy results from the meaninglessness that is spawned in this atmosphere. Administrators praise teachers for surgically precise data informed lessons while somehow failing to see how turned off the kids are to this. Teachers are taught that students are 'consumers of education' instead of youth in need of initiation. If students are 'consumers of education', then we have been in a recession in education for the past 50 years – because school has become the mall – and our 'consumers' are drifting from store to store but they just aren't buying much.

Stop for a moment and voice the ways your life has become meaningless in our modern society.

If I do not teach you about faith while you are in high school, I cannot help you complete your education. You cannot become a healthy and properly educated adult until you have a healthy relationship to power. I can only fill your heads with more and more information. Without faith and a healthy relationship to power, that information will not be useful except to encourage further imbalance and to confuse you even more about your purpose and your place and your true identity.

Your teacher must be able to give you the needle of wisdom before he sends you out to the haystack of information on the internet. That was a message from a man named Huston Smith. When we send kids out to the haystack to find the wisdom we should be giving to them first, they never find it and they only get more lost out there. Or worse yet, they are taken in by all the misinformation and lies that can be found out there.

If you want to find the courage to let go and have a healthy relationship with power, you are going to need the greater vision of faith. You need a center and a solid grounding and a balance.

Faith is the tiny needle of wisdom you need before you get lost in the haystack of information. I am going to teach you about faith because without it the path of your education is blocked by a loss of meaning causing a serious educational disability. Diagnosticians label this as one of our current popular diagnoses for teens. Faith is a better way.

All the teacher techniques in the world practiced perfectly every day still cannot provide the missing ingredient in education. The missing ingredient is passion. Passion is only ignited by soul in a community that is grounded, centered, and balanced in a very conscious way that is recognized by every teacher and every student every day. Without it, I am afraid it will be another year of poor test scores and data analysis for teachers along with more another boring year of school for you.

Teaching Faith

These themes and stories will not deal directly with either religion or God. If you want religion or God, this is not a bad thing. But you must go find them somewhere else. If you do believe in God already, these themes will not interfere or mess with whatever your conception is about God. If you are an atheist, these themes are designed to stretch your ability to see without ever questioning or challenging your beliefs about not God. So, then, these themes on faith are about vision, not religion. I am going to try to give you the vision that Brad gave to me. Let me give you an example.

The Ocean as a Great Mystery

The ocean is a great mystery. The oceans are mysteriously connected to the moon through the tides. The ocean is beautiful and blue. It is also dark and deep and full of mysteries we can sense but cannot fully understand. The waters of the ocean are what gave birth to life.

Without the ocean, there would be no life. The salt content in the water of your mother's womb had the same salt content as the waters of the ocean. The ocean incubates life and sustains life. The ocean is also an energy that can be seen through the waves. The unseen energy that powers the waves causes visible ripples.

The same energy powers my life. My life rose up out of this power just like a wave. The wave is just the visible manifestation of the power, but it is not the power. We cannot see the power but we know it is there.

So ocean is part visible particles of water and also non visible energy that powers and creates waves. There is a lot more about the ocean, but I have made my point. Science can continue to study the ocean forever and it will never find all the facts and all the connections to you and me and the moon and the universe. The knowledge that we accumulate eventually disappears into mystery, a great mystery that we can feel in our bones and that science can hint at and that it can point us towards, but that we can never completely figure out or have power and dominion over.

All the knowledge is so vast that it can never be contained. At some point in education, science must intersect with poetry and imagination. The ocean is a great mystery.

Much like the Delaware Bay Story, the metaphor of the ocean is all about connections. When you understand that your life is connected to things both seen and unseen then you are in a place where faith can be born. The ocean is full of connections of the visible ocean at surface level to the invisible ocean at a deeper level beneath the scope of my naked eye. Understanding that there is a lot you don't see no matter how smart you are is very important to the development of faith.

So, my perspective on the ocean acknowledges a visible aspect at surface level; an invisible aspect consisting of microscopic realities unseen by the human eye as well as invisible creatures and realities deep down in the depths of the ocean far beyond the scope of my surface vision. In addition, the ocean also presents a non visible aspect in the power that creates the waves. We will briefly discuss the non visible aspect next.

Looking at the Night Sky

Here is another story about the great mystery and about how science intersects with poetry and imagination at the point where science's facts disappear into the hazy unknown. The ocean metaphor was about visible and invisible phenomena that make up the ocean and its mystique. The next story deals with the non-visible. Invisible things are there in front of you but cannot be discerned with the naked eye or with the brain at the surface level. Many of the ocean's mysteries had to be discovered by science since we could never see all these mysteries at the limited vision of a surface viewpoint. Invisible connections are deeper than the apparent surface visibility.

However, non-visible phenomena are even more mysterious. Non-visible phenomena are not apparent to the human eye and also not understandable by science either. We call these realities non visible because materially, they are not there. Instead of the ocean we are going to look at the night sky this time in our exploration of the non-visible.

Science does not acknowledge the non visible. You will have to go to poetry and imagination and your own 'bones' to 'feel' it. God would be part of the non visible world if we could talk about him, but we can't so we won't. What we will talk about is the ability of humans to have 'gut feelings' and to sense things that can't be proven or seen. Have you ever heard anyone say, "I just have a gut feeling about this"? Have you heard the expression, "I can feel it in my bones". If you have heard these statements or made them yourself, you were paying attention to the non visible world.

Shepherds on a Hillside

Try to imagine a time before cars and electricity and cell phones and air conditioners and airplanes and cable television. Back in the days of the village, none of these things were present. The villagers back then had an acute sense of how much they needed one another. This was because the village back then had to be self subsistent. This means that whatever they had and whatever they wanted had to be produced right there.

When you went to buy a pair of shoes, you actually knew the guy who made the shoes. You knew how important that guy was and how much you needed him. You could not just go to Wal-Mart and buy some shoes that were made by someone on the other side of the world. Your shoemaker was your neighbor. When you ate some food, you knew the people who were growing the food for the village and you knew how much you needed them. When a baby was born, you understood that the baby was going to arrive with a gift to bring to the village. Some need was going to be fulfilled by the birth of that child. The baby was more than cute and cuddly. She was a vessel that needed to be cherished in order to bring out the gift that the village needed so badly.

The same was true for all the rest of your daily needs. Everything had a connection and you were acutely aware of how important each person was to you. The village had a center where all of these connections were nurtured. At the center, all the people would gather to celebrate, to discuss plans of action and political issues, to grieve and to mourn.

We don't seem to have a center to the village anymore. If you go down to the downtown green in my city today, you will find homeless people pushing carriages full of everything they own. The homeless person carries his entire universe in that shopping cart. He is disconnected from everyone and everything. No center is a sure sign that a village has lost its sense of connection and faith.

One of the most important jobs back in the days of the village was the job of shepherd. I am not talking about a German Shepherd dog. I am talking about the guys whose job it was to guard the flocks all night long on the hillsides on the edge of the village. These guys were very important to the village. They guarded the sheep from predators all night. The village needed the flocks in order to provide clothing and food. Thus, shepherd was a very important job.

Being a shepherd was not the most exciting job on earth. It consisted of sitting still all night on the hillside. The shepherds never went to high school or college like us. They did not have a sophisticated science background like us.

Think about being on one of those hillsides all night long. The shepherds had no cell phones, no video games, no television or laptop. They just sat on the hillside quiet all night listening to the beating heart. As they sat there, they would gaze up into the vast night sky at the millions of stars that were visible. Back then, there were no city lights. The sky was filled with so many visible stars that in many areas they seemed clustered like clouds of stars stretching on forever. If you have ever been out west in the desert at night far from all cities, you have seen the beauty of the night sky that I am referring to in this story.

Well, it came to be that the shepherds would sit on the hillside with nothing to do but listen to the beating heart. As they sat there all night, they began to tell stories to each other as they gazed at the night sky and wondered where all the stars came from. The very constellations that we recognize today in astronomy originally came from the imagination of these uneducated shepherds as they gazed at the night sky.

There was little communication back then between villages. It was the time when you had to literally send a 'runner' to bring a message to the next village. If there was another village just 100 miles away from you, you might live your whole life and never know the other village was there.

But it came to be during these times that shepherds all over the world were gazing at the night sky and wondering the very same things: Who are we? How did we get here? How did the stars and the moon and sun get there? What is going on? Whatever it is, it is big, really big! And it is obviously all connected.

Joseph Campbell who studied the stories of different cultures and villages around the globe made the astonishing discovery that the stories that people made up to explain their origins and the mystery of life were very similar even though these cultures were thousands of miles apart and the people had no way of communicating. None of the stories was exactly the same, but they all had a basic root to them. Here is an example of a story that might have been told by shepherds in a typical village.

In the beginning, the shepherds imagined that there was nothing at all, but then they told a story about how a great explosion occurred from the empty void that flung all the stars across the night sky. The stars were very much connected and they were telling a story. When the shepherds began to see the constellations, it was their way to see that all the stars in the night sky had connections that were mysterious. The stars were related to one another and they were interacting together.

The shepherds had no scientific facts. They were simply in the presence of the beating heart and they looked up at the night sky with the wonder of the poetic and imaginal eye and they 'felt things in their bones' and they got 'gut feelings' about what was going on.

The 'gut feeling' and the 'feeling what is in your bones' and the imagination are all part of the non visible world.

Because they lacked education and a lot of factual information, the shepherds were very much in touch with these non visible elements to their lives. They respected the non visible phenomena very much even though they couldn't see it or prove it. They looked at the night sky honestly and simply and in the presence of the beating heart. They 'felt' the night sky 'in their bones'.

Why am I telling you all this? What does it have to do with growing up in America in the 21st century? What does it have to do with our group? And what does it have to do with faith?

I am about to read you some scientific facts along with some scientific theories that are a long way from proven, but still, show much evidence to being true. These items are taken from a book written by a scientist named Brian Swimme. This is the scientific story that has evolved after years and years of scientific research and study. Here we go.

We are on the planet earth, eight light minutes from the sun. The sun is a million times bigger than the earth. Our solar system resides in the Milky Way Galaxy which is 100,000 light years across. At the center is a BLACK HOLE.

Our solar system revolves around the center of the black hole at the center of our galaxy every 225 million years.

Andromeda Galaxy is two million light years away from our galaxy. Both Andromeda Galaxy and our galaxy, the Milky Way, have galaxies circling around them. Some galaxies thousands of light years part seem to be pin wheeling in a manner that suggests they are connected in some way.

Einstein's revelation was that the universe is expanding and that it must have all come from a certain point. Before that, there was emptiness which was cracked open by the big bang. The big bang was potential realized and we are embers in the explosion.

The universe is expanding infinitely and it is all moving away from one central point at the speed of light. The big bang is ongoing. This means that the big bang did not actually happen millions of years ago. It is still happening right now and we are still in it. The big bang is a story and we are in it.

If the movement of these super clusters of stars is reversed by scientists, they all come back to a single place and point in time. Everything came from this central point, or singularity. In our group, we call this point the center of the stone. Just like the universe has a center that tells a story of purpose, so inside my heart there is a spark that is waiting to break open the stone to release the energy to do my life purpose. And it is all intimately connected in very mysterious ways that can never be completely uncovered by science. The mystery can be felt at times. And it can be expressed by poets or artists.

Scientific Theory now fully entertains this idea of a "Big Bang" or explosion that occurred out of this empty central point. The universe is the result of that explosion as the galaxies and stars and solar systems and planets like earth are all part of that original explosion. The universe we live in was flung across the new frontier of time and space where our earth eventually took its place as the 'third rock from the sun'. And here we are now. And there were the shepherds on the hillside so many years ago. All of us are riding at the speed of light in a non visible spark of energy at the heart of being.

Science was thousands of years coming up with these theories about how we got here. Tremendous effort and time went into the lives of many great men of which Einstein was only one. All that research all these years, and the final theory they have come up with matches the basics of the imaginal story that those shepherds told each other all those years ago.

The shepherds listened to the simple beating heart in silence and they felt the night sky in 'their bones' and they got 'gut feelings' about what the story of the universe was about. They came very close to the same story that science is now pondering and trying to prove. This is the great mystery. There are connections that I cannot see or prove, but can only imagine. I have just taken your education way beyond the tight constrictions of data analysis into the open space of wonder and awe. Wonder and awe are where soul can be created and where passion can be reignited in the young. Our public schools will never rise from the dead until wonder and awe are given prominent attention that is at least equal to the current obsession with data and its analysis. Modern education has become stuck in a world of unrealized potential and unused energy that leaks daily.

So, what does this story have to do with faith? And what does it have to do with letting go? Well, let's leave it at this. Something is going on. And it is big, really big. And it is all connected and each particle and wave of energy within it is connected to the mystery of it all. And I am in it. I have a part to play in it. I am not an isolated accident in this story. The universe is a story. And I have a part to play in the story. It is my job to get passionate and burn my ember in the big bang of my earth walk.

Faith is when I stop seeing my own life as an isolated and separate thing. Faith is when I realize the story of the universe is the story of me. Faith is when I realize that this story of the universe has the energy of a train that will not be stopped. Faith is when I realize that I have been given the gift to write my own chapter in the story of the universe. I am free to join the glorious story of life in time as a part of the universe, or to write my own personal, egotistical story that fights the train. The train will thunder through to its destination. Faith is choosing to get off the tracks. Faith is a story where I learn to let go and to ride the train.

Faith Activity

As we pass the Talking Stick today, talk about what you think faith is. Did you ever have faith? Did you lose it? Do you have it now? What is faith?

Why is faith so important for letting go? Are you aware of the things in your life that you need to let go of? Are you aware that you have a seat reserved on the train of the universe? Will you take your seat and do your part? Or will you do your own thing and act as if the universe is all about you and what you think and want today?

Will you let go to the movement of the great mystery? Or are you going to live your life trying to manipulate and control people and things that are beyond your control?

How has your life worked so far? Where are you now in relation to the train? Are you riding the train? Are you on the tracks with your hand up trying to stop the train? Are you out of it all together trying to ignore the tracks and the train and the purpose of your life? Are you out smoking bones instead of the warrior's work of 'feeling what is in your bones"?

Infinity

In the next section, we are going to explore the relationship of infinity and faith. We are going to look at science as it has explored the topic of infinity in relation to black holes and quasars that are found in the universe. Remember our own reality here on earth is revolving around a black hole at the center of our Milky Way galaxy. So, our lives are very much related to the black hole.

A black hole is life disappearing back into emptiness or formlessness. Could there also be a black hole at the center of you where your body will disintegrate and your formless energy will make a mysterious passage to an unknown place. Ancients called this place 'the other side'.

Infinity extends outward from the empty point of centrality or singularity that was the big bang. It is forever expanding as I write this. It is forever expanding? Now that takes an imagination for the non visible!

We are also going to look at something called quantum physics which is the study of the tiniest particles of matter and the tiniest sparks of energy that science is able to study. The scientists studying quantum physics have also discovered that infinity does not only disappear outward away from us forever, it also disappears inward inside of us forever. So infinity does not only extend outward, it also extends inward.

We seem to be woven into an awesome tapestry. There could be another whole universe right on the tip of my finger. Now that takes an imagination for the non visible world!

Faith understands that it all has no beginning and it all has no end. You and I have no beginning and no end! Am I talking about God now? Damned if I know! So, let's leave him out of this since we are in school and let's just keep going with our exploration.

Black Holes and Quasars

I am holding up a picture of a galaxy. Notice how it seems to be spinning around a bright center. The center is a black hole? Why is the center so bright if it is a black hole? It is bright because as matter is sucked into the drain of the black hole, it gets very hot and it starts burning.

Now if there is a black hole at the center, and if it is being filled with matter that is spinning down the drain of the black hole, shouldn't there be a bottom to the hole where a lot of dead junk resides from the galaxy? It would seem that way.

But the truth is scientists can't find the bottom of the black hole. It is not there. Matter gets sucked into the black hole and it is gone!!! Where does it all go? It is a mystery. Could it possibly be the same empty or formless place that caused the big bang in the first place?

As we gaze into the rest of the infinity of the universe, scientists have also discovered something called 'quasars'. Quasars are like the opposite of a black hole. They seem to be bursts of pure white light, of energy exploding outward from a somewhere. Well, like the black hole, the quasar seems to have no point of origin. It just explodes out of the emptiness much like the inside of the black hole just disintegrates back into emptiness..

I am not a scientist. I am a storyteller. I am creating a myth by which teenagers can build soul. I ask scientists reading this to forgive any technical error in relation to strict scientific research. The black hole is a mysterious descent into certain death. But when we look inside the hole, there is no death to be seen. A quasar is a mysterious birth of energy pushing its way outward into our visible world of matter. But where does it come from? It is not to be seen.

Infinity is the subject of this story. It is an infinite universe? Infinity either exists or it doesn't. Science overwhelmingly agrees right now that it does exist. So if nothing ever ends, where does dead stuff go? The truth is held by the black hole. I don't know where it goes, but it goes somewhere. There is nothing dead inside the black hole. Life just moves on through it.

There is nothing there to bury in the heart of a black hole. Material sucked into the black hole is not dead because it is not there. IT IS GONE! The death of the black hole is an illusion. You and I never end. The black hole is a bridge. The story goes on and never ends. Death seems to just disappear into a non visible world that we just can't see from here. And life bubbles up out of some unseen emptiness into our universe just as mysteriously.

Maybe the visible and non visible worlds are connected in a mysterious equation. An equation has an equal sign. When something passes over the equal sign into the other side of reality, then maybe something from the non visible side needs to bubble up on this side of the equation. Something arrives here out of seeming nothingness. But it is an infinite universe so it has to arrive from somewhere because infinity is everywhere. It just seems to bubble up from a non visible place that is there but cannot be understood or measured. But it is there.

So in this infinite vision, neither birth nor death really exists. What if the black hole of the visible universe is nothing more than a birth canal into quasars of another side I can't see, a non visible energetic side of life? And what if the quasar in this universe is nothing more than the material birth point from the canal of a black hole from an energetic universe I can't see from here? What if our most prolific scientific facts disappear into a dream that never ends?

What exists is transformation from visible to non visible along with transformation from non visible into visible. Energy keeps transforming itself into matter and matter transforms to energy.
The point in between matter and energy is the great mystery of life.

How is all this movement being powered and directed and by whom? That is the great mystery of life. It is a mystery because I can't prove any of this. I am like the shepherd on the hillside now using my imagination. Gazing at the stars and imagining the story in my bones.

If you are learning to gaze with wonder and awe right now as you learn, you will see that the purpose of your life is embedded and encoded right inside the empty potential of your soul. Helping you to break open the stone is to unlock this potential and to put it into the motion that is required by your life purpose.

Have you ever heard anyone speak about a near death experience where a person actually dies but then is resuscitated? All of these people tell similar stories when they come back. The story goes something like this - "I felt myself going down a long black tunnel. Then, I saw a very bright light in front of me and I wanted to move toward the brightness." Well, it sounds like sliding down a black hole toward a quasar of pure energy to me.

What about the day you were born? It is a very similar story. You were in one world one minute, then you started to slide down a black hole. You were actually dying to the world of your mother's belly. As you slid down the black hole, you saw a bright light. Someone was here to greet you when you moved into the light of your earth life.

Faith understands the story of the universe is also the story of me. Living my personal story only takes place within the context of the mystery of the bigger story. Since the universe is infinite and keeps transforming itself from visible to non visible, then I too am infinite and will only transform myself from visible to non visible on the day I die. The day I die is the day I am born - just like the day I was born on earth was the day I died to my mother's womb.

Perhaps, the villagers were not so stupid all those years ago when they used to say that the ancestors were present among us but could no longer be seen. Perhaps they understood something we forgot about the power of the waves that the ancestors left behind that go on affecting us long after they had disappeared to the other side. They understood connection between visible and non visible. They respected the mystery that cannot be measured. They had faith.

If you can see yourself in this bigger story, you will have the faith you need to let go and live your life on purpose in the presence of the train of the great mystery of life. If you find this through religion, great! But whether you find a religion or not, you have to return to the sparkling eyes that see the deeper wonder of life before you can accomplish your goals as an adult. Otherwise, you are condemning yourself to a perception of separation, isolation, and anxiety – the very things that plague a faithless society and a failing school.

Quantum Mysteries

In the last section, we looked at the story of life through the wonders of the universe expanding forever in a never ending journey of birth and death and rebirth in an outer expanding infinity. Now we will explore a story of life through the wonders of the tiniest particles of matter and the tiniest sparks of energy as they disappear within themselves into an inner infinity.

Scientists who study the tiniest particles of matter and the tiniest sparks of energy that man can detect are known as quantum physicists. Quantum physics is one of the places where science accepts that there is a non visible universe that we cannot see or measure.

Scientists have been able to reduce matter to the tiniest particle that can be studied. When they look inside this tiniest particle, what do you think they see? They see a spark or a wave of energy inside the particle. When they look at the wave or spark of energy inside the particle, what do you think they see? Well, they see particles floating in the wave.

And when they pick out one of these particles and look inside of it? You guessed it - they see another wave of energy. When they look at this wave of energy, they see particles of matter. When they pick out a particle and look inside of it... it just goes on forever. Matter converts to energy and energy to matter in the last story I told about black holes. The transformation back and forth goes on forever.

In this story about particles of matter and waves of energy, we find that the material world has a non visible inner core directing it in a wave. That wave is a like the wave in the ocean or the train in Brad's Story. I can't see it just like I can't see that the earth is traveling around the sun right now, but it is there and it has its reasons and it is connected to everything else in the universe.

The most amazing discovery of the quantum physicists is this. They understand that when they are studying the particle of matter, they cannot experience the wave. And similarly, when they look at the wave that the particles are floating in, they cannot experience the individual particles. The best example I can think of to explain this is to compare it to the fact that we are on earth and we see the particular matter before our eyes that constitutes earth perception. But we have no concrete knowledge that the earth is spinning and revolving around the sun that is also revolving around a black hole. We just can't see that from here.

In order to witness the 'wave' that the earth is riding in, we would have to travel far into outer space. But once we got there and we saw the arc and the spinning waves that our earth is riding within, we could no longer see all the particulars that we see in front of us each day. Looking at the particle, I can't see the wave the particle floats in. Looking at the wave, I can't experience the particles.

This is not being taught to you as science. This story should humble you to the fact that when all is said and done, you really don't know much. What does this mean? Apparently there is always another side that we cannot see at all times as we live here on earth. And the other side is intimately connected to the side that we can see at all times. Both sides of reality are part of one whole that is bigger than I can know. I can only imagine it. It is a great mystery. It inspires awe.

Faith understands that life is an infinite story where all things, seen and unseen, visible and non visible, alive and dead, energetic and material, are in a constant state of transformation that apparently has no beginning and no end. All we can do as human beings is ride the train. Riding the train is another way of expressing acceptance of your powerlessness over particular people and situations and to trust that you are here for a reason and that you will go through the things you must go through for a reason and that there is something that you must do while you are here. Let go. Trust the beating heart. Own your story. Tell your story Live your story. Your life is a story. Write it well.

YOUR LIFE AS A STORY
Step 3
12 Steps of Growth

If you have been brave enough to accept your powerlessness and if you have found the faith it takes to begin to let go, you are well on your way to mature adulthood and to warrior status. But the job is not nearly completed yet. So get ready, kid! We are going in! We are going in to your story. The last section tried to relate you to the bigger story. That was just an imaginal eye opener to get you ready for this. Just like the universe has a story, you have a story. And your story follows the pattern of the universe since you are living in the universe and the universe is living in you.

Your story is unique in two ways. First, as we have stated, you have a purpose and it is your job to find your purpose and to stay true to it on a daily basis. Something as simple as saying hello to someone may be on your purpose. You never know how much your simple hello might mean at that moment.

Second, as we have stated, you can make choices. Your choices either flow with the wave or the train of the bigger story, or they try to control or take power over the bigger story. There are only two life positions in human experience. Either you are flowing with the wave of the bigger story as you fit into it, or, you are trying to be the big story.

If you believe in God, this statement may be expressed as you are either serving God, or you are trying to be God. If you believe in Not God, then you would read this differently. You are either riding the train or you are trying to be the train. It is all the same whether you believe in God or Not. There are only two possible life positions for humans.

Trying to be God or the train can be fun for a while sometimes, but it ultimately will get you killed before your time, or sent to prison, or at the very least, sink you into an inevitable unhappiness because you are not the train and you are not God.

Trying to be the big story is trying to be God. And we aren't allowed to talk about God, unfortunately. But fortunately, we are allowed to talk about trains. So learn to ride the train, or get on the tracks and try to demand that the train stop for you. Get flattened every morning by life. It is up to you, but please remember, as we have learned, the train always wins because the train has the power and you are a passenger that needs to find your seat. Accept it. And enjoy the ride!!

Trying to be the train always leads me into a situation like the invisible glass whose illusion killed the butterflies as they smashed themselves to death trying to go through. Something I cannot see is blocking my way and I go into my God frenzy like a spoiled little brat trying to force the situation the way I want it or the way I think it should be. It gets me exhausted or even killed if I cannot calm down and let go of control and listen to the beating heart.

Although I am going to give you the elements of your story right now, I do not want you to try to tell your story yet in group. We have more ground to cover. But I want you to be aware now that you have a story and that you are making your story come true as we speak. I want to make you aware that your story fits into the big story of the universe.

If you have risen above the life of consequences with more intelligent choices and behavior, if you understand you have a purpose and a gift to bring to your village, and you have begun to perceive your relationship to power in a more mature way, then you are ready to understand that you have a story to tell.

Telling the story in an honest way is the act of breaking open the stone that will unleash the wave of energy needed to accomplish your life purpose and to bring your gift to the village.

On the next two pages we will outline the elements of your story. You will not attempt to tell your fully integrated story until closer to the end of this group. But it is time to understand you have a story and that your story has common elements with the stories of other humans. You story has common elements with the story of the universe.

Life is a story
The universe has a story
Everybody has a story
You have a story
Yours is a microcosm of the bigger story
Birth is innocent
The journey is of time
Time creates a wound or betrayal
Loss and death are encountered inside the wound
Wound or betrayal ends innocence and creates separation
Separation cuts you off from the universe
You try to be your own universe
You get lost from your ground and your connection
You get lost from your self
You create a new you – a new myth about yourself
You wear a mask to try to make your myth come true
You stand on the train tracks
The train hits you hard
You get very angry
You get lost
You don't care
There is a jolt of lightening like a crisis
It cuts you down
Someone finds you or you find them
You go through hell
You tell your story
Forgive yourself and others
You go back home
Home to your heart
You tell your story to know yourself
You tell your story to forgive yourself
You tell your story to free yourself
You write the rest of your story on purpose
Life is the Story of you
Learning how to find your way back home
So you can do your purpose

The Elements of Your Story

- You were born innocent and beautiful
- You were whole. You didn't even realize you were separate from your mom yet
- Time became your teacher
- Time taught you to separate all the bits of human perception into particulars
- This was good. You got good grades in school and you could name all the particulars
- Slowly you began to lose sight of the whole.
- You separated yourself out into a particular. You felt alone.
- You were confused because you thought you were special
- A wound or betrayal or loss happened shattering your innocence
- Your sense of separation and loneliness increased.
- You began to wear a mask to protect yourself so you would not be wounded again
- Your mask helped you survive but it slowly got you lost from your self
- You forgot who you were. You became someone else.
- You needed someone to help to face you with your loss
- You needed an educator to help you see the whole again
- You continued to drift away from your center – your self
- You got really lost from your heart
- Power was the thing you now needed to survive. It was you against the universe in a lonely daily battle.
- One day while you were trying to be God, you had a bad fall
- Crisis happened either formally through education or by its own means
- You humbled yourself. You knew you couldn't be God
- Your relationship to power was examined and altered
- You told your story and started the hard journey back to the heart
- You got real and present. You reconnected to the wonder.
- I brought my gift to my village and family
- You were blessed as an adult by an elder
- You write the rest of your life story comfortable with loss and death
- You are connected to the whole and at peace with the particulars
- You become a responsible young adult

These are the elements of the story. To condense this story - There is a child who was whole and on purpose with a gift to bring to his village. Time brought a wound to the child. The wound ended the innocent connection to the whole and the child set off on a journey to find happiness out there somewhere.

The child was smart and he began to categorize, and particularize, and separate everything he came upon. He got good grades. But then, after the wound, the child separated one final thing that would change his life – he separated out himself and then he labeled himself. And with the new label, the child lost his sense of wonder and he forgot who he was. He became the label. The hell of adolescence had begun. The separation and the label made him lonely, lost, and feeling like he needed to control the whole universe in order to survive. He made many mistakes and wrong turns on this part of his life journey. Separating and isolating your disabilities in school reinforces the loneliness and isolation. You lose the passion to learn.

The journey ended like a butterfly smashing into the Plexiglas. There was danger. A death occurred. It was the death of the adolescent conqueror. Education by an elder or by life itself started the child back home to the key to happiness in his own heart. When the journey home was completed, the story made sense because the story fit the pattern of the story of every man since Adam and Eve. The child was an adult who could live the human story with both the beauty of the whole and the confusion of the particulars. Loss was accepted as part of the human condition. Purpose was embraced with love and devotion.

Acceptance of loss is very hard to master. A small child is kept in innocence for as long as possible. And it is good and right. But loss and death and betrayal come into every child's life one day. This is one of the most difficult tasks of your crossing to adult warrior status. It is part of your story. Everyone got the wound, not just you. Many great warriors have had the wound before you did. It is what you do with the wound that will determine whether or not you ever become a warrior or an adult. Let us explore this wound of loss and sorrow now through a story called the Tree of Sorrows.

The Tree of Sorrows

A story was once told many years ago by a man named Baal Shem Tov. He was a wise man from the Jewish tradition in Poland.

Once there was a huge meadow. This meadow was so huge that it could contain every man and woman on the face of the earth. No one had ever seen a meadow so big.

In the middle of this meadow was a huge giant oak tree. Now this tree, like the meadow itself, was quite extraordinary. It was so big that it had as many branches on it as there were people on the face of the planet earth. Imagine a tree so big that it had one branch on it for every man and woman walking the planet.

The people of the world cry many, many tears. They long to gain control of all sorrow and sadness. Oh yes, they take pills and cures prescribed by the doctors. They take drugs sold on the street. They try denial. They find diversions to make the sorrow fade for a while. But still, no matter what they had tried, sorrow stayed. And so it has been since the beginning of earth. Ever since men and women left the garden of pure happiness, sometimes called the Garden of Paradise, they have struggled to gain control of this thing called sorrow and its annoying child, suffering.

A story told many years ago said that men and women had to leave the garden of happiness because they were given the gift of choice by the great mystery that oversees all being. Once given that gift of choice, one day two of them, (named Adam and Eve in a great story from the past), chose not to follow the law of nature that kept all things in perfect harmony and balance. Once this choice was made, the humans had to accept a life of opposites and a life of consequences. Now where there was once only joy, there was sadness. Now where once there was only peace, now there was war. Now where once there was only light, now there was darkness. There were no neutral acts on earth. Every choice had a consequence, good or bad. Oh yes, I forgot, now there was good and bad, two more opposites. Men and women had to live with good and evil. They struggled with good and evil all the days of their lives.

But still, they longed for sorrow to be eradicated forever. They did not want to suffer anymore. For really, who wants to suffer? None of us want to suffer.

One day the great mystery that rules all being called all the humans out into the great meadow that could hold all humanity. And so every man and woman on planet earth arrived into the meadow. They saw the huge tree with so many branches that there was one branch for every man and woman there. They sat around the tree and they waited.

Soon, they heard a voice. It was the voice of the great mystery. The voice did not seem to be coming from the sky. It seemed to be coming from somewhere deep in the gut of each person there. And so, there was no language problem at all in the great meadow. Each man and woman heard the voice in his own language. The voice spoke softly, yet it was such a powerful voice that human ears could not help but listen. The voice asked the humans to find their faith. It asked them to follow these instructions.

This tree was called the tree of sorrows. The voice asked each man and woman in the field to walk up to the tree. Next, they were asked to find an empty branch on this tree. Finally, each man and woman on the face of the earth was asked to take all his own personal sorrow and hang it on an empty branch on the tree. And so, with some anxiety, but with complete bravery, each man and woman hung his sorrow on a branch of the tree.

When the instruction was completed by everyone, they were asked to step back from the tree. There was silence. All of humanity stood by the tree of sorrow and gazed at the big tree in silence. There was a tree that held all the sorrow of all men and women. They could see all of the sorrow on the face of the earth. And they could not speak because the sorrow they gazed upon was so great. Some people wanted to run away. There was no place to run. So there was only stillness and silence before the tree of sorrows.

As they gazed at the tree, some people started to find a new faith and forgiveness they could not seem to find before this day. People looked at their friends and said to themselves, "Oh my! She has experienced all that sorrow and still she gets up every morning and tries the best she can to take care of her children." "Oh my! That man has been through all that sorrow and still he gets up every day and goes to work to try to give his children a good life." Despite all the sorrow, people began to realize all the courage and love that existed in the world. That no matter what people have been through, most get up out of bed every morning and try again. Grudges were forgiven in front of that huge tree. Faith was rekindled on that day because it was so clear that so many people were obviously trying so hard to be good people in spite of all this sorrow. Mercy permeated that meadow in stillness and silence. And humanity was humbled by reality.

Then, in the total silence, the voice of the great mystery spoke to the people one more time. The voice said, "You are human. Sorrow is part of the human condition. You must live with sorrow if you are going to be human. Accept sorrow and live a good life and you will one day again earn the garden of happiness that your ancestors Adam and Eve chose to leave so many long ages ago." "Take care of each other"

So now, finally, the voice of the great mystery of all being spoke these last words:

"You must now go back to the tree of sorrows and you must take sorrows because sorrow is part of human life. BUT, YOU DO NOT HAVE TO TAKE YOUR OWN SORROW BACK. IF YOU HAVE SEEN ANYONE ELSE'S SORROW AND YOU THINK YOU WOULD RATHER BE THAT PERSON, YOU MAY TAKE THAT PERSON'S SORROW AND LEAVE YOUR OWN BEHIND'

The people of earth stood in silence and gazed at all that sorrow. It seemed for a second like the stillness and silence would last forever. But then, slowly, people began to approach the tree of sorrow. On that day, each man and woman eventually walked back to the tree and accepted sorrow. And not a single man or woman chose to be someone else. In the end, each man and woman walked up to the tree and took back his or her own sorrow and walked away.

And that is the story of the tree of sorrows.

This is the most important lesson on sorrow and the wound that I could ever teach you. No matter how much you hate the wound, you must accept it. Because if you were given the opportunity, you would still choose to be you and keep your own wound once you saw everyone else's wound. So, now the wound becomes your friend. If you can take hold of the wound, it becomes part of your story. Now, you don't have to sit around and wonder why things happened to you anymore. You are not special. You are just another wounded warrior candidate with your own personal sorrow on the branch of the tree of sorrows- like everyone else. We will discuss how to take hold of your wound more fully later in the course.

The purpose of telling your story is to hold and then release your story while keeping the honey or the gold that is at the essence of the story. In this way, the most hurtful event in your life also becomes the 'twist of fate' that marks your survival. It marks the creation of your strength of character. The more you have been through in your life, the more gold you can claim. It is the gold that you will need in order to bring your gift and do your life purpose. The best parts of your character and your humanity are forged out of your pain.

Thus, the sorrow you once thought would kill you now becomes the source of your strength once you accept it and then draw the gold from the experience through the telling of your story.

Summary

This challenge has covered a lot of material. More than that, the challenge has asked you to make some courageous moves in your life. It has asked you to accept powerlessness, to let go of what you do not and cannot control, to become aware that the universe has a story, that you have a part to play in the story, that the story of time is the story of feeling wounded and separate, that the outcome of the story is up to you and whether or not you can accept and embrace your wound, tell your story, and become a warrior who writes the rest of the story on purpose for his village.

The steps to remember to do are simple but very challenging:

- RECOGNIZE what you are powerless over
- ACCEPT what you are powerless over
- LET GO of what you are powerless over
- TAKE HOLD of the wound and your story so you may move on and do your purpose like the other brave warriors who came before you who did their purpose so that you might have a better life.

If you are unable to accept your powerlessness, there will be repercussions in your life. They are:

- PHYSICAL -You get sick and you need meds
- EMOTIONAL - You get consumed by your feelings or you choose not to feel
- SPIRITUAL - You lose your sense of connection and purpose and meaning.
- COGNITIVE - You picture yourself as an isolated victim and you try to be God and take power over daily life
- MYTHOLOGICAL - You live out your story drifting away from center forever looking for happiness 'out there' somewhere where you can never find it.

Grief Ritual

The challenge will end with a formal grief ritual. Grief ritual is a way to own a loss, to acknowledge something you must accept and to let go so that you may grieve and mourn like a brave warrior. Grief ritual frees you. It allows you to accept, feel, grieve, and to go on and live to do your purpose on earth for your brothers and sisters.

Grief ritual is a way to make yourself feel your sorrow inside a safe container so your feelings can't consume you and you won't get stuck or sick. Sorrow and loss are not optional. To be fully human, sorrow and loss must be accepted and felt deeply. The closeness you feel when you grieve with others makes you feel close and connected to others even though you are going through sorrow. You do not get isolated because your whole village is there to grieve with you as you will do for them. Your myth sees yourself finding the courage to go inside your own heart for the truth even if it hurts so that you will not have to live out your life as an isolated victim drifting away from center and seeking happiness in all sorts of unhealthy ways.

What do you grieve today? First, grieving is not a requirement. You may pass. However, I would warn you that loss and death are not optional in life so I hope that you at least understand that you will need to grieve at some point if you want to be an adult warrior.

Here is a story to help you understand what to grieve and let go of today. It is a story I heard told by Tino Plank. I believe Tino heard this story from Sobonfu Some.

The One I Couldn't Save

Once there was an African village. It came to pass that a terrible flood swept into the village from heavy rains in the mountains above. The villagers had no time to prepare for the rushing waters.

There was a young mother who had two children in the village. She panicked as she heard the flood waters sweeping through because her two children were out playing out of her site.

She called out the children's names but they were nowhere to be found. She was desperate to find them. She ran to the edge of where the water was rushing through the village. She looked up and coming toward her in the swiftly moving current were her two children. She wanted to save them. She loved them both so dearly.

As they got closer, she realized that she could not reach in and save both of them. The water was moving too fast. She would have to reach in and save one. This filled her with horror and she screamed. But there was no time for anything and no solution to the problem. The children were upon her. With no time fort hesitation, she reached in and pulled one of her children from the water. As she held him up, she looked down stream at her other child being swept away. Their eyes met for the last time. And he was gone. She wept for the child she couldn't save.

What you grieve today is the child you couldn't save. Pick the sorrow or loss or betrayal in your own life that you could not change and that you must accept. That is what you grieve today.

Here is the procedure for our grief ritual today.

1. I have passed out a tiny piece of paper to everyone in the group. Take a moment to think about something that you know you are or were powerless over that you know you must let go of. On the piece of paper, write down the intention of what it is that you are letting go of. It does not have to be a lot of writing. You are putting an intention on the paper. As long as you are clear about what your intention is, all you need to write on the paper is a short symbol or phrase about the intention.

2. Next, I will teach you a short African Grief Song that was taught to me by a woman from the country of Burkina Faso in Africa. Her name is Sobonfu Some. It is a short but deeply emotional melody. Let us learn it together now after I play it for you. It comes from a set of compact discs entitled. "Women's Wisdom from the Heart of Africa". Your teacher or group leader may choose any short melody of grief to begin the ritual.

3. We will begin to sing the song together in our circle until it is strong and full of the deep feeling of grief. Then, the elder will begin to pass the burden basket around the circle as we sing. Each person in the group will hold the burden basket until the song is sung through once to them. During the singing, the person holding the basket will place his burden that must be let go inside the basket and pass the basket to the next person

4. The song will be continuous until the basket has completed its journey to every group member.

5. Any group member that does not want to participate may pass.

6. When the song and the exercise are complete, we will have a short discussion before going outside with the basket full of burdens. We will place the burdens in a small pile on the ground and light them on fire

7. As the fire burns the paper, the burden will transform from matter (paper) to energy (smoke). This is our way to give the wound or problem or loss to the great mystery

8. We will leave the ashes as a way to accept loss as part of human life.

9. We dig a shallow hole in the ashes and earth. We plant an acorn to symbolize our growth into mature 'oak trees' that are energized by the ash we leave behind.

The teacher should process this grief ritual with you. It is not good to analyze it. It is very important to discuss the emotion you felt around the activity of grieving and then letting go.

Conclusion

You have just passed through a very challenging part of this course. If you feel like you could not follow all the theories and stories, don't worry. These issues and stories will come up again and again during the course of our journey as we tell our stories to each other.

In any case, the core goal of this challenge is not measured by how well you understood them, it is measured by your willingness to accept powerlessness now and to let go as you enter the adult world.

The themes presented simply taught you that you don't know much. When the little you have learned of the visible experiential world is combined with all the facts of the invisible world and the mystery of the non visible world, you have three choices.

- Let go and flow in the mystery doing your part in life.
- Live your life in a fearful or shallow way avoiding real life at all costs.
- Make believe you can know everything as if you could be God.

If I have taught you something about the great mystery at all, it is that I don't even know what I am talking about. Letting go is allowing the great mystery to humble your power seeking ego into its proper place where it can do its life purpose.

Humility in the presence of the great mystery is what these first three steps of the Steps of Growth were about. Humility allows you to find your small part in the story of the universe instead of trying to be King of the universe. Once you are in your proper place in relation to the ground, to your own beating heart, and to the great mystery, you will be balanced and in a place where your ego can begin to make smarter choices from a place of inner strength.

In the next challenge, we will now explore your personal story more fully. What was the wound that took away your innocence? How did you go off purpose? What have been the consequences?

QUESTIONS FROM HEROIC JOURNEY CHALLENGE THREE

1. List the things that you truly have control over? What do you notice about this list? What do all the items have in common?

2. How have you been slamming yourself into the Plexiglas like those butterflies in The Butterfly Story? What is the immovable Plexiglas in your life that you have tried to fly through?

3. Write about an issue in your life where you have successfully acknowledged your powerlessness.

4. Why is 'letting go' so difficult for most human beings? Why is it difficult for you?

5. In Brad's Story, what did Brad mean when he said, "There is a train coming through and I have to get out of the way"?

6. Brad had 'faith'. What is faith and what does it mean to you?

7. Have you ever stood on the railroad tracks and demanded the train stop? What happened?

8. What is the great mystery and what does the concept mean to you?

9. What does faith have to do with 'letting go?

10. What is a 'gut feeling'? Have you ever had one? Talk about it.

11. Can you accept your branch on the tree of sorrows or would you rather be someone else?

12. What are the elements of your story and how does your story fit into the bigger story of the universe? Use the list on Page 141 as a guideline

13. What is the difference between visible, invisible, and non visible perception?

14. How many of these perceptions have you utilized in your life?

15. What is 'the wound' and who gets it? When?

16. Were you able to grieve and let go during the grief ritual? Write about it. Why did the teacher encourage you to grieve in community?

Bridge to Challenge Four

Before we begin the next challenge, we are going to do the Group check up that we did earlier when we explored trust in the group.

Answer the following questions during group today when the talking stick is passed to you:

- What is it like for you to be part of this group?
- What have you contributed?
- Who is the person in the group that you feel most connected to? Tell them about it.
- Who is the person in the group who you feel least connected to? Tell them about it
- What can this person do to help you feel more connected to him?
- What do you suppose it is like to be in a group with you? Well, you are about to find out!

At this point each group member lets the student know what it has been like to be in a group with her. Students are not allowed to make personal attacks during this exercise. You are to let the student know what they say and do, and how it affects you. Try to be specific rather than general in your comments.

Heroic Journey
Challenge #4

Locate and Respect
The Source of Happiness

Message to Group Leader:

This challenge deepens awareness of the personal story within the context of the larger story of the train racing through time in the realm of power and mystery. Now that the inevitability of sorrow and loss has been introduced, the story needs a hero – and a villain. Participants will play both parts in their own stories. In this challenge, group members are introduced to the concept of 'the wound'. The wound is a loss of innocence that is naturally provided by time. Life looks totally different to the wounded child. He is acutely aware of loss and betrayal. He puts on a 'mask' and creates a new self to protect himself from further wounds. This is where every child's journey 'off track' has its origins.

Group Leader's Outline

- ## The Wound and the Separation

  - What is the 'wound'?
  - How do you 'take hold of the wound'?
  - Healing = Light and Air and Attention

- ## Creating a New Self to Replace the Wounded Self

  - The Mask(s)
  - The Journey Away from Home
  - Finding a Special Friend

- ## Mental Slavery

  - Attachments
  - Cures Become Consequences
  - The Mental Slavery Story
  - The Chains of Mental Slavery
  - Loosening the Chains of Mental Slavery

- ## The Courage of the Empty Cup

  - Learning from the African American Experience
  - The Long Journey Back Home
  - Resting in My Own in Skin in My Own Heart

Introduction

This next challenge will be much less of an intellectual challenge and much more of a personal challenge. It is one thing to understand about powerlessness, and quite another thing to personally accept it in your life and to begin to let go. This challenge is an application challenge. Talking about it is nice but doing it is what it is all about in our village.

What is the wound in your story? What did you do with this wound? How did you experience it and where did you search for relief and happiness? What mask did you put on to avoid the wound and avoid your own feelings and heart? Where did your search for happiness lead you and what were the consequences?

Do you have the vision yet to embrace and tell your own story. This is the trip back inside to your own heart. Your story is the story of a long journey away from your own heart along with another long journey back home to your heart.

That is the subject of this challenge. Let's Begin!

The Wound and the Separation

As we learned in the story of the Tree of Sorrows, suffering and loss are part of the human condition, which is the condition of consciousness in time and space. Sorrow is not optional in human life because we experience the normal transitions and transformation of life as losses. There comes a day in every child's life when time provides the child with a 'wound'. This may be a physical wound, but it is also a psychic wound. It happens very close to the heart, the very same place where the source of all happiness is located.

Even though everyone gets the wound and feels the pain of loneliness and separation that comes with it, most people in our society try to keep their wound a secret. The result is that they end up experiencing their wound very personally. Many people today have no knowledge of the necessity and prevalence of the wound in every human life.

When you personalize the wound, you feel like you are a victim and that you are the only wounded person who got hurt like this. The wound is a very natural part of the long journey that every human makes, first away from the heart, and then back home to the heart.

What is your wound? Can you remember a certain incident that became your wound? If you cannot, can you at least remember a day when you woke up in the morning and looked in the mirror to find that your life had been changed forever? As you look into the mirror on the morning that you have the wound, it feels like everything has changed, like nothing is the same anymore. Your eyes lose their shine and life makes you anxious or depressed or very angry. You feel alone and different and cut off from everything and everyone around you. Your innocence is gone.

If you can remember a specific cruel instance that became your wound, you may talk about it in group if you want. In our village, this is called 'taking hold of the wound'. Some people do not have a clear memory of their wound. That is okay. What is more important than the physical details of your wound is that you remember a time when your innocent happiness was interrupted by your experience of death or loss or betrayal. Taking hold of the wound is acknowledging that you once were innocently happy and now you have become separate or disappointed in life or angry with rage at life. If you can remember this day and acknowledge it, you are taking hold of the wound.

Taking hold of the wound is your way to admit your powerlessness over circumstances in your own life story.

Now that you are holding and acknowledging the wound, there is more to understand and to do. The wound has happened to every human, not just you. Time provides the wound and no one who is human escapes this wound because humans live in the realm of time.

Being unable to escape the wound might be upsetting, but there is a bright side. Although you cannot escape the wound, young warrior, you are not a victim. You are a young warrior embracing the wound like all the brave warriors that came before you. Every young warrior has had to pass through this place. And now it is your turn. Take hold of the wound. It is yours.

Healing = Light and Air and Attention

Why take hold of the wound? Why not ignore it or find a diversion or think about something else? Taking hold of the wound is not just some psychological or psychiatric psycho-speak. It is an essential part of every human's journey or passage from childhood to adulthood. You don't grow up and become an adult unless you master this part of your life no matter how many academic competency tests you have passed and no matter how many college degrees you get. Many a Harvard graduate is still a child at the heart level because this work is left undone. What happens if 'taking hold of the wound' is left undone?

Let us once again use the metaphor of an actual physical wound as a way to show why it is important to take hold of your psychic wound. If time one day provided you with a big gash on your arm that began to bleed, it would be very important that you not ignore this matter. The universe would do its part as parts of your body rushed help to the injured arm to try to heal it, but if you did not take hold of this wound and do your part, grave consequences would follow.

What would happen? If you ignored the gash completely and the cut was deep enough you could die. If it was not deep enough to kill you, and you ignored it and failed to attend to it and clean it, it would get infected. The infection would not go away even if you tried to hide it with a bandage.

The infection would eat into your skin, enter your bloodstream, and eventually begin eating right into your bones. You would get very sick and you would suffer. You would find it very hard to live a happy life. It would infect and affect every part of you. You would be labeled with a disability or a disease.

Just like this physical wound, your psychic wound must be acknowledged and attended to if you want to heal. The wound must be acknowledged, cleaned, and it must be given light and air in order to heal.

Taking hold of your wound is giving it light and air and attention. Ignoring the wound will have grave consequences that will affect every day of your life.

Back in the days of the village, people did not have such a wide variety of toys and diversions, and screen names and ways to avoid experiencing the wound as we do today. They understood that acknowledging, and surviving and healing the wound was the most important part of an adolescent's education. Without this experience, the adolescent would not pass through the gates to mature adulthood.

Nowadays, the wound is not seen as a normal part of life in time, nor is dealing with the wound seen as part of a child's education. The price we have paid for this as a society is very steep. Children, especially young males, don't seem to grow up anymore. A well educated brain with an uninitiated soul is no more than a smart lost person. Smart lost people are very preoccupied with themselves and their childish needs. The wound gets ignored completely or it goes off to the psychiatrist to be diagnosed as an abnormality or deformity to be medicated or amputated.

THERE IS NOTHING WRONG WITH YOU!

YOU ARE NOT SICK!

YOU HAVE THE WOUND LIKE EVERY OTHER HUMAN HAS HAD THE WOUND SINCE ADAM AND EVE OR SINCE THE APEMAN LEARNED TO TALK AND WALK UPRIGHT.

TAKE HOLD OF THE WOUND. IT IS YOURS.

The Mask

So far, we have discussed what the wound is and we have discussed when it happens - in time. Next we will discuss where the wound happens. The wound happens in your heart. Even if you are physically or sexually abused on the surface, the gash that wounds you happens in your heart. The heart is the very essence of who you are. When it gets wounded, you are not the same. You try to ignore or wish the wound away but it is there and it does not go away.

The result of this makes a lot of sense. You choose to separate or abandon your own heart. The wound happens in the heart and you don't want to acknowledge or feel it, so you abandon it. Trying to abandon the wound makes sense. Unfortunately, abandoning your heart leaves you cut off from the real you, from your own happiness, and from the power and desire to do your life purpose.

If it is too painful to be you anymore, who will you be? Herein is the core of every problem you have developed in school and out of school. When you cut the connection to your own heart, you could not be yourself anymore. You were changed. You put on a mask for the world to see. You created a new you.

What kind of mask? Well, people choose different masks. It might be a 'failure' mask and you begin to fail in school, usually between 7th grade and the first year of high school. It might be a bully mask. It might be a criminal mask and you begin to get into trouble constantly with the police. It might be a withdrawn, lonely mask where you sit all by yourself in the cafeteria and have no friends. It could be a party mask where you act happy all the time and have many friends outwardly while feeling very lonely and cut off inside.

It might even be a 'Straight A's" in school mask where you make all seem fine to the outside world while you suffer from anxiety and depression under the surface. The masks are all different but the result is still the same. You feel cut off and separated from your own heart because you just don't feel like you can go there anymore. It hurts too much. You wear a mask and forget who you are. You try to forget the wound - but it is still in there. Your heart goes with you no matter where you go or what mask you put on your face.

Mask Activity

Draw or make a mask that shows the person you chose to become once you were wounded. If you are very artistic, spend some time being creative, but truthful. If you are artistically challenged by this assignment, at least write a bit about the mask you chose to wear after you were wounded. Tomorrow we will discuss these 'masks' in the group.

The Journey Away From Home

In the days of the village, the elders ripped you from your parent's home in the middle of the night and you were taken out to the countryside to make your long journey to adulthood. Out there, you were put through the grief of taking hold of your wound. You were put through the most vigorous physical, mental, emotional, and spiritual tests all designed to bring you down. That's right! Bring you down - into your wound, and back through your story and the story of your ancestors into your own heart - home. Your power is in your heart. Your gift is in your heart. Your sense of meaning and connection and community is there. Your happiness is there. Your wound is there. Are you ready to go in, young warrior?

If this initiation is not completed, the young adolescent does not come home, she does not get educated no matter how many tests she takes, and she does not grow up and become a mature adult in her community. Where does she go?

Some people never come home to the heart ever again. They spend the rest of their days wearing a mask, avoiding their real feelings, and searching for happiness out there somewhere in possessions, people, emotions, thrills, college degrees or other things. The elders would say that they will live a life drifting further and further away from center for the rest of their lives until they either crash or die out there.

Initiation was the elders' way to cause the crash in the safe container of initiation so that the journey back home to the heart could be completed and a mature adult could be produced.

If you have taken hold of the wound in group this week and if you have recognized the mask you put on after the wound, you have come a long way on the journey already. But there is still a long way to go. As you drifted away from center far from your heart, you probably found a special friend. That is the next part of every man's story that we will explore next.

Finding a Special Friend
Step 4
12 Steps of Growth

Go back now and read Step 4 of the 12 Steps of Growth with your teacher. After you read it, take a moment to reflect on it and share any question or reaction you have after doing the reading.

The search for happiness out there is insatiable. It takes people to some very strange places. It takes others to more normal places. But the bottom line is that the journey does not produce satisfaction nor does it find the happiness that it is seeking. Searching for happiness 'out there' a long way from your heart is like trying to fill a big sinkhole that can never be filled. With each new purchase or possession, the hunger only grows and the sinkhole gets deeper and the feeling of emptiness increases.

This search outside for happiness has become a way of life in our country. I can remember as a child looking at a Christmas catalog and picking out the gifts I wanted for Christmas. When Christmas finally came and I got the gifts after months of longing and waiting, I played with my presents for a few days. But by then, I already had my eye on something else that I wanted. I was very young but I was already introduced to the world of the sinkhole.

Attachment

In Step 4, you read about attachments and the part that attachments come to play in our lives. An attachment is like finding a special friend on your long journey away from the heart. It is a long lonely journey when you are far from your own heart. A friend comes in handy. You attach yourself to that friend in hopes of finally finding some peace and happiness.

Let's explore the attachments again briefly. You might attach yourself to stuff or possessions or shopping for stuff and possessions. You could get attached to a substance as a special friend. Some people get attached to emotions like anger or sadness or even a sort of phony happiness that seems too good to be true. Some people find an attachment to perfection, or being right all the time, or winning. Many people find their attachment in another person where they pin all their hopes and all the pressure for their own happiness on another human being. Some get attached to sex. Some get attached to gambling. There are as many attachments as there are things in the world. The problem with an attachment is not the thing itself. The problem is your relationship to the thing or person or emotion. It is your way to cling on to something that becomes an addiction or habit that might provide the happiness you have wanted so badly.

Attachment Activity

Today we are going to pass the talking stick around the group. What has been your tendency in relation to attachments? See if you can own your own shortcoming and weakness by identifying the attachments in your life.

What is your attachment?

How did it help you at first?

What are the long term consequences if your attachment becomes a habit or addiction?

After we have all taken the stick and spoken, we will compare and discuss the attachments we have chosen and what the benefits and the consequences have been or might be in the long run.

Cures Become Consequences

An attachment starts out as a neat way to control the world and to feel good for a while. It works so well at first. It brings you relief.

It brings you a bit of pleasure, or anesthesia for the pain of loneliness from wearing a mask for so long.

But as this special friend takes its hold in your life, sometimes addiction is born. What started out as a special friend that helped you cope with life is now your master controlling much of your time and activity. This happens at the expense of other things that you know you should care about and attend to in your life. You become a slave obsessed with the friend you thought would help you. You get stuck in a repetitive behavior or thought pattern that is hurting you but you just can't seem to stop some days, and you don't want to stop other days. Though you live in a rich and free country, you have become a mental slave.

Mental Slavery Story

We are very fortunate that we live in a free country. Although all human beings have been imbued with consciousness and the freedom to choose what they say, think, and do, many countries in the world do their best to place tight controls on what their citizens say, think, and do.

However, living in a free country has its burden as well as its blessing. A folksinger named Phil Ochs once wrote "Freedom will not make you free". I am not going to take us into a lengthy discussion on the word freedom. Let's just leave it at the fact that freedom is the ability to choose what you say, think, and do. Freedom will not make you free? What does that mean? Next, we will talk about something called mental slavery.

Mental slavery is a condition that occurs when a person uses his freedom to choose to find an attachment or addictive way of acting or thinking or doing. Even though the mental slave can still vote and speak and do as he pleases, he has used this freedom to chain himself to the slavery of an attachment in his life.

Today, I have just passed out the floor plan to the base of a slave ship that was used to transport Africans to America in the 1800's.

You may be disturbed to notice that the slaves were chained together in the most debasing and inhumane way for the long journey across the Atlantic Ocean.

Place yourselves on one of those slave ships for just a minute. Use your imagination. You have seen other people leave on these ships before. You know that once they leave your home in Africa that they never return. You are chained like an animal on a ship and you will never see your family or your village or homeland ever again. You do not know where you are going, but you do know this is not good. You are being treated as if you were a piece of garbage. Some people do not survive and they are thrown overboard. Some people are very sick and they are thrown overboard as well. There are too many slaves to let everyone go to the lavatory so you are chained in the dark with the stench of urine and excrement for the entire journey.

There is no hope. There is no reason to go on living. You have a wound that is more than you could ever imagine having to bear in your life. But somehow, you survive the journey. You are taken off the ship on a small island off the coast of South Carolina. You are on an island prison camp. They are feeding you now and trying to make you look good for auction. You are still a slave but now at least you can walk around and talk to others.

As soon as a small group of you get together, you suddenly find yourselves trying to construct makeshift musical instruments out of anything you can find. Back in your village, people sang songs and felt their grief deeply. You felt deep grief at your plight and you knew it was time to do a grief ritual so you found a way to make instruments and you sang your grief in a group.

The slave masters are first very amazed that you are singing songs. But then, they feel threatened by your singing. Why? They can feel the power in the spirit of your song. One thing they do not want you to have is power. They quickly take away the instruments but that does not stop you. You begin to make beats with your feet, with your hands, and with your mouth. You go right on singing your songs. The instruments are gone but your song cannot be killed.

You do not stay on the island very long. New slaves are coming in everyday. They are moving you out. You are just a beast of burden to them. You are sold to the highest bidder. You work for a large plantation owner for the rest of your life. You live in subhuman quarters. You have little in the way of freedom to choose anything about your life. You learn to say, "Yes Sir" and "Yes Ma'am" and live a hopeless existence with no hope that anything can change for you for the rest of your life.

Mysteriously, the song that you began singing when you got off the ship continues on the plantation. You find an old guitar and you make it sound like an instrument from West Africa called a kora. You sing whenever you can with your brothers and sisters in slavery. The music you make is very sad, but it is also very soulful and full of spiritual strength. The music comes to be called the blues. The blues is your way to sing your story and to keep the human spirit in your heart alive.

This is not a history class. So why did I tell you that story and why did I ask you to imagine yourself as a slave? I have told you this story to demonstrate a fact that African Americans have proven not just to themselves, but to all mankind. They have shown us that a people can be inflicted with the most horrible wound from which no recovery could be apparent on the surface experience level. Through the singing of the blues, they never lost the spirit inside their own beating hearts. Those slaves had no reason to hope, no reason to care, and no reason to want to live and to go on. Yet, they did remember from the village that they should sing the songs of the deep heart in a community ritual when it was time to grieve.

The root of this music was so full of power and spirit that it has become the root of all the wonderful music that has followed in American culture. Whether you listen to rock n roll music or rap or R&B, you are listening to music that has its roots in the blues of those slaves.

If African Americans can survive a wound so deep and grievous, if they can rise from the ashes and go on to a glorious future, then you and I can survive our own wound and rise from the ashes to a glorious future as well.

There is something in the very deepest heart of you that nothing can stop or kill no matter how deep the wound.

Before you can rise from the ashes, you first have to sink into the blues of your story. Your story is also a story of a long journey away from home where you got very lost and hopeless. You must find the courage to go within and feel it and bring it up to consciousness in a grief ritual, a song that everyone else knows and understands when they hear it. In the truth of your story, the spirit and power to rise up from the ashes will arrive mysteriously. That is the African American story. That is every man and woman's story. Everyone has within them the power and spirit to survive the wound. But first you have to get real and sing and feel the blues.

Fortunately, slavery was abolished long ago. In addition, the Civil Rights Act of 1964 and the Voting Rights Act of 1965 righted more of the injustices left over from the days of slavery. Slavery and discrimination are now against the law.

What does all this have to do with our group and the initiation to adulthood? Although physical slavery has been wiped out in America, something I will call mental slavery is still very much alive. People make the chains of this slavery by some of the choices they make in the long journey away from the heart. They feel lonely and lost and far from their home in their own heart. The community that used to encourage grieving in community has been fractured and seems to be disappearing. Grieving has gone out of style. In this atmosphere people tend to choose attachments that quickly become habits and addictions.

Our culture of commercialization actively encourages this attachment based way of living. There is a quick cure for whatever ails you. Buy it. Take it. Feel good. You are fixed. Singing the blues in deep grief in community has gone out of style in a society that has declared it unnecessary.

The early African Americans were not trying to make a big hit on the radio. They were singing the deep grief of taking hold of the wound in the deep heart.

Some of these chains of mental slavery are attachments to illegal substances, but just as many of these attachments are addictions to perfectly acceptable things. These attachments chain people in the bottom of the slave ship just as surely as the physical chains that once chained the slaves from Africa. People willingly choose their chains. And they become mental slaves.

What are the chains of mental slavery?

MENTAL SLAVERY

CHAINS OF THE PAST

CHAINS OF THE MASK

CHAINS OF THE PILL

CHAINS OF THE WILL

Explanation

The chains of the past are the things from your past that you have not been able to face. These chains also emerge from all the stuff you put in your bag. You carry this bag of unfinished business from the past on your back. It can become very heavy and burdensome.

The chains of the mask are the disguises you have used, the personality you created once you got wounded. This personality with its choices of style and behavior has been like a mask you wear. The mask was just great at first but now you have worn the mask so long that you can hardly remember who you are anymore. You have become a slave to the mask.

The chains of the pill represent all the attachments you formed to try to help yourself. They include drugs and alcohol, but really also include anything else that you have used to try to make yourself feel better and avoid your wound and your shadow. These are the chains of the pill.

The chains of the will are all the ways you have tried to control what is not yours to control. People, events, and things that are beyond your control become chains everyday because you want to control what is not yours to control. You have gotten so frustrated at your inability to control all these people and things that now you have lost control of yourself too. These are the chains of the will.

Self Awareness

Taking hold of the wound, getting honest about attachments, and telling your story puts you in a place where you can undo the chains. You have to calm down. You have to stop struggling. Willpower is no good here. It's too late for that.

Calming down and being aware undoes you from your chains much like one would free himself from 'finger handcuffs'. The more you struggle and pull, the tighter the enslavement becomes. The more you relax to the situation, see it as it is, accept it, the looser your fingers get until you can finally get free again.

Again this getting free means you need courage. You may not realize how much you prefer your slavery to your freedom. Freedom brings self responsibility. It brings choices. It can be scary. Some people never uncover the shadow, never acknowledge attachments, and remain in their chains forever. Many of us, however, get sick of our selves, or at least the selves we have created through our attachments. We have a chance to examine the wound, the shadow. We have a chance to be free.

Thus, telling your story becomes your way to go deep into the wound, to sing your blues song in a powerful and soulful way, and finally, to break free of the mental chains that you created in a misguided attempt to survive your wounds.

Mental Slavery Activity

As we pass the talking stick today, see if you can identify which of the chains of mental slavery are present in your life. All of us are involved in some way with the Chains of the Will because this struggle is the struggle of human growth to adulthood and successful elder hood that all people struggle with in their lives.

Talk about the chain that you identify with most. How do you identify with this chain? What are your attachments and which of these chains are your attachments linked to?

Compose a blues poem or a rap about your story in the chains of mental slavery. Let the poem reflect your faith and your willingness to go on even in hard times. Inside the bravery of this poem is the energy that taps the strength of your soul.

Loosening the Chains of Mental Slavery

Step 5
12 Steps of Growth

Recognizing the attachments that have made you a mental slave is a very hard task. Denial is a very big part of any attachment or addiction. "It's not a problem for me". It's not affecting my life at all". "I don't do it that often" The list of rationalizations for attachments is huge. Any person who finds the courage to start to examine and own an attachment is taking a big step toward freedom and fully mature adulthood.

Read step 5 with your teacher. Relate it to the 4th step of the 12 Steps of Growth. Relate it to the chains of mental slavery that we just studied. While recognizing the existence of an attachment is a big step, an even bigger step is to 'let go' of an attachment. Even after you have recognized an attachment in your life, the idea of letting it go is scary. Your attachment fills a big part of your daily life now. Letting it go is crossing a border to the unknown, or crossing the border back to the place you were when you chose the attachment in the first place.

Although your heart longs for freedom, you are also a creature of habit who doesn't like change, especially sudden change. Many times you have lived your life with a chain of mental slavery for so long that it is hard to imagine life without it even after you realize that is not good for you. Your attachments have been trying to fill a big empty hole in your life for a long time. But this empty hole is a sinkhole. The more you pour into it, the more it begs to be filled. You are trying to fill the emptiness so you don't have to remember or experience the wound. But it is not working anymore and you know it. You are not happy. Freedom has not made you free. You have made your own chains of slavery and now you are stuck.

Just like the African Americans in the story of slavery, you have the courage and strength to get free. You have the same strength of soul in your own heart to sit in the emptiness until you rise up from the ashes. But how do you do it? First, you have to be brave and feel and sing the blues.

The Courage of the Empty Cup

We live in the richest and the freest country in the world, but still, as Mother Theresa noticed once, people don't look very happy here. People use their precious freedom to choose a chain of mental slavery.

Finding the courage to let go of your attachments is to find the courage to sit with the empty cup. Let me explain.

I am holding a cup of water in front of me. It is full. I am thirsty so I take a gulp. Now I am pouring more water in the cup. But what am I doing? I am pouring the water into the cup and it is overflowing and spilling all over my pants and all over the floor. The cup is already full. What am I doing this for?

I don't know why I am doing it. As ridiculous as that may seem for me to spill water all over myself onto the floor, that is exactly how I behave when I have developed an attachment in my life. I can't be satisfied.

I fill the cup day after day until I am pouring so much into it that my life is a mess. And still, I am not happy or satisfied. I can't get enough of more and more but it is still not making me happy at all. My cup is full and overflowing with my needy hunger for more and more. My life is a mess.

Finding the courage to let go of an attachment is to find the courage to sit with your empty cup. This is totally foreign to American culture of the 21st century. Sitting with the empty cup is not profitable to anyone so it is never encouraged any more. When you sit with your empty cup you have nothing to cling to. You are alone with your feelings and the truth of your heart song, your blues song, your story.

Now this seems very irrational and very depressing. It is depressing, but it is more than depressing. Pay attention, children. The blues song in your story takes you straight to your heart where your wound is. That is not pleasant. But that is not all that you find in the courage of the empty cup in your heart. You also find your desire, your strength, your power, your purpose, your happiness. At the core of the real and true beating heart is where you rise from the ashes.

When you listen to the African American blues or to the roots country music of the dirt poor white people of the South, it is not an experience of wallowing in depression. There is strength in the melody. There is spirit in the rhythm. There is faith in the harmony. This is why the roots of the blues and the roots country music in our modern culture have never died. It is full of the spirit at the very heart of all of us.

Now, young warriors, it is our turn to confront the chains of our slavery, to sing the blues with the empty cup of soul and faith, to rise up from the ashes of the very wound where hope had been lost and left for dead.

This is your next challenge in your warrior training. Giving up the 'special friend' of an attachment is never the hard part. Sitting with your own beating heart and feeling the blues in your heart is the hard part. Doing this is to sit with your empty cup.

The Long Journey Back Home

Sitting with the empty cup is to realize that happiness is not 'out there'. It is the end of the long journey away from home. And it is the beginning of the long journey back inside to your own heart, your own center, your own home. The journey is your blues song. It will take you back through the story of all the mistakes you have made while you were lost and desperate for happiness that you couldn't find or control. It will take you into the wound where you will acknowledge it, give it light, give it air, and begin the process of healing that will complete the journey home to the heart.

There at the core of the stone is the spark of the heart that has remained alive in you throughout all of the wounds of time. Nothing can change that place in you. Your happiness and your purpose and the knowledge of the whole universe are alive there. It is for that noble reason that it is time for you to break open the stone.

There is still work to do. Our celebratory banquet is still months away. But now you are pointed in the right direction if you want to proceed. It is already expected that you take care of this business of your daily school life, or the daily life you must deal with wherever you may be as you read this. Nor is this group about coming to a group everyday to complain about your friends or your enemies. It is not about complaining about teachers. It is not about blaming others for your problems. IT IS ABOUT YOU AND YOUR STORY. IT IS ABOUT YOUR JOURNEY BACK TO YOUR OWN HEART.

All of our remaining challenges will be about the signposts you must follow to complete this courageous journey back to the center of the stone, where that spark in your heart is still alive.

QUESTIONS FROM HEROIC JOURNEY CHALLENGE FOUR

1. What is the wound? What is the cause of the wound? Who gets the wound?

2. Why is the wound often located near the heart?

3. What happens to a psychic wound when it is never given light, air, and attention?

4. Why is 'letting go' so difficult for most human beings? Why is it difficult for you?

5. What is the mask? Describe the mask(s) you chose?

6. Can you identify and discuss an attachment that you cling to?

7. How did your attachment help you at first

8. What were the long term consequences of clinging to your attachment?

9. What is mental slavery?

10. Can you name the chains of mental slavery

11. Which chain(s) can you identify with?

12. What does the history of African Americans teach you about yourself and about human nature?

13. What does it mean to sit with your empty cup? Why would you choose to sit with your empty cup?

14. Why is it so hard to get honest about an attachment in your life?

15. Are you ready for the warrior's journey back home into your own heart? Write about it.

Heroic Journey
Challenge #5
Realize My Potential Through the Portal Of Forgiveness

Message to Group Leader:

This challenge covers the last six steps of the 12 Steps of Growth. It introduces students to the concept of forgiveness. Like each phase of this unfolding story, forgiveness has a cognitive aspect, and an application aspect which challenges students to put stories and themes into their daily lives. The "King of Trees" is a story of rising up from the ashes. It is a story where a tree apparently dies and disappears and then mysteriously reappears growing right out of what appears to be solid rock. However, the solid rock has a crack. It is broken open. And out of the small crack has emerged a tree that had been left for dead. The challenge ends with students examining the concept of relationships and boundaries in relation to forgiveness. Students are now ready to bring their life purposes to the world.

- ## Forgiveness as a "Baby with Bright Eyes"

  - o What is forgiveness?
  - o Why is it Important to You?

- ## Story of "The King of Trees"

  - o How Does this Story Impact My Life?
  - o What does the Story have to do with Forgiveness?
  - o Putting Yourself into the Story
  - o Forgiveness as a Form of Freedom
  - o Learning how to Practice Forgiveness

- ## The Burden Basket – A Tool of Forgiveness

  - o The Meaning of the Burden Basket
  - o The Use of the Burden Basket
  - o Staying True to My Deepest Heart

- ## The Box of Perception

  - o Vision as a Key to Living
  - o The 3 Ways of Seeing
  - o If I Only Believe What My Eyes Have Seen......

- ## Sacred Space and Sacred Path

  - o Sacred Space and Your Boundaries
  - o The Story of the Hollies and the Grapevine
  - o Walking Your Sacred Path
  - o Taking Your Purpose to the World

Introduction

Forgiveness is the gateway to the final four challenges of this course. Without it, you will not be able to carry out the challenging tasks of the rest of the curriculum. As with the rest of this course, understanding forgiveness is only half the task. You must learn how to do it if you want to become an adult warrior. Whether you realize it or not, if you have worked the challenges well on powerlessness, you have already begun the process of forgiveness.

Forgiveness is a function of the present moment. So, as we approach this present moment experience, this is a good time to review the distance we have come so far in order to be clear about where we are now with our understanding, meaning, and purpose.

When our circle opened, it was still a totally new experience. Becoming a group member and experiencing the birth of this group was a very big accomplishment. It did not happen by accident. It took trust and willingness to step outside of your zone of comfort.

As we proceeded, you understood that you came to earth with a purpose, a mission. Forgiveness is the spot where you will now be asked to start bringing that gift of purpose to the village.

We next began to explore our personal relationship to power. This was an intense exploration into your ability to accept and let go to the things and people that you are powerless over. Mastering these steps is showing your ability to stand on your spot and do your thing without the childish demand that circumstances, people, and things go the way you think they should go.

During the past few weeks, we have begun to delve into the specifics of your personal story in relationship to your wound, your mask, your attachments, and your examination of the chains of mental slavery. Again, this was a challenging and brave exploration.

We are now proceeding into new territory. Our job is not to walk into the wound and get consumed by it. Our job is to walk in and to stand in the emptiness with the faith that we can rise from the ashes just like the slaves were able to do.

You have been asked to explore the cold, dark places in your story. Now that the black hole of winter is here, we are going to be taught to accept and hold this space patiently like the squirrel in the squirrel story. Like that squirrel, forgiveness is waiting faithfully in the dark and in the right place for the dawning hope of the warm sunshine.

The cold and dark has its beauty. It is time to gather around the fire and tell our stories to each other, to look into each other's eyes across the flame with honesty and openness. Living through hard times in a group builds character and dignity and most of all, deep respect for one another.

Sitting honestly and openly on this spot with character and dignity, without denial or avoidance, brings us quite naturally to the next leg of the path of the warrior - Forgiveness.

Let's Begin!

The Baby with Bright Eyes

Forgiveness is a newborn baby with huge innocent eyes.

This story is based on an ancient story.

On the coldest, darkest, most hopeless night of the year, there was a family that was homeless for the night. The woman was pregnant. Her husband tried desperately to find a warm place for her to stay. Everywhere they went they were turned away.

Finally he came upon a barn on a hillside. It wasn't much but it would have to do. There the man and his wife spent the night among the animals in the hay trying to stay warm. The situation was brutal and cruel and it seemed that all was lost. But the man and his wife lived the truth of their story and kept their faith there in the hay in a smelly barn. They made the best of it and waited for morning.

As if things weren't bad enough, now the woman began to give birth. At first the husband panicked, but again, he found the courage and strength to live in the truth of the moment. His wife gave birth right there in the barn.

This is not the end of the story. The King of the land, who was severely attached to his own self importance and power, heard that a baby was born. He got so threatened by the birth of this baby who might replace him as King that he sent men to try to kill it. But the baby survived.

It was a beautiful baby with huge big bright eyes. The eyes burned with hope, the hope of an innocent newborn about to begin his journey in earth life.

The lesson of the story is this. On the coldest, darkest night of the year, when all hope is lost, right at the moment of the deepest despair, a beautiful baby is born with big, bright eyes. That baby has eyes so innocent and true that the parents can't help but love the child and they find the strength and courage to go on.

The birth of the child in the middle of the dark winter is a mystery that you can repeat in your own life if you keep your faith and do what needs to be done even on the darkest night of your life. Right there in the barn of your hopelessness, the beautiful baby is born and you will be amazed at the power of love in your life.

What is Forgiveness?
Step 7
12 Steps of Growth

Read step 7 of the 12 Steps of Growth with your teacher. Discuss any initial feelings or reactions that reading this step might bring up for you.

This step tries to present you with a different perspective on the word forgiveness. Most people today tend to look at forgiveness as 'letting someone off the hook". In this way, they tend to see forgiveness as promoting injustice, the injustice of telling someone it is okay when they have done something wrong or harmful.

What is forgiveness?

According to Wikipedia:

"Forgiveness is the mental process of ceasing to feel resentment or anger against another person for a perceived offence, difference or mistake, or ceasing to demand punishment or restitution. Forgiveness may be considered simply in terms of the feelings of the person who forgives, or in terms of the relationship between the forgiver and the person forgiven. In some contexts, it may be granted without any expectation of compensation, and without any response on the part of the offender (for example, one may forgive a person who is dead). In practical terms, it may be necessary for the offender to offer some form of apology or restitution, or even just ask for forgiveness, in order for the wronged person to believe they are able to forgive."

This definition of forgiveness demonstrates my point. The definition talks of forgiveness as letting someone off the hook for something they did. The 7th step of the 12 Steps of Growth gives you a different perspective on forgiveness.

First of all, forgiveness is not something you do for someone else. You do it for yourself to free yourself from the burden of carrying a grievance with you. A warrior grieves fully and then lets the matter of his grievance go. He does not do this to give someone else a break. He does it to give himself a break from carrying the grievance with him. Carrying the grievance is like trying to run with a lead weight strapped around each ankle. If you cannot forgive, you are making your life run right now with these weights on your ankles.

When you forgive someone, it does not mean you will allow them to hurt you again. It may well mean you don't choose to see that person ever again. It is still forgiveness. Forgiveness is something you do in your heart. It means to surrender to the facts, it means to let go and release something that is going to hold you back and hurt you if it is not released.

Last, forgiveness is done for an even more important reason. If you cannot forgive the other humans who have done wrong to you, you also will not be able to forgive yourself. You are also human. You also have gone off purpose like all the other humans. You also have been selfish and hurt someone. The most important person that you will ever forgive in your life is you.

When you own your whole story, you are not just going to talk about the things that happened to you, you are going to talk about your own shortcomings and mistakes as well. You went off purpose. If forgiveness is not given to all other humans, it also is not given to you. You need forgiveness to release your mistakes in order to get on with your life today - free. So forgiveness is about freedom. And a warrior cherishes his freedom because freedom allows him to search his own heart and bring his own gift to the village. When forgiveness is practiced successfully from inside the heart, it finds the key to happiness.

Forgiveness allows you to stand on this spot right now free from the past and the future. You are carrying no guilty burden from the past and no anxious worry about the future. You are here on this spot now being true to your own heart and owning all of you, forgiving the good and the bad and waiting for the baby with big bright eyes to be born.

In religion, this would be called being in a 'state of grace'. In this book, we just call it breaking open the stone.

Talking Stick Activity

In group today as we pass the talking stick, answer the following questions:

What is forgiveness to me?

Have I been a forgiving person in my life? Explain

Is there anyone in my life that I still cannot forgive? Explain

Can I forgive myself? Explain

Everyone should take the talking stick and explore forgiveness thoroughly. In a way, our exploration about forgiveness is once again a crucial junction where the remainder of the journey of this course could be derailed by the debris on the tracks. This time, it is the debris of anything that remains un-forgiven in your life.

Forgiveness is a place of power where you stand in the present moment totally freed from the past and totally freed from worry about the future. Author Ekhart Tolle's recent book is entitled, "The Power of Now". Forgiveness is the power of now in your life. It frees you to make a purposeful and present journey. It is a stone broken open to free the flow of passion and purpose from a powerful place that is balanced and focused. That place is at the very core of your human being.

The King of Trees

A Story of Forgiveness

When I was a child of about seven years, my father would give my mother a ride each week to an appointment on Hamilton Avenue near my home in Waterbury, Connecticut. There was an open field near the place where the appointment took place each week. The field was full of overgrown grasses which spread all the way to the base of a hill. The hill was called Pine Hill. In addition to the grasses in the field, there stood a giant oak tree. It loomed high and mighty above anything else around it, a huge tall twisted trunk with its branches rising high and wide.

While my mother was at her appointment each week, I would wait in the car with my Dad and my younger sister who was about three years old. One day as we sat there, my sister sat transfixed gazing at the tree. After gazing for a long time, she said to my Dad, " Nobody can't climb that tree, hah Dad?" My dad looked at the tree and saw the wonder in my sister's eyes. He responded to my sister, "No, Rose, nobody can't climb that tree. THAT'S THE KING OF TREES." He said the words 'king of trees' with much emotion like this - "The KINGGGG OF TREEEEEES"

My sister's young eyes ballooned as she sat transfixed gazing at the King of Trees. I thought the whole conversation was stupid and I said nothing. All I wanted to do was to get back home to play with my friends. I wished my mother's appointment would be over. I wished I didn't have to sit in the car and wait for her each week. Every week, we would return to Hamilton Ave. and we would wait in the car for my mom. Every week, my baby sister would notice the tree and then say to my father, "Nobody can't climb that tree, hah Dad." My father would reply again, "No Rose, nobody can't climb that tree. THAT'S THE KINGGGG OF TREEEEES." Every week my sister's eyes would balloon wide with wonder while I sat there bored at the whole ritual.

The story would unfold in exactly the same way every week. Although I was initially bored with this, I eventually started to look at that tree and think of it as a huge immovable object, like something that was solid, something that could be counted on to be there. The King of Trees was like a symbol of strength and stability. Although I was beginning to be quite skeptical of everything even as a seven year old, somehow the size of the tree, the look of wonder in my sister's eyes, and my Dad's proclamation of the tree as the King of Trees made me feel very safe. It felt like the tree was something sacred that could always be counted on to be there.

A few years later, the interstate highway project in the United States was well under way. The great coast to coast connection of highways did not exist before the late 1950's and early 1960"s. The system of highways was built so that goods could be shipped coast to coast quickly. Before the system was built, travelers and truckers had to travel on roads with traffic lights through town after town. It was a very slow way to travel. The highway system was built to get us to distant locations more quickly. Two main highways, I-84 and State Highway Route 8 intersected in Waterbury. I-84 was about to become a main national thoroughfare between New England-Boston and New York-and points west and south. The project in my city, Waterbury, was a huge endeavor. Crews blasted through the side of Pine Hill in Waterbury. They wanted the highway to be straight and fast with no steep hills. Our region was very hilly so crews blasted deep into bedrock leaving sheer steep rock cliffs along the highway's path. As they prepared the terrain for the highway, they wiped out everything alive in their way. They cut right through Pine Hill leaving a sheer rock cliff.

My Dad took me to Hamilton Ave. to watch the big Euclid trucks that were so big they "could not be driven on a paved road without damaging it." I can still remember the trucks backing up the side of Pine Hill removing masses of blasted rock ledge. While I was there, I saw something that was to affect me greatly. Within what seemed to be a very brief time span, I watched as a bulldozer, scoop, and a Euclid truck approached the King of Trees.

The men got out of their trucks and bulldozer and they looked at the King of Trees. And then it happened. They jumped back into their heavy machinery and went to work. I watched as they 'took out' the King of Trees. It took them all of 10 minutes to mow down, chunk, and load the King of Trees into a Euclid truck and carry it away. It happened that fast. Or so it seemed to me. My Dad did not even notice this, or, if he did, he said nothing about the quick end to the reign of the King of Trees.

But I couldn't believe it. It touched me very deeply. I began to cry quietly, careful not to let my Dad see. It was gone. The great and kind King of Trees was nothing at all to the power of their machines. But why was I crying about this? I tried so hard not to let my Dad see me cry.

It was not until years later that I realized why I was so emotionally affected by this. In fact by the tender age of nine years old, some things that should never have happened to a kid of nine had happened to me. My innocence was ended at this tender age by a sexually abusive Catholic priest. The church had been as solid as that tree in my childhood. My faith in God had been shattered by that priest. And I was only nine years old. Just like the King of Trees on Hamilton Ave, the King of Trees that was in my heart was torn out and carted away in a matter of minutes. I lost my faith in anything. I had no faith and I was alone in the world though I went through the motions every day like all was okay. It wasn't okay, for all I could see was the hillside of my life blasted away like Pine Hill, and the King of Trees in my heart was as shattered and dead as the King of Trees on Hamilton Ave. My outside shell looked fine to the world, but my head was severed from my heart and it seemed that my heart was dead. I was wounded by a predator, but worse, I was wounded by my own thoughts that God had betrayed me.

Unfortunately, I lost my faith for years and years as my life was given to rage and sadness - rage at anything I perceived as being unfair - sadness at the loss of all that I believed in as a child. I grew into an angry, young man that soothed his anger with many obsessive attachments. My life was a mess.

Eventually, twenty years later I went to a 12 step meeting and met a guy named Brad. Things changed for the better and I started to get my faith back again. First, I had to forgive myself for 20 years of hurtful rage and paralyzing depression. Many years were wasted. And my faith was still not very strong. But then, something strange was to happen one day as I was stuck in a traffic jam. When it was over, my faith was fully restored and it has remained strong ever since then.

One day I was stuck in traffic on I-84 right near Pine Hill. The highway they had built for speed was so clogged with traffic that nothing was moving. I was in the very spot where the work crews had taken out half the rock hillside and all of anything that was alive. As I sat in the traffic tie-up, I reminded myself not to get upset. I could do nothing about this. I had no control over the traffic. It calmed me enough to just relax and notice my surroundings. I looked over at the cliff to my right, sheer rock rising above me. I looked about at the other cars stopped on the highway. But my eyes finally settled back on the steep rock cliff that descended to the highway.

Then I noticed something. I could hardly believe it. I blinked my eyes once to see if I was imagining things. I turned away but soon I had to turn back toward that cliff. I blinked again, still thinking I was seeing things.

What do you think I saw coming right out of the rock and doing its best to grow up toward the sun? Growing sideways right out of the rock where it would not appear that anything could possibly grow, there it was - The King of Trees. It was as if the solid rock cliff had somehow broken open. And something that had been left for dead reemerged alive and intact.

Tears filled my eyes. They were happy tears. They were tears of understanding. They were tears of gratefulness that I had survived all the mistakes I made in my life to experience this day. The King of Trees never died. It couldn't be killed. It made a comeback. It probably started growing back up as soon as it was cut down.

While I was off on two decades of hopeless drug and alcohol induced self destruction, the King of Trees just quietly did its purpose and made its slow, quiet recovery near Pine Hill.

It's been here for years - but I never had the eyes to see it until this moment. I was too busy in my anger and depression to notice it. I had surely driven up and down this highway hundreds of times in twenty years but I just never had the eyes to see it. I wasn't looking for it. I was focused on speed and on darker things all the time.

Tears of faith streamed down my face. I realized that if the King of Trees survived here on the side of Pine Hill, then the King of Trees survived in my own heart as well. If the King of Trees could not be killed on Pine Hill by the wound from a bulldozer, then the King of Trees could not be killed in my heart from the bulldozer of my terrible wounds. The King of Trees survived the wound. And I survived my wounds too.

My faithless, dead heart was healed and it once again became a place of passion and wonder and awe. The potential of the person I was meant to be was at my disposal again too.

I had become a man. It took me a long time but here I am standing on my own two feet, a faithful survivor, a stone broken open, rebirthing the King of Trees.

All these years I just didn't have the eyes to see it. I was looking in other places for happiness and never finding it. But the King of Trees was right there doing the best that it could and slowly growing up toward the sun one faithful day at a time. And now I am here also - writing this story - doing the best I can and growing one faithful day at a time.

I have suffered such terrible wounds. And I made so many self destructive trips to the liquor store. I hurt so many others along the way as well. Thank God for forgiveness. Faith is mine once again.

And faith will be yours as well if you can stand still in the open empty space and pay attention. If you do, the King of Trees will appear. You will be amazed to find your passion rekindled and your potential intact and ready to be realized.

How Can You Learn To Forgive?

The story of the King of Trees was a story about faith and a story about vision. There is a saying that I have heard that goes like this "You cannot find light by analyzing darkness over and over again". Not being able to forgive is like analyzing the dark over and over.

Such a person never sees the baby with bright eyes or the King Of Trees. He is too busy wallowing in the analysis of darkness, repeating the story over and over, failing to see the King of Trees sitting right there in front of him. Be careful of what you are searching for. If you are analyzing the same darkness day after day, then darkness is all you will see and it is what you will find. There will be no King of Trees for you.

Forgiveness has been the goal of this whole self exploration we have done so far. If you are doing the warrior work, you are getting there. Next, I will present you with a good aid to help you to remember forgiveness because forgiveness is only good to you if it is active and present.

The Story of the Burden Basket
Step 8
12 Steps of Growth

Go back and read Step 8 with your teacher. The burden basket which sits in the middle of the circle is an excellent tool to remind you of the need for forgiveness. Remember, forgiveness gives you maximum usage of your present energy. If you can remember forgiveness, you will have your relationship to power aligned properly, you will be raised above the life of consequences, and you will have the energy and desire at your disposal to do what you must do with your life to achieve happiness.

The story of the burden basket has its origin in Native American culture, although other cultures have similar tools. The burden basket can be placed anywhere such as the center of our circle. Native Americans used to place one outside the entrance to their home. You can put a tiny basket anywhere in your house as a way to utilize the power of the burden basket.

Now the basket has no power in and of itself. You give it the power by the power of your intention. Here are some of the possible uses of a burden basket:

Definition: The burden basket is a tiny basket but it is strong enough to hold any burden that is too big for you to carry right now. If you consciously place the burden into the basket, it is your way to give it to the great mystery of life, your way to accept your powerlessness, and your way to trust that if you stay true to your own heart, the situation will see its way through to a new beginning.

- The burden basket was left at the entrance to the home so that friends celebrating could enjoy themselves by leaving their burdens outside the home at the door. In this way, a person could let go of his troubles for a while so he could enjoy time with his friends and relatives and family. You and I can use the burden basket in the same way. There is a time to discuss problems, and there is another time to be less self involved and more open to fun and closeness. That is when you use the burden basket.

- You can privately use the burden basket yourself at any time. Just take the problem or burden that is pressing down on you and put it metaphorically in the basket. It does not make the problem or burden disappear. It aligns your relationship to power. You give what you cannot change or control to the great mystery and you wait with faith and hope for the king of trees. That is forgiveness.

- Last, you use the burden basket to place your own shortcomings and mistakes into it so that you don't carry the burden of your human tendency to mess up. Own your shortcomings and habitual excuses. Put it all in the basket. Life is short. There is a lot to be done. You are forgiven. Get on with it.

Burden Basket Activity

Today as we pass the talking stick around the room, talk about a burden that you would like to place in the burden basket. Talk about how this burden has prevented you from enjoying the present moment. Talk about how it may be affecting your ability to perform your daily obligations. Place the burden in the basket and unburden your own heart and brain so you can be who you need to be today. Who do you need to be today? You always need to be yourself, your real 'in your bones' 'deepest heart, self with all of your burdens, masks, and excuses cleared away.

The burden basket is an aid to help put you at the doorway to forgiveness. Forgiveness is a vast empty space of infinite potential. When the past or future is not burdening you, all that potential is present in you. In that infinite empty space of potential, you are like a mini big bang about to create the reality of the gift you came here to bring into the realm of time and space, the gift of your life purpose. You become the stone broken open, the reemergence of the king of trees

You will find exactly what you are seeking, and nothing more. What should you look for? Be patient, be true, and look for the king of trees. You will only see what you are trying to see in that empty space of infinite possibilities. So be careful for what you are expecting to see because that is exactly what you are going to find, young warrior. If darkness is your master, the darkness is your life. If you are conscious and forgiven and forgiving, the darkness becomes a place of potential where your life purpose unfolds. It is finding the key to happiness that the God, or the Not God, challenged us to find on our journey through time on earth.

Forgiveness leads us right into the 9th step of the 12 Steps of Growth. It is your job and responsibility to always be conscious enough to 'feel what is in your bones' and to stay true to your deepest heart. The rest will be given to you in its own time as it has been prepared for you by the story of the universe.

Let us proceed!

Stay True To My Deepest Heart Today
Step 9
12 Steps of Growth

Staying true to the deep heart is what it is all about. Bring yourself here successfully and all you need do for the rest of your life is to keep getting still and to keep moving forward. You are a warrior and a mature adult. As we learned earlier in the story of the Key to Happiness, happiness is right here in your own heart everyday as long as you stay true to your center. As step 9 says to you, "Happiness happens forever every moment I stay true to my deepest heart without trying to demand that this world go the way I want it to go."

In this space, you will hear the small inner voice that gets the birds to Delaware Bay on the right day at the right time. You will experience the very real blessing that is the gift of forgiveness if you can hold this space and just listen.

How do you achieve this state of mind with all the ugly things going on in the world? It is not always easy. And you will find yourself at times giving in to the hopelessness of the headlines or the sadness that happens in your own family and circle of friends. But it can be done. That is the function of forgiveness.

Story of the Box of Perception

The story of the box of perception is perhaps the hardest of my stories to try to tell in writing. It is very much a story that needs to be spoken and demonstrated. I will speak it and demonstrate it today, but I am also making an attempt to write it down so that you may take it with you.

Achieving forgiveness and faith in your life is a matter of achieving a higher awareness. There are three levels of perception that we will talk about. A child is only capable of the first one most of the time. Many people eventually become capable of the second level of perception, but many do not. Even fewer people make it to the third level of perception in their lives.

Our current public education system only recognizes the first two levels of perception at this time. That is a pity since you need all three levels of perception to be an initiated warrior and a fully mature adult. Education is not complete without the higher order third perception.

First of all, what is perception? Literally, it means to "see through" something. Your perception is your 'point of view'. It is how you see something initially, and how you interpret what you see through your own thought process. Perception is very important because as we have said, you only see what you are looking for. That is why two people can be looking at the very same thing where one sees only hopelessness and negativity, while the other sees hope and opportunity. Perception is what you choose to see and how you choose to see what you are looking at.

So then, what are these three levels of seeing through something?

- CONCRETE - the first level of perception is concrete. It is a self centered way of seeing things. Everything you see and all that exists to you are what you have seen and experienced in your own material life. Nothing else really exists to you. This concrete seeing is 'self centered' because it revolves around you. You are not open to other ways of seeing in this position. This is childish perception because it is a very limited way of seeing things. For a child, this way of seeing is quite natural. For an adult, it usually describes someone who is all for himself and thinks he knows it all. Since the only thing that exists is what he has seen, then other people and other views appear to be quite stupid to this person. This person is innocent as a child, but when this perception is carried over into adulthood, this point of view cannot help but be very negative. At the concrete level of seeing, people are dying and things are falling apart constantly. This person becomes angry, or depressed, or anesthetized from all that he has seen. Many people get stuck at this level of seeing and do not move on.

- EMPATHY BASED - the second level of perception is called empathy based perception and it is achieved by many people. I call empathy based perception community centered perception. This person gets beyond his own personal viewpoint and begins to listen and understand that different people have experienced different things. He understands that he can learn from these other people. And he can also teach them about what he has seen and done. Empathy based perception is more democratic. It is better than concrete perception because if everyone on earth stayed at the concrete level, each person would think he knew the truth and everyone else was a moron. There would be no community.

It would be each man as a truth and a country unto himself. At the empathetic level, you recognize there are other ways of seeing. You pool your point of view with the points of view of others around you. We respect each other and we try to get something done in life together. It insures you do not get stuck in your own self-righteousness. Think about what is going on in our Congress in Washington right now. They have been unable to get to this second level of perception. There is no pooling of perceptions to reach a consensus or agreement. Blind partisanship is limited to concrete perception. It is immature seeing. Apparently, we are currently being ruled by the half blind and the immature. At the concrete level, there is only one acceptable way to view things – 'my way or no way'

- NON VISIBLE - The third level of perception is called non visible. It is faith centered perception. Fewer people ever get to this level of perception, but some do. By faith centered, I do not mean necessarily that these people are religious. They may belong to a religion. However, there are many religious people who are still stuck at the concrete level of perception. So this is not about religion. It is about recognizing that, even if all of us empathetically share all the knowledge that we have, there is still a lot we don't see and understand. On my best day of optimum brain functioning of my life, I still only have a thimble full of what is the story and knowledge of the universe. I can't see it all from here at my human point of view in time and space, and neither can my brothers and sisters. It takes faith to function at this level of perception. Without faith, this level of perception is too scary to contemplate. But, again, you do not necessarily have to go to church or believe in God to see in this way. It is a great mystery if you are an atheist. And it is a Great Mystery if you believe in a formal, personal God. If you have achieved this level of perception, you have achieved a mature relationship to power in your life. The power of the universe is a force bigger than you can imagine, and you are a part of it. The Lord is the Golden Rule! Or, if you prefer to view this in a non-religious way, "The golden rule is lord"

The Demonstration of the Box of Perception

Let me now hold up this large painted box in front of you. Each side is painted a different color. I am holding it up in the center of the circle. I need for you to use your imagination as I explain the story of the box.

Please imagine yourself as very small in relation to the box. You are so small that, as you stand on your side of the box, all you can see as far as you can see in any direction is the color of your side of the box. Your side of the box is a metaphor for all the experiences and all the things and places you have seen in your human life. Nothing else exists for you beyond this side of the box because it is all you have seen and done. This is concrete perception.

Now, I will ask you one at a time what color the box is. "What color is the box, John?" John says, "The box is red." I say, "Of course the box is red. Any idiot can see that can't they? It is therefore a red life, isn't it John?" John says, "of course, obviously". Next I go to another person in the circle and I say, "Crystal, what color is the box?" Crystal says, "The box is green." I then say, "Of course it is green. Any idiot can see the box is green, can't they? It is therefore a green life, isn't it, Crystal?" Crystal says, "Yes".

Next, I say, "What is wrong with John over here? He thinks the box is red. Crystal, is he stupid or what?" Crystal says, "He must be stupid or blind. The box is green. It is obvious" This goes on around the circle. Students see the box and the concrete reality of the experiences they have been through as the totality of what life is about.

They do not acknowledge other points of view as having any validity because they have never seen the other sides of the box. As far as the concrete level perceiver sees, there are no other sides to the box. The other people do not perceive correctly. They all need to adjust their perception to see what he is seeing.

Great battles are fought in life over concrete perception. They happen in the hallways, cafeterias, and lavatories in school. Sometimes, the battles get physical. Congress gets bogged down in lack of humility through partisan concrete vision. Countries also have wars over concrete perception. Families have domestic disputes. A world full of concrete perceivers would be a world where you stand alone and feel like no one else on the planet knows what is really going on, but you do. The results of this are not pretty. Pick up any newspaper.

People who can make the leap to empathy based perception can eventually understand that it is a big box and there are different sides and each has a different but valid point of view from the side of the box where you are viewing life. At this level of perception, people can learn to get along, countries can use diplomacy to work things through, Congress would find a way to compromise, and families can learn to tolerate differences of opinion on matters without coming to blows. A world of empathy is a more fluid world unlike the world of solid concrete perception.

But finally, there is a third perception. Spatially, the box only inhabits a small portion of this big room we are in. So now, we go on to non visible perception. What exists beyond all the sides of the box that is far beyond all of our human capacity to see and to experience? What is out here and out here? And what is within you in the infinite depth of your heart?

The infinity of the great mystery exists within you as well as far beyond the universe of the sides of the box. This is faith centered perception. At this level of perception, you must 'let go' and have faith in the truth inside your own heart. You need to forgive your own side of the box to be here. And you need to the maturity to forgive everyone else's side of the box to be here.

There is an infinite universe out there and it is a great mystery that it is somehow mysteriously all held together like it appears to be held together as it disappears beyond the viewpoint of the most talented astronomers and quantum physicists into the mist of mystery.

If it is a mystery and it can't be known, why acknowledge it? You acknowledge it because when you are in the forgiveness state of mind, you can 'feel' the truth of this non visible world in your bones. The village elders used to call the stones "the bones of the earth". They used to say that the knowledge of the whole universe was at the center of the stone. So the truth is in your bones. That is what happens when a person has an intuition and says "I can feel it in my bones". The heart at the center of the stone is your heart. When you can sit quietly in a forgiven frame of mind, you are here now. You are approaching the center of the stone. Be true to this place. Let it speak and act through you. There is something you have to do to fulfill your life purpose. This is the sacred place from which the courage and the energy will come. It is very powerful once you learn to access it through your new faith based perceptive skills.

Drawing Activity

Use a piece of paper and imagine it is your side of the box. Make a drawing of all the important things that happened that shaped your concrete perception as a child. Try to include happy times of youth, but also your wound, your mistakes, your mask, and any ways in which your concrete perception changed as you got older and saw all the problems in the world and in your family and community. If you have trouble drawing, you may write in some symbolic words that depict your concrete perception.

We will discuss the drawings during our next group. Keep in mind that concrete perception is not 'bad' perception. You have to live here on the planet in the muddy reality of earth in time and space. You have to live in the limited experiences provided by your side of the box.

Concrete perception, therefore, is not 'bad' perception. It is 'limited' perception that leads you to conclusions that may not be true. It also leads you to distrust the 'truth' of the mystery living in your own heart. Without trust in that deep heart, you can't hope to fly to Delaware Bay on Delaware Bay day. You will be too self involved to be there on purpose on that glorious day. You will be somewhere else, lost in the battles and losses and temporary triumphs of your side of the box.

The closest you get to the truth is when you drop your mask and your excuses and complaints, and your attachments, and you just get real with yourself about what it feels like inside your bones today. That honesty takes you to the heart at the center of the stone of earth life. And that is as close as you and I get to the truth of the whole universe. That's as good as it gets on planet earth.

In community, the closest we get to the truth is to gaze into each other's eyes and to respect the truth as it speaks through each individual. It is tricky because all of us tend to drift between perceptions, sinking into totally concrete perception when we are afraid or threatened. Still others get caught up in a faith based perception that tries to rise above earth life so that the mud of real life never has to be acknowledged or experienced again.

Effective faith based perception respects the lord of mystery at the same time that it demonstrates the willingness to live every day in this mud and concrete world. This is what we are trying to do right now in this group. This is earth life. We have to live on this planet on which we are apparently trapped. Don't question and don't try to escape it. Get in touch with your deep heart and live in it. Live in community from the center of your being, from your heart.

And then you just do what you do and say what you say in deep respect to the mystery, in deep respect to your community of brothers and sisters, and in deep respect of your sacred and vulnerable mortal self.

If All I Believe Is What I Have Seen

If all I believe is what I have seen on my side of the box
I project what I have experienced as the whole truth

If the wound happens on my side of the box
I project my wound as a very personal wound

If I project my wound as personal
I see myself as a victim

If I get stuck in this victim stance
I lose my core and my center and my connection to the mystery

If I lose my core and center
I lose balance

If I am not balanced and not centered
I drift from my own heart

If I drift from my own heart
I am alone and unhappy even when I am around others.

If I am alone against a hostile world of wounds and death
I need an attachment to make me feel good

My attachment changes me more and I get more lost from my heart
I make a new personality based on the wound and my side of the box

I keep drifting away from center
Until someone or something cracks open the stone of my personality

I return to my own deep heart
Accept earth life as it comes to me
I live centered and balanced
Real
Forgiven
Forgiving
True

If you are working yourself through this challenge successfully, you have passed our village's version of the State of Connecticut's CAPT Test. But our CAPT is a different test. **CAPT - Coordinate A Perceptual Transformation.** Now there is a test that can turn around public education.

I am honored to be your teacher. If I have taught you something, it is only because I have no idea what it is I am even talking about. And neither do you!

If you can remember the steps we have traversed so far, you are ready for the final forgiveness concept in this challenge. This is the 'maintenance lesson' Once you are in your own heart and on track with your purpose, you will constantly drift off purpose. You need a warrior's consciousness. We will talk about what that is a bit later in the book as we approach the banquet. For now, I want to discuss the next step on the 12 Steps of Growth.

Sacred Space-Sacred Path
10th Step
12 Steps of Growth

Read this step with your teacher. If you have any initial reactions or impressions about the step, share them with your group.

Once you have achieved the vision of perception and the patience of faith, you are ready to rock, young warrior. I am going to teach you to ride three horses as we approach the end of the year and our village celebration at the banquet. Before you can ride any of these horses, I need to make sure you know how to walk. That is the subject of this 10th step

When you are staying true to your deepest heart, you are in sacred space and you are walking your sacred path. You are like a bird flying to Delaware Bay. You are right on the money in your daily life, focused and on your spot, here and now.

First, let's quickly deal with this word sacred and its religious connotation. The literal meaning of the word sacred is to designate something to be worthy of reverence and deep respect. If something is sacred, it is inviolable and not to be messed with.

When you treat something in your life like it is sacred, you are devoted to that activity. So then, your sacred path is the life purpose you were sent here to accomplish. It is sacred for all the reasons stated above. Your sacred space is the personal boundary of your personhood. In order for you to walk your sacred path, you need to be in sacred space. That space is sacred because it is from this place that you will find the courage and power to do your purpose. It is the place where the unstoppable king of trees emerges from the broken open stone.

Sacred Space

In order to be within your sacred space, you have to be free of your mental chains, free of your mask, and solid in the balance and center of the heart at the core of the stone that is you. The layers of stone are the chapters of your life story, but that story is now being written, not from the wounds and losses, but from the spark at the center of your being. That spark is sacred. It is the real you. Protect the sacredness of this spark in you. Let no one mess with it.

Boundaries

Your sacred space is boundless inside your heart. But on the outer edge of the stone, you need to develop and maintain boundaries that protect your inner being. Without these boundaries the world will enter and hurt you over and over again.

What are your boundaries? Your boundaries are physical, emotional, mental, and spiritual. Physical boundaries allow you to demand respect for your body. With this, you must develop respect for the sacredness of other people's bodies as well. Hold your arms out at arm's length in all directions. That is your personal space. Anyone who enters this space needs to do so with your permission. It is your sacred space.

Many people who want to be loved very badly allow other people to crash their boundaries hoping people will love them if they do. Anyone who crashes your boundaries does not love you. They are too self involved at the childish level of perception to love anybody. Close the door and make them respect your boundaries. Also, of course, develop a deep respect for the boundaries of other peoples' personal space.

Your emotional and mental and spiritual boundaries are also very sacred and need to be respected. Only you know how it feels to be you inside. Place yourself in the company of people who can respect the real you in your heart. Move away from people who cannot accept you for how you feel or for what you need to maintain your own self respect.

You need to be able to understand that people will disagree with you and may even confront you. That is part of life on all sides of the box of perception. But once they personally attack you or try to force their way of seeing or feeling on you, they are crossing a line that you need to protect. Your boundaries are being crashed. Your space is sacred. Don't let anyone violate the boundaries that are important to you.

So then, your job is to first establish your boundaries for yourself. Then you demand respect for your boundaries. Move away from anyone who constantly needs to crash your sacred space.

You also have to respect the boundaries of others. If you became a father and had always dreamed of having a football playing son, what are you going to do if God has given you a passive, artistic son? Are you going to try to turn him into a football player? You are going accept and bless him as he is and you are going to nurture him to be the best he can be while accepting his core and his heart exactly as they are. He has a gift to bring and a life purpose. Your job as a parent is to open the space for the gift to be delivered.

It's hard work and it is impossible unless you can get your small self out of the way by accepting what the mystery of life has given to you. The sacredness of each human heart must be respected.

Relationships

Relationships can be tricky. We all want to make another person happy. That is one of the joys in life - to love someone and know you are the reason they choose to be happy today. But a relationship requires balance just a like a person. Abusive relationships are not balanced. The needs of one person take precedence over the other person's needs. One person drops all boundaries and self respect trying to remain in the good graces of the abuser. And it seems the more the violated person gives up in self respect and self boundaries, the more the abuser wants. The abuser is never happy. Clinicians call this a codependent relationship because each person is feeding and dependent upon a relationship that is not healthy.

Here is a story about relationships and boundaries that I call The Hollies and The Grapevine

The Story of the Hollies and the Grapevine

Relationships make life worth all the trouble. Despite all of the problems, being with people you love and care for is why most of us get up every morning. But what makes a good relationship? Relationship comes from the word relate. Relate comes from the word 'relay'. Relay means to communicate, to connect in a meaningful way. Relay is similar to the word 'real'.

A good relationship is one of respect where I can be real with you and you can be real back. In this act of open communication, love is born. I know you and I love you. You know me and you love me. I am energized and affirmed when I know that someone loves the real me just because I am me. I feel supported in this love and I find the strength to get up each day and do my life purpose. In the end I get back only as much love as I have been willing to give.

Yet many people get into relationships that hurt, where all the giving is one way with no return, where they get put down and injured every day instead of getting energized and affirmed. Often, people in these poor relationships stay together either out of habit or because they are afraid of the unknown and prefer their daily poison to the uncertainty of life without their current relationship.

How can you tell a good relationship? It does no good to make up a list of positives and negatives. The truth about whether you should be in a relationship or not is in your own heart. You already know if the relationship is good for your life or bad for it. You do not need a list of positive traits and negative traits, nor do you need anyone else's opinion. The only question you must ask yourself is whether your life is being energized and affirmed every day or whether the relationship is just dragging you down every day. You already know the answer to that question and you already know what you should do. Listen to that voice in you. That's the challenge of your life!

I thought of this story one day when I was sitting in my backyard. I was looking at the big tree in my neighbor's backyard. It was slowly being covered over by a giant invasive creeping grape vine. The grapevine had climbed the trunk and was now busily creeping and covering every branch and every leaf on that giant tree. It seemed that the grapevine loved that tree so much that it needed to cover every inch of its existence. It was taking possession of the tree because it loved it so much.

Yet I knew that this process would not have a happy ending for that beautiful tree. The grapevine would not stop loving that tree until it smothered it to death. It would kill the tree it loved it so much. This was possessiveness really. It was not love. And possession in a relationship is smothering. It is so smothering that it actually kills the object that it supposedly loves so much. A possessive relationship sometimes feels very nice at first because it is paying so much attention to me. But a possessive relationship eventually crosses a line and becomes annoyingly clingy. Finally, it crosses another line into the territory of suffocation and abuse, and sometimes, even murder.

Right next to my deck are a line of holly bushes that I planted many years ago. I planted these hollies in a line side by side, one female plant and one male plant in a line. The male plant sends its pollen by way of the breeze to the female holly. The female holly responds by producing beautiful red berries. The female plant thrives and grows and is quite beautiful, yet she remains totally independent of the male plant. The male plant is not smothering her or killing her or abusing her or possessing her. He is energizing her and affirming her. And the female plant is doing the same for the male. As she sits by his side, she does not try to smother or possess or kill the male plant. She is energizing his life and affirming his life every day. It is a beauty that I witness every year.

But, what happened to the grapevine and the oak tree?

Oh yes, the grapevine succeeded in his desire to totally surround the big tree. The big tree died last year. What a shame. I guess the grapevine thought smothering the tree would win its love. Instead it suffocated the very object of its desire. There was now a big problem for the grapevine. . Without the nutrients from the tree, the grapevine could not live either. It didn't matter in the end. My neighbor paid a tree service to cut down the tree and its invasive lover, the grapevine.

Are you in a creeping vine relationship or a holly relationship?

Demand respect for your own sacred space and be tender and respectful to the sacred space of everyone you meet. In this way, you grow side by siding affirming each other's existence and growing in a way that is both loving and liberating

Sacred Path

Once you have the sacred space thing in order, all you really need to do is listen to your heart and keep walking. The path will open before you. Beware! There are many tempting side roads along the way and some of them lead to big trouble and consequences galore.

If you stay balanced, you will know when you are off on a side road. If you have good friends and relationships, your loved ones will remind you when you seem to be going off purpose.

Pay attention. Confrontation and friction are not necessarily a violation of space. As long as the confronter is respectful, he or she may be noticing something that you really need to pay attention to. Loved ones usually know we are going off purpose long before we know it ourselves. It is not love if there is never any tension or friction.

A relationship is a balancing act. Listen to your heart and pay attention to how you are coming across to others at the same time. Let your loved one's know how they are coming across to you as well. Encourage and affirm and spur each other on to growth and the liberation of being the best you can be in your life. The result will be beautiful red berries.

Relationship Activity

When the talking stick is passed around today, talk about a relationship you have been in that has been like the grapevine's relationship to the oak tree. What was it like? Are you still in it? Talk about the characteristics of this relationship. How did it help you at first? How is it dragging you down and preventing your growth in time?

Relate a time in your life when you felt like the smothered, suffocating oak tree in a clingy relationship. Now, also relate a time when you were the grapevine trying to possess another in a needy way that was unhealthy.

Next, talk about a relationship with someone that is like the relationship that the holly plants had. What is that like? Talk about how the relationship started. Talk about how it grew and how it now affirms you and helps you grow as a person. Talk about your part in helping the growth of the other. How is this relationship helping you? What are the beautiful red berries this relationship is producing?

Touching the World with Your Love
Step 11
12 Steps of Growth

This sounds a little like a hallmark card so I hope sometimes hallmark does get it right because I can't think of a better way to say it. If you are on your sacred path, you are going to do your life purpose. You may not even think about it or know you are doing it while you are doing it. It will just come natural. Now the next sentence does not sound like a hallmark card. Love is dropping your sheen of excuses and your mask and giving your real self to another. Love is living your story and creating a life story you can live with inside your own heart. Love is what you do when you are whole and on purpose in your own heart. When you are comfortable in your own skin, everyone can feel it and they are drawn to you.

This is touching the world with your love. You are making a ripple in the ocean of life and your ripple or wave is in concert with the waves around you. It is very powerful. It is very life affirming. And it is very natural once you start to flow with it.

Taking my Place in Our Group and in the World
Step 12
12 Steps of Growth

We are covering these final steps faster because they all require forgiveness as a prerequisite. If you can get to an expanded awareness and consciousness of forgiveness and flow in that state of being, you will do these final few steps quite naturally, almost automatically, though they are best enjoyed when you do them consciously.

This final step has a specific meaning. We are now over the hump on this train ride. You should be at the point where you are ready to start taking a leadership role in this group. Are you here for others as well as yourself? Are you giving of your time to someone or some cause in the community?

In criminal court these days, judges sentence kids to community like it was a punishment. I know the intention is good, but I want to make sure you understand this - **Community Service is not a punishment. It is noble and needed.** Even if you are not currently under arrest for something, I hope you will find a way both inside our group and outside our group to find a way to contribute to the well being of the village. Community is what makes your life meaningful and purposeful. Without it, you get quite lost, off center, ungrounded, and out of balance.

Community Activity

As we pass the talking stick today, talk about a community project you are involved in. If you are not involved in anything, talk about a project you might volunteer for, or even one you might create yourself. Give back to the community. The community has given you much. Be grateful.

Also, talk about extending and deepening your role in the village of our group as we begin to approach the second half of our journey. Right now as we speak, there is another kid like you down at the middle school or about to come into the venue of wherever you are taking this course.

When he arrives in one of our groups, it is you who will help him by your example. He will come here with a blaming attitude and a victim stance approach to his own problems. You will understand because that is the way you arrived here. You will also know every bit of the new kid's excuses because you have already tried it all and have surely been in his shoes once upon a time.

You are the future of this village much more than you realize. Without a core of top leaders, the teacher cannot get the new kids to take the program seriously for months. If you are serious, and you are a leader, it takes a few hours for the new kids to know they need to take the village of our group seriously.

Conclusion

This has been a very arduous challenge. It could easily be split into two challenges but it is important you see the connections in the journey we have traveled thus far. At the beginning of this challenge, we were not yet at the midpoint of our journey. The train was chugging slowly uphill. With forgiveness, this group is in a new place on the journey. Now we are over the hump. We are well on the road to the final destination.

We have arrived at the spot where I can put you through the final test. If you have a handle on your own story in the context of the bigger story, you are ready to navigate the troubled water, to explore your myth and possibly establish a new myth by which to live your life, and you are ready to bring the train into the station at our banquet.

The waters of our lives are red, black, and white. Learning how to navigate these waters is one of the final skills of the journey of this group. It is a formidable skill, but I am certain the time is right and that you are ready to ride the rapids.

Let's begin!

QUESTIONS FROM HEROIC JOURNEY CHALLENGE FIVE

1. What is forgiveness to you?

2. How is the description of forgiveness in the 7th step different from most people's perception of forgiveness?

3. Who is the most important person that you will ever have to forgive?

4. Why is it so important for you to forgive others?

5. What does the phrase "You can't find light by analyzing darkness over and over mean?

6. Why wasn't the storyteller able to see the King of Trees for 20 years?

7. What is a burden basket used for? How could you use the burden basket in your life?

8. What are the three levels of perception described in the box story? Describe the difference between the three levels. Which levels of perception do you use?

9. What is your sacred space? Describe what physical and non physical boundaries are.

10. How clear and strong are your own boundaries? Explain what you mean?

11. What was the meaning of the story of The Hollies and the Grapevine? What did it teach about relationships?

12. Describe a relationship you have had and compare it to a holly relationship or a grapevine relationship.

13. What is your sacred path and how do you know when you are on it? How can others help keep you on the path?

14. What are you contributing to the community you live in? What can you do to get involved?

15. What is your role in our group now? How can this role evolve into one of leadership if it is not already?

Heroic Journey
Challenge #6

Learn to Recognize, Accept, And Navigate My Emotions

Message to Group Leader:

This challenge marks the place in the journey where the application aspects of this course take precedence. The lessons have been taught. The stories have been told. It is time for the young initiates to show that they can keep their vision active at a mature level while diving 'in' to the muddy reality of every day. That muddy reality is full of opposites, of conflict and friction, of confusion and of moments of clarity, and of deep sorrow and joy as well. The truth of daily living is felt through our emotions. In order to traverse earth life successfully, you must learn to be in the moment. In the moment you must develop the ability to recognize emotions, to walk into the truth of each emotion, and to learn to ride these emotions like a warrior.

- **Living the Story in Colors**

    o Reviewing the Story
    o The Purpose of Water
    o The Intelligence of Digestion

- **The Truths at the Center of the Stone**

    o Emotional Alchemy
    o The Process of Heating and Freezing
    o The Shadow Aspect of Emotion
    o The Pin that Puts Me to Sleep
    o Break Point or Boiling Point

- **The Circle of Feelings**

    o Red Desire – Red Anger
        ▪ Recognizing Red Desire and Anger
        ▪ Navigating Red Desire and Anger
    o Black Darkness – Black Sorrow
        ▪ Recognizing Black Death and Sorrow
        ▪ Navigating Black Death and Sorrow
    o White Light – White Joy
        ▪ Recognizing White Light and White Joy
        ▪ Navigating White Light and White Joy
    o Yellow Vigilance – Yellow Fear
        ▪ Recognizing Yellow Vigilance and Fear
        ▪ Navigating Yellow Vigilance and Yellow Fear

- **The Process of Red-Black-White as a Process of Initiation**

Introduction
Are You Ready To Ride?

Have you ever looked outside in the middle of winter at the frozen ground? It would appear that everything is dead. Trees are bare. Flowers are decayed. Nothing is growing and thriving. But then in March, you notice when days start getting longer. The sun is arcing higher in the sky slowly coaxing the new life of the spring. Birds chirp a song of rebirth. And so, the lifeless, barren winter does come to an end. Can you put this truth into your heart?

If you have been paying attention to the concepts introduced on forgiveness, you have learned to appreciate that there is a certain beauty to the coldness of winter. It is in the hard times of the cold and dark that we bond together so that we can survive. Out of the survival of the hard times your character gets built. You recognize yourself as a survivor and a warrior.

The pilgrims celebrated the first thanksgiving only a few weeks before the long cold winter was to begin. It was a celebration of gratefulness even though they knew that many of them would not survive that first brutal winter. The English villages where they had come from had never experienced a winter such as the ones we have here on the east coast. But, they were grateful, nonetheless. They did what could be done to help each other through. This was the price of freedom from the slavery of religious persecution. They willingly chose the dangers of the winter in New England over the slavery of a life with no freedom.

This is our thanksgiving in our village. You are a courageous warrior navigating the cold winter of your story because you know it will make you free. Just like you believe that spring time will arrive in a few weeks even though all life outside seems to be dead now, you can also believe in the spring time of your emotional life, and the spring time of your life story, even though the wound and the hopeless winter that followed made you feel frozen and dead.

If you have had the courage to follow the journey of this train ride all the way to this point, you are ready for the spring time of your life story. But, unfortunately, the spring time of your life is not without its own challenges and dangers. The snows melt, and the rivers rise and move swiftly. Sometimes they overflow their banks with the melting snows of winter.

Your next challenge in your warrior training is to learn to navigate the troubled water. There is an old African American spiritual song that goes like this:

Wade Into the Water
Wade Into the Water, Children
Wade Into the Water
Jesus Is Going To Trouble the Water

We have to leave Jesus out of this introductory talk if we are in a public institution. So we will insert 'great mystery' in where they sang about Jesus. The great mystery of life troubles the waters of our life. As author Karla McLaren pointed out, either we learn to navigate these waters, or we don't learn to navigate them. Ignoring them completely is an option, but it is not advised. Why? Have you ever had your back turned in ignorance to a powerful wave while you were standing in the ocean?

The waves of our waters are Red, Black, and White. In order to do this together, we need to put into practice everything we have done so far.

We need:

- A functioning group with all internal issues out in the center of the circle. Our ability to live in the muddy truth of our daily group process must be a daily commitment by now.

- We need an understanding of our relationship to power. Our intellectual abilities must be celebrated for their smarts yet humbled to their human limitations.

- Finally, we need an understanding, and more importantly, a daily consciousness and focused application of vision that respects concrete, invisible, and non-visible realities. Faith and willingness to accept, to let go, and to forgive must be in our daily consciousness even if forgiveness is too difficult to do at times.

We are not looking for solutions as we begin the journey of the next two challenges through the Red, Black, and White and through the examination of myth in the story of our lives. What we are looking for is truth as we experience it in our bones. We are now approaching the homestretch of the journey to break open the truth at the center of the stone.

Let's Begin!

Living the Story of the Universe

Before we venture out into the waves of our daily lives, let us briefly review the waves of our universe one more time. Our daily lives are connected to the story of the universe and reflect the story of the universe here at our level of being. It is a wise move when we learn to flow with this story since it is also our story.

Astronomically, our universe is expanding outward infinitely from a fixed center. Your life and the waves of your life are also expanding outward infinitely from a fixed center. It behooves you then to get in touch with your center because the center will provide the balance you will need to expand your life into adulthood successfully. I hope by now, whether you go to church or not, or believe in God or Not God, that you have broken open the stone enough to be with your center.

From the perspective of quantum physics, your center disappears within itself into the infinite heart of the great mystery. Stay true to your deep heart and you are staying true to the great mystery that powers this universe of infinite expansion and infinite implosion.

On earth we live in the world of energy and matter. Einstein brilliantly came to the conclusion that E=MC squared. This formula stands for ENERGY = MATTER X THE SPEED OF LIGHT SQUARED.

Now, I am not Einstein for sure. But I am a storyteller. In my story, energy is the unseen force that powers the waves. Matter is the concrete world of particles that I perceive everyday with my eyes. The speed of light brings mystery into the equation. We live in a reality where energy and matter keep transforming back and forth across the equal sign of Einstein's equation. Waves of energy eventually become matter. Matter becomes the fuel to spark new energy - in a perfectly balanced equation of moving visible, invisible, and non visible phenomena within an amazing constant called the speed of light.

This makes the equal sign in this equation very interesting indeed. What does it mean to a storyteller like me? First, it means that apparently there is no death. Particle transforms to wave and wave transforms back to particle - infinitely. Secondly, it asks the question who or what is the power or commander at the point of transformation in the equal sign of the equation of life? Now there is a question we are not going to answer. Find your own answer in your church, or in your heart. For us in our village, it is a mystery and that is where we leave it. But it is a mystery that induces faith and recognizes a center where my life and all existence are perfectly balanced in an equation that is a dance of life.

Hold this center to keep your balance as we proceed. We are going into the troubled water of human life right now. Find your own center, not someone else's center. Be balanced and comfortable in your own skin.

That is the story of the universe. That is the story of your life on earth. And that is also the story of all the days within the story of your life on earth. Navigating the troubled water is learning how to navigate the waves of your energetic life, your emotions, in a way that allows your life to flow and unfold. Without this skill, you are overwhelmed by your emotions or you tend to deny or hide them.

Either way, inability to express emotion leads to symptoms and consequences as well as a reduced capacity for quality of life.

Prerequisites for Emotional Navigation

The Purpose of Water

We need to make sure you understand the element that your navigation will take place within. Water is the essence of life as we know it. As the story goes, the very first signs of life crawled up out of the wetness.

Science tells us that 80% of our body content is water. It would be wise then, since it is the essence of life and since it is the substance that we will be asked to navigate ourselves through, to take a look at water. How does it operate? Where does it go? What does it do? What is its purpose?

I am holding a small cup of water. I am going to spill just the tiniest droplet on the floor. Can everyone see the tiny droplet of water here on the floor?

Okay, now we are ready to see what we can learn from the intelligence of water. Forget about the droplet while we have a little discussion.

When I spilled that tiny droplet out of the cup, which way did it go? Yes, it went down. It seems like a silly question but I have just demonstrated that water is smart enough to follow the laws of nature, of gravity. It didn't demand to go sideways or up. It just surrendered to its powerlessness over gravity and down it went.

Can anyone now use her imagination and try to tell me where the water tried to go when it went down? There are a lot of good answers but the answer I am looking for is that the water tried to go home. The water tried to go home? Where is home? Let's just say that for water the ocean is home. So that tiny drop hit the floor and did the best it could to get to the ocean. That is as far as it got.

All water does its best to get to the ocean. That is where it came from and that is where it wants to go.

Now the poor droplet I spilled on the floor didn't get very far. Too bad, huh!! Just down the street from here, there is water in the brook that we call the Mad River that is making real progress in its journey to the ocean. It is flowing on down through Waterbury, past the mall to the Naugatuck River. The Naugatuck flows into the Housatonic River. And the Housatonic flows into the ocean into Long Island Sound at Westport.

So it is with all water. If we look at a map of the United States, we will find that all the water in all the brooks and rivers east of the Appalachian Mountains, runs down to the Atlantic Ocean. All of the water on the other side of the Appalachians runs down into the Mississippi River and down into the Ocean in the Gulf of Mexico. Likewise all the water on the eastern side of the Rocky Mountains flows down to the Gulf as well. On the Other side of the Rockies, there is some water that gets trapped in a great basin on its way to the ocean. But the rest of the water all flows down to the Pacific Ocean on the west side of the Rockies and the Sierra Nevada Mountains. It is a law. Water wants to go home to the ocean.

Let's briefly look at how the water travels to the ocean. At times the water surges and rages with rapids. It is very powerful and passionate. The energetic color that goes with passion and raging is red. Red is full of action and power. The red fire of electricity comes from raging water.

Some water stagnates or seems to be going nowhere in whirlpools for a while. Stagnant water is somewhat depressing. The energetic color that goes with this is black. It looks pretty hopeless for the black water. It is stuck in stagnant pockets or whirl pooling with no visible progress.

At other times, water moves peacefully and contentedly on its journey to the ocean. The energetic color for peace and contentment is white. So, then water can make its journey in rage at times, depressed at times, and at peace at times. But it never stops trying to get to the ocean because that is its purpose.

There are two prerequisites that must be remembered consciously in order to do the red, the black, and the white successfully. The first has to do with your relationship to power.

The important thing to notice is water's relationship to power. Water does not resist. Its relationship to power is in perfect alignment. It rages when it is time to rage. It stagnates and accepts this when it is time to stagnate, and it flows contentedly and peacefully when it is time for that. Water is on purpose and it accepts its powerlessness to the great mystery of life. It just does what it does.

This is true of the water in the ocean as well. As powerful as the ocean waters are, they obey the laws of the tides which in turn obey the laws of the moon and its relationship to earth, the sun, and the black hole at the center of the galaxy. Water is very powerful, but still, it knows its place and has its relationship to power perfectly aligned to the power of the great mystery of life.

Now, let's get back to the tiny droplet of water we left here on the floor. That poor water cannot get to the ocean now because of me and my victimizing decision to spill it on the floor. It went as far as it could get and it could get no further. If that water could talk, it would probably be cursing me. It would probably be blaming me. It would probably be very depressed because it could not get to the ocean because of my actions. I killed that water and stopped it from doing its purpose.

Look down now at the droplet of water. Ummm... wait a minute! Where did it go? Anybody, where did the water go? It is gone!!!

That's correct. It is on its way to the ocean. It has evaporated back into cloud and it is heading for the ocean right now as we speak. It didn't die here on the floor at all. It is doing its purpose like water always does its purpose.

Notice the water never complained. It did not take a victim stance. It did not let me have power over it. It was patient and just did what it does to complete its life purpose. When it couldn't get to the ocean in liquid form, it found a way to get there as cloud.

Water does its purpose and has its relationship to power straight.

Our emotions are meant to flow just like water. Water pushes forward in red with passion and action. It flows peacefully and lazily at other times in the white. And, still other times, it gets hung up or stuck in stagnation and blackness like the water on the floor.

Water is also like me in that it has a visible material presence and a spiritual invisible presence. The water on the floor did not die. It transformed from visible to non visible. It also flows in the non visible presence of the power of the great mystery that controls the tides and the pull of the universe.

You and I need to learn from the water. After all, we are 80% water. We are trying to go home also. The ocean that we return to is also not visible from here. Our ocean is inside our own hearts and beyond the concrete facts in front of us. It is vast and endless and small and simple all at the same time.

In order to do the red, black, and white like a warrior, you will need to learn and remember the intelligence of water. Respect your own power in the redness, blackness, and whiteness of your daily life. Use it. Respect the larger laws of the invisible and non visible power of the great mystery of life as well. Now that is smart water. And that is a smart human too. You need to have your relationship to power aligned, balanced, and in focus to do the red, black, and white in your life.

Water has transformational power when it is smart enough just to be water and do what water does. You and I have the same transformational power too when we are smart enough to just be ourselves and do what we do.

The Intelligence of Digestion

The second prerequisite for doing the red, black, and white successfully is to be able to live in a state of forgiveness. Forgiveness can navigate the waters of the red, black, and white successfully because it knows how to find and stand at the still point of the present moment.

It is free from the guilt and wounds of the past, and free from the worry and anxiety of the future.

So now you are probably going to laugh at me, but I am going to ask you who has urinated or had a bowel movement in the last few days? Everyone, I hope. I would like to look at the natural intelligence of the digestive system. What does it have to do with forgiveness and the ability to do the red, the black, and the white?

Quite simply, the digestive tract is intelligent enough to take the food you feed it and to make a number of important decisions. First, it will evaluate and expel upward anything that it perceives as being poison or toxic to you. It refuses receipt of alcohol, for example, when too much arrives at the portal. And up it comes.

Second, it takes the food that it does accept and makes another important decision. It decides what should be extracted from this food that is of use to your body. It takes all the nutrients, all the vitamins. That intelligent decision gives you another day of life. It sends the nutrients into your bloodstream where they are transformed from matter into the energy that powers your day.

Third, it takes the unused part of the food that it cannot find a use for and it sends it down the river and back out to the material world. Brilliant!

If we could learn the intelligence of the digestive system, we could do forgiveness to perfection. First, we would expel anything from our boundaries as soon as we perceived that it was poison for us. Next, we would be smart enough to take the food of our past life experiences and to extract whatever lessons and strength could be taken from it. We would release that good into our bloodstream so it could be turned into energy to power our life purpose and our emotional day.

Last, we would be smart enough to eliminate whatever we don't need, and whatever is not useful. We would not hold onto the parts of the past that could back up and make our emotional lives unpleasant and toxic. Not being able to eliminate what is not helpful will cause repercussions - life threatening repercussions.

If you don't believe me, just ask the digestive system what happens if your body cannot eliminate.

So then, learn the intelligent forgiveness of the digestive tract. You have to be able to stand in the forgiveness of the present moment in order to successfully traverse the waters of the red, black, and white in your life.

Both the story of water and the story of digestion are stories about transformation. Water does its thing and successfully transforms to cloud when it is time to transform. Digestion does its part in the transformation of matter into energy right inside of you every day.

Now let's see if we can apply this intelligence to the daily lives of our emotions in the red, black, and white. What are the truths we must traverse in life red, black, and white?

Truths at the Center of the Stone

When the elders of the village said the knowledge of the whole universe was held at the center of the stone, they were looking at that stone with a simple depth that provided them with answers that are perhaps no longer possible in our complex age of parsed specifics.

They were not looking at the stone and making a superstitious conjecture. The center of the stone told a story to them. It is my story and your story. It is the story of the whole universe. There is mystery at the center of the stone that is shrouded by the passage of time. Every tiny particle that makes up the stone of your life happened in time. In time, the mystery at the center was covered over. What was that mystery that the elders simply accepted as mystery?

Telling your story in our village is like cracking open the stone. Removing the protective shell that time has created is at once exciting and scary. It brings you back to your own heart which provides the exhilaration of letting go and being real. It is scary because you are wounded by time. Going back to the center brings you back through your time wound.

That is scary and perhaps you would never make this journey on your own without insistent elders who knew that making the journey was an unavoidable part of education and the passage to adulthood.

So then, what were the truths at the center of the stone cracked open in the adolescent stage of life? As a child, you were protected from these truths because innocence is the essence of childhood. But now your childhood is over. Experience has extinguished innocence. The only way back to the truths at the core of the mystery and its infinite flame was through your story.

The elders saw three truths at the center of the cracked open stone:

Truth number one is WHITE. At the center of the universe, at the center of my heart, at the center of the stone, there is pure joy. It is a joy so great that it cannot be explained in the human realm. It can only be felt at certain times when the heart is opened and free and willing to be real and to feel. It is the joy of purpose and meaning and connection. It is the joy of community. It is the essence of love. The story of Delaware Bay depicted the beauty and connection inherent in this story before human consciousness and choice came into being. The universe is a joyful place to experience and it is good. Experience the joy at the center of your heart fully and willingly and you are showing the skill of the initiated warrior able to face adult life. Faith gets you through this experience. This experience, like all experience, eventually dissolves like a wave hitting the shore and dissipating quite naturally if you are brave enough to ride the truth of it fully with eyes wide open.

Truth number two is BLACK. At the center of the universe, at the center of my heart, at the center of the stone, there is pure sorrow. It is a sadness that is so great that it cannot be explained in the human realm. It can only be felt at certain times when the heart is opened and free and willing to be real and to feel. It is the loneliness of all the empty space of the universe. It is a black hole that is the truth of human death and loss. It feels disconnected and alone. The universe is a lonely place to experience and it is good. Experience the sadness at the center of your heart fully and willingly and you are showing the skill of the initiated warrior able to face adult life.

Faith gets you through this experience. This experience, like all experience, eventually dissolves like a wave hitting the shore if you are brave enough to ride the truth of it fully with eyes wide open.

Truth number three is RED. At the center of the universe, at the center of my heart, at the center of the stone, there is pure desire. It is a desire that is so great that it cannot be explained in the human realm. It can only be felt at certain times when the heart is opened and free and willing to be real and to feel. It is the explosion of all the creativity and movement of the universe. It is a star shining brightly as it gives itself with love to its offspring, its precious planetary children.

It burns itself up slowly and brightly and purposefully and willingly to fulfill its role in the great mystery of the universe. The universe is a place full of desire and longing to experience, and it is good. Experience the desire at the center of your heart fully and willingly and you are showing the skill of the initiated warrior able to face adult life. Faith gets you through this experience. This experience, like all experience, eventually dissolves like a wave hitting the shore if you are brave enough to ride the truth of it fully with eyes wide open.

These are the truths at the center of the stone. These are the truths at the center of your heart. This is your unfolding story that you are now telling and accepting and writing through the gift of choice one day at a time for the rest of your adult life. Only fear can stop you. And only love and faith and a willingness to be real can provide the means to transform fear to courage.

You are a burning ember, a particle of matter and a wave of energy that is part of the big bang. Yes, you will burn out someday. But first, you have to live here on earth in the energy of the red, black, and white to fulfill your purpose before you can go back home like the water. It is so sad, so beautiful, and it is so full of desire. It is the energy of earth life. It is meant to be lived to the fullest. All you need to do to be successful is to ride the waves in balance and focus in relationship to the ground and you will create a story that will leave behind a ripple that will live on for years and years as your legacy. You will be a cherished ancestor.

A Warrior's Journey for Teenagers

The Village Is Where I Find

Purpose

Place

Meaning

EMOTIONAL NAVIGATION

**THE ALCHEMY
OF
THE RED - THE BLACK -THE WHITE**

Student Text

Emotional Alchemy

Alchemy was the very early study of chemistry. Although the alchemists had very little knowledge about the details of all the elements, they were the first to understand that, in fact, there were elements, that these basic elements were at the core of all being, and finally, that the elements could be heated up and transformed. For instance, when we heat up the elements that make up water, it becomes steam.

Our emotions are like the parts of an elemental chain we call our feelings. The basic sub elements of feeling are four:

Happy

Sad

Mad

Scared

From these four basic feelings are derived many other variations of feelings, but these are the basic four we are going to work with in this group.

Just as with the chemical elements, our emotions can be recognized, heated up, and then transformed. So therefore, just like water can be heated up and transformed to steam, so can anger be heated up and transformed to sadness etc.

So emotional alchemy is a method by which we can recognize, heat up and transform our emotions. Once you learn to be an emotional alchemist, your feelings can never overpower you for very long. They can never own you again. You are about to learn the warrior's way which is to say that you are going to learn how to recognize a feeling, walk straight into the feeling like a warrior which will heat the emotion up, feel it fully until you bring it to 'boiling point' and then watch it simply dissolve and transform itself into the next emotion on the chain.

So, therefore, you are no longer going to try to learn how to **solve** your emotional problems, rather you are going to learn to **dissolve** your emotional problems.

This process encourages you to walk into an emotion, to feel it deeply to the core, and to watch it dissolve into the next emotion on the chain. The process recognizes emotions as energy. This energy can be compared to waves on the ocean. Each wave can be met, can be navigated, and can wash itself out in time as it breaks on the shore. The waves on this emotional ocean are red-black-white waves.

Picture a circle with a center and three outer circles. The center is still and it is perfectly balanced. The middle circle is where emotion bubbles to the surface in our group. At the edge of the outermost circle, group members learn to accept and acknowledge feelings. When confusion and wobbling occurs at the outer edge of the circle, we consciously dump all emotion into the center of the circle where we sit with it until the circle regains balance.

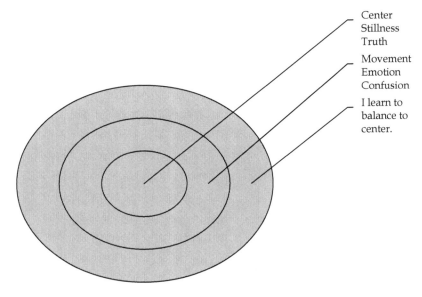

Center
Stillness
Truth

Movement
Emotion
Confusion

I learn to
balance to
center.

At the center point or core of the circle is the stillness, the balance, and knowledge needed to learn how to experience and navigate any feeling. That is why we value the stillness in a group. Once a group is established, the center speaks to us and it corrects imbalance.

As group members we are confused by the movement and massive feelings that swirl. But as we mature, we learn to identify a feeling, walk into it, and dump it into the center where we achieve the patience, balance, and acceptance to navigate the feeling. In this way, feelings are navigated and transformed as they hit the shore.

The transformation moves in a circular way that never ends. You can't be fully alive without feeling. At the human level of being, which is where you and I are, the red-black-white circle of emotions is our reality. You can't have human life without happy (white), sad (black), and anger (red) along with the feeling of fear that we experience in finding the courage to feel our emotions.

Our feelings are like the colors of the rainbow. We experience them as quite real in the human realm where we live even though scientists know that pure white light (joy) is the only real color. The others only appear to be colors to our eyes because the white light gets refracted through the prism of human perception. Nonetheless, we are human. We think like humans. We perceive like humans. We will have to do the red-black-white like humans as well.

Emotional Navigation

The navigation of emotions leads the elements of our feelings in a circular journey where the forms (our feelings) seem to change all the time, but the elements themselves never change at all.

Just as matter is in a constant state of transformation where the basic sub elements of life never change at all, so the energy of our feelings are in a constant state of transformation where the basic core of our human being never changes at all.

Your job, then, is to find and hold your center, your core, your soul. Next, you must stay true to this core while you trust yourself enough to experience all the feelings around the edge of the wheel that is your life. You cannot be fully alive without feeling all the human emotions. Every feeling is a valid feeling as long as it is real.

So an emotional navigator does not see sadness as a problem to be solved or as an illness to be cured. She does not see anger as an evil to be avoided. She does not look at happiness as a thing to cling to or to try to hold onto. She is not ashamed or afraid to be afraid either. She identifies the emotion she is in and rides it through until it dissolves.

An emotional navigator understands that there is a process by which each emotion can be accepted as part of human life, a process by which each emotion can be experienced and felt very deeply and intensely, and a process of transformation that dissolves each emotion in its own time into the next emotion. The motion of this process resembles waves on the ocean. They rise and roll and then dissolve on the shore. It takes quite a bit of courage to learn these navigational skills. That is why you must grow up now. It takes faith to do this. That is why you have a group, a village, to help you through the truth of each experience.

Freezing

Before a person can learn to ride the energy of his emotions, he first needs to recognize his emotions, accept his emotions, and be willing to walk into the wave of that emotion. A person could also choose to freeze his emotions as hard as a rock to try not to feel anything at all. The result of this choice is a person who no longer feels happiness, sadness, anger, or fear. Some prefer this. It is a choice you can make. I would only warn you that at the core of the frozen rock, there is still the truth of how you feel whether you let yourself experience it or not. This truth denied has repercussions. You develop symptoms, both mental and physical. It is not possible to be fully alive, to be fully human unless you are willing to feel. You have come to this earth with a gift to bring to us. You are probably not going to be able to bring it unless you are fully alive.

Nonetheless, many people choose to freeze or deny their emotions. In doing this, they cut themselves off from their own soul as well as from all the human joy, sadness, and frustration-achievement that make life worth living for most people.

The Shadow

Each emotion on the circle of feelings has a self contained 'shadow' aspect which might be designated as the more negative tendencies of that feeling. The shadow is like a monster that must be befriended in order to take away its power over our feelings and actions. If you are going to find the courage to fully explore the Red-Black-White, then you are going to have to own the shadow parts of yourself which are found within each of the emotions.

The shadow has been described by others as 'the bag you drag along behind you' or as the bag of hidden or unacceptable feelings and urges you carry in the heavy bag over your shoulder. Shame must be shed and you must find the courage to own your shadow.

Shadow feelings must be acknowledged, accepted, and allowed to dissolve as well. A shadow tends to follow you when you run from it. It also tends to get bigger if you try to ignore it. Turning to face or meet the shadow takes away its power, and thus, becomes the way a warrior is encouraged to deal with his shadow.

The Pin

Freezing an emotion effectively cuts off your heart from your head. In many fairy tales, like Snow White, the image of falling into a deep sleep occurs. A pin is placed in the neck to put you into this deep sleep. The sleep helps you avoid experiencing the pain of the wound, but it also pulls you out of the real world where you have to bring your gift.

In myth, this pin separates your head from your heart. It is your heart that hurts. And your head wants to get away so it doesn't remember or feel the pain of the wound. Your heart was innocently searching for love when it got hurt. But your head is searching for power. Once the pin is placed in your neck, you are cut off, not only from the wound, but from all the love in your heart. After this separation, all that is left is your head and its unquenchable search for power.

Your exploration of the Red-Black-White will help you see the places where your emotions may have caused your head to dissociate from your heart, thus putting you in a deep sleep. The sleep helps you avoid the emotion, but unfortunately it is also the same sleep in which we drift off purpose in our lives. If the process of initiation through the Red-Black-White does not occur, this sleeping state can cause a person to fail to grow into her life purpose. A person in this state of mind will drift away from center the rest of her life.

Your job is to 'wake up' from the sleep so your soul and heart are reconnected to your brain and body.

Without the ability to navigate through all the emotions, the pin can cause a person to get stuck in an emotion for years. Thus, in the circle of the red-black-and white, many people who are angry all the time are seen as 'stuck' in red. People who are depressed all the time are 'stuck' in black; and people who try to make everything seem just great all the time are 'stuck' in white.

Break Point

Each of these emotions also has a break point. The break point is reached when an emotion is felt fully and deeply in a warrior's way. When an emotion is navigated in this way, it reaches a crest and a break point just like a wave where it dissolves itself on the shore. The waves are red, black, and white. You must learn to ride all of them if you want to be a true adult warrior in your village.

Successfully learning to walk into each emotion and to ride that emotion like a wave until it dissolves on the shore is to become a full warrior capable of living a full emotional and physical life in the real world. A person who is unable to ride a wave through to breakpoint is destined to get stuck in one of the colors, or, perhaps, is destined to deny and avoid all emotions for the rest of her days. In either case, warrior status is never achieved and a person never learns to successfully navigate the Red-Black-White.

The Circle of Feelings

The circle of Emotional Navigation consists of three basic colors from which each has several offshoot colors. In emotional navigation, fear as a fourth major emotion is found in each of the colors and at the point of dissolution of each color wave:

White - pure light, pure energy, innocence, wonder, happiness, joy

Red - desire, movement, anger, achievement, reaching out, frustration

Black - absence of light, hopeless, death, grief, loss

White - Out of the ashes of black will come the dawning to white

Yellow fear floats through all the emotions and is found at the transition point between the colors as well. The fear must be navigated as well in order to find the courage to keep crossing the bridge to the next color.

None of these colors is the good one.

None of these colors is the bad one.

While happiness may seem to be the most desirable, trying to cling to happiness or trying to recreate old happiness will only make you unhappy fast.

While sadness seems like the least desirable, accepting loss and grief is part of life. It also brings us closer to one another as we feel our grief. Most importantly, living through your human sadness is what builds your character and makes you a warrior prepared to do your purpose and bring your gift. Many times the gift is born out of the courage it took to feel deep sadness.

Anger seems bad, but when you learn to accept and feel your anger appropriately, it can be turned into wonderfully creative achievements and accomplishments.

Finally, the very fear that makes you feel so inadequate and weak is also the key that reminds you it is time to be brave, to sit with your village, and to find the courage to feel and transform to the next color in the circle of emotions.

This circle of feeling never ends as long as you are alive on planet earth. As long as you are human, you will have to experience the red, the black, and the white. You can learn to do it willingly and with dignity like an adult, or you can use all your life energy trying to ignore it, avoid it, or complain about it.

Becoming an emotional alchemist is learning to dance. The dance is the dance of life. Some steps are joyful; some steps are sad; some angry; some fearful. Once we learn to dance in our village, all you need to do to do your purpose in life is to KEEP DANCING.

Summary

Here, we do not encourage you to 'get your anger out'. If all you do is to 'get your anger out' without going to the very core of your anger, you will only need to get your anger out again and again every day. Your group is here to help you feel your anger to the core.

In this way you will actually watch yourself go 'through' the anger. When you go 'through' it, you will probably come to ashes, fall apart, and break into tears. You will pass into black.

We cannot and do not prescribe medication for sadness and depression here. We are not a hospital. Nor do we worship sadness or depression like some people who dress in black every day. Sadness and depression are not problems to be solved. They are real, valid emotions that need to be heated up and then dissolved. Dissolved black, felt fully to the core, brings the first new glimmer of white light in its own time.

Do this alchemical circle once and you have passed the test. Find the courage to do it again and again in your life and you have become a full adult, a true warrior.

WHITE	RED	BLACK	WHITE
Birth	growth	death	rebirth
dawn	day	night	dawn
innocence	anger	sadness	joy
beginning	achievement	loss	starting
liberty	busting out	imprisonment	freedom

In our village, fear is the emotion that is felt between the emotional crossings. Since happiness can never be recovered unless one is willing to do the dance of the red, black, and white, it is therefore very important that the warrior face the fear so that he will be able to cross to the next color. That is what the group is for. It is an emotional support to help students feel each emotion, and then ride the wave through to dissolution.

One of the best ways adolescents have developed to avoid the fear is to take drugs. Drugs are a wonderful temporary return to white without the experience of all the other emotions. But the white feeling is as temporary as the effect of the drug. It is an attempt to return to white without walking through the rage of red and the desert of black. When the drug wears off, the student finds himself still stuck in the color he was in before he took the drug.

Without any knowledge of the red, black, and white dance that is required for real happiness, all the student can do is take the drug again for another phony trip to white. A drug addict is only a person who has forgotten how to do the dance. He stays stuck in red, or black, or both, and he returns to white temporarily each night with the attachment of his choice. But when he wakes in the morning, the rage and depression are still there waiting to be felt. The wave of color is still waiting to be acknowledged, felt fully, and dissolved in its own time on the shore.

Teaching students the red, the black, and the white is the job of the teacher. Doing the dance of the red, the black, and the white is the job of teacher and students.

The Dance

1. Ground yourself in stillness in the center of your head

2. Just like an electrical ground, you can run excess energy into ground

3. Feel your emotion. If you cannot name it, call it red, black, or white.

4. Understand the dance and flow of the red, black white.

5. Move further IN to your feeling in community with your village.

6. Now move your feeling out into the center of the circle where you can talk to it.

7. Your village can now see your feeling too while it is out in the center.

8. Your feeling can be felt fully without owning you if you stay grounded

9. Your feeling can be felt fully without owning you if it stays in the center.

10. The circle is your container, your vessel. Now you have a tool of navigation.

11. Navigate the waves of your feelings. Let them flow. Ride the rapids too.

12. Feel each emotion, and let it go as it passes into the next color.

Now you are dancing in the red-black-white. Now you are a warrior.

Red

Black

White

I learned The Red, the Black, and the White through a tape of the same name that I heard from the poet, Robert Bly. His understanding that a boy or girl must **grow down** into the muddy waters of human experience is a central focus of this course. The journey of growing up toward a palpable adulthood is not completed without this parallel growing down. This growing down is the element that is missing in public schools.

The muddy depths that we will traverse in our journey and story will take us deeply into our emotions in an experiential way that teaches us that emotions are teachers of truth that will allow us to grow and strive if we can find the courage to identify our emotions, accept our emotions, and most of all, to feel our emotions. For more in depth knowledge regarding the recognition and navigation of emotion, refer to Karla McLaren's work entitled *The Language of Emotions: What Your Feelings Are Trying to Tell You*, 2010, Sounds True.

RED

Desire
Anger

Achievement
Growth
Movement
Action
Struggle
Excitement
Passion
Striving
Reaching

Hatred
Fury
Rage
Jealousy
Envy
Resentment
Disgust
Murder

What is Red?

Fire is the symbol of red. It is a mystery. It is good because it is real and it is part of human life and the life of the universe. It is pure desire. It is the reason you get up every morning and try again even when all seems lost. Red keeps on going and keeps trying to make right even in the face of the morning newspaper headlines.

All red, no matter how destructive or how productive eventually comes to ashes. There is no special deal for you, young warrior. This is your life and mine. You will accomplish your purpose in life in the glow of your red fire. You will also make most of your mistakes and do your measure of evil while in red when you lose your way.

Boundaries in Red

Boundaries are very important in red. Since red is fire, it is capable of warmth and creation as well as terrible destruction. Learning to burn the fire of red within the boundaries of the fireplace is very important. Without this ability, you may well burn down the house, or the whole forest. Using the container of the fireplace of your group is a safe way to burn your fire where you can still feel its fury without damaging others or yourself.

In this way, you are now free to explore the truth of red in the safe container of the group where you can be sure the fire is tended to within our fire line or circle. When red anger is out of control or unacknowledged, it can cause you to violate the boundaries of others. It can lead you to try to force your will on a situation.

Being unable or unwilling to uphold and defend your own personal boundaries from the violations of others also causes your red anger to overwhelm you. It is important in red to feel the passion fully, yet to always ride the wave in such a way that you respect the boundaries of others, and in such a way that you make sure your own boundaries are not violated by others.

Red anger is quite appropriate when your boundaries are being violated. You need red passion and anger to do your life purpose.

The Pin That Can Freeze You in Red

A person stuck in red is angry all the time. This person is afraid to truly acknowledge his anger because the anger is so intense he is afraid he may kill someone. His solution - 'the pin' - is usually to try to control other people or things beyond his control. It makes him feel safer to try to do this but it also makes him feel angry all the time.

Another way the pin may manifest itself in anger could be an attempt to deny or to stuff down the anger. The result of this solution is very explosive and unpleasant for the people who must live with this angry person. Stuffed anger explodes outward onto unsuspecting strangers. When someone opens fire at the burger line, they are often heard shouting things like, "I will show you" Stay away from me." "Now you are going to pay." Of course, the people being shot are usually innocent bystanders who never met the shooter before.

Frozen or stuffed anger is also directed upon the loved ones that we cherish the most. Repetitive, habitual anger and abuse of loved ones is often the result of a person's inability to learn to ride the red wave.

Another solution or pin for an angry person is to try to 'get their anger out'. While this solution does not try to avoid or deny the anger, it usually does little to dissolve the anger either. This person ends up needing to 'get his anger out' every time anything is not in his control.

Without, vision, faith, or a path through the red anger, a person finds a never ending fountain of rage that just seems to bubble and bubble day after day.

Finally, one other way a person gets stuck in red is to place the pin in his neck every time he gets near the point of transformation from red to black. This is the 'fear pin'. This person wants to stop being so angry, but at the same time, this person is very afraid of ever letting himself spill through red to the sadness of black. So he sticks the pin in his neck to prevent spilling into black.

Without realizing it, he chooses to stay stuck in red. He much prefers his anger to the sadness he knows would follow. This person will think he wants to stop being angry all the time. But as the bridge to grief is about to be crossed, he pulls back and retreats into the safety of his anger.

In the community of the village, with an elder present who has made the journey, the youth can find the faith, courage, and vision to descend to the heart of red, examine the wound, and break through to black. There are some very scary aspects to red. And we will examine them next.

The Shadow in Red

The other side of your ability to do red fully in the fireplace is that red is capable of much destruction and boundary violation. Red can be quite evil if it is not acknowledged in the fireplace of your life. Hatred, fury, rage, jealousy, and even murder are all part of the shadow of red. If you acknowledge the redness of these feelings inside the fireplace of the group, they can be respected, yet still safely contained.

Inability to acknowledge shadow red can result in unwarranted attack, or attack that violates boundaries and tries to force your will on a situation. In these cases, unacknowledged and uncontained shadow red can destroy good relationships, or even get you arrested. The most extreme case of shadow red out of control would be the act of murder. All of these shadow feelings must be acknowledged and befriended. In this way, the shadow never overtakes you. A shadow always loses its power when light is shined on it. If a light is not shined on the shadow, it looms bigger and bigger until you are overwhelmed.

In the course of warrior training it is always remembered that the goal is always to acknowledge the shadow, and thus take away its power. A shadow brought into light loses its power and allows you to be in the driver's seat of your decisions and your life. You are human and you have human reactions and tendencies, some of which are not all that noble. Acknowledgement is the key to dissipation and dissolution.

Breakpoint in Red

Disintegration
Coming to Ashes

Red spills into black at a breakpoint we might call 'disintegration' or 'coming to ashes.' After the fire burning kitchen work of red, we come to ashes. What came together in the red falls apart in black. What rose to life will die. Desire, like all fires, burns itself out when its purpose is completed.

To do red wholly and deeply is to be a warrior capable of a great purpose and tremendous good to the village. It is also the ability to respect and contain the shadow side of red until it too is disarmed and quieted through acknowledgement. Red always burns itself out. Before it does, it is the adult's job to burn it brightly and to channel it into creative endeavors and passion for the purpose of life.

The consequences of the fire you make in your life will ripple for years and years in the lives of your descendants. It is for love that you burn this fire clean and true in the fireplace of your life today as you courageously go forward in time to breakpoint.

Breakpoint is the place where one emotion, felt fully, dissolves in its own time into the next wave or emotion that comes along. Your job is to ride these waves with dignity, and respect for yourself and others.

- Acknowledge the emotion
- Accept the emotion
- Descend into the emotion in community
- Ride the emotion fully and sanely through to breakpoint
- The emotion dissolves and dissipates at breakpoint
- Repeat the process -acknowledge the new wave that rises up

Questions in Red

Red is learning and building and separating. It is creating and achieving, but is also capable of tearing down and destroying.

Red is moving slowly away from center. Red is rising to the heights of your life. Red is movement and struggle. Red is excitement and passion. Red is angry at times. Red is young and restless and ready to fly from the nest.

THE SHADOW IN RED: The shadow must be disciplined not to demand control over things that it has no control over. It must be watchful of greed, violence, and other violations of boundaries of others. It must be brave and stand firmly, but appropriately, in the face of the boundary violations of others.

RED IS FIRE

1. Describe the fiery red, passionate person in yourself? Talk or write about what brings you to life.

2. What good things have you accomplished in red? What are your achievements? Talk or write about your interests and your creativity as a person.

3. How have you gone off track in red? Talk or write about times, or periods of time, in your life when you know you were out of control or off course in your life.

4. What are the traits of the shadow side of red that you must acknowledge and learn to burn respectfully in the fireplace of your heart? Talk or write about the impulses in you that frighten you.

5. Write or talk about a time when 'you burned the whole forest down' when in red – a time when you went overboard and did some serious damage?

6. How have you burned a productive warm fire in the fireplace of red – how have you used your red energy to passion or fuel yourself to get something productive done? Talk or write about a time when you followed through and persevered to complete a project or an important endeavor.

7. Have you ever been stuck or pinned in red for years? What are the consequences? Do you know anyone stuck in red right now? Talk or write about times of your life when anger became habitual. How long were you stuck? What were the consequences of being stuck in red? How did you get unstuck? Are you still stuck?

8. How have you used anger to successfully protect your boundaries? Talk or write about a time when you had to make a stand against an emotional or physical violation of your boundaries.

9. How have you used red to violate the boundaries of another? Talk or write about a time when you know you stepped over the line and tried to force your will on a person or situation. Own the shadow and it will not control you next time.

Walk straight into the truth of red like a warrior.
Sit with it in your group. Acknowledge it and feel it fully.
You are responsible for what you do in red. Act responsibly.
You are an adult now.

RED ALWAYS COMES TO ASHES. IT IS GOOD BECAUSE THIS IS THE WAY IT IS. WHEN IT IS TIME, FEEL THE COURAGE TO CROSS OVER THE BREAKPOINT INTO THE BLACK ASHES

BLACK

Sadness
Death

Community
Cooperation
Character
Support
Hope

Depression
Crying
Isolation
Loneliness
Separation
Hopelessness
Apathy
Emptiness
Grief
Loss
Suicide

What is Black?

Ash is the symbol of black. It is a mystery why ashes are part of our lives. It is good because it is real and it is part of human life and the life of the universe. It is pure sorrow. It is the time of your life when you cherish the community of your village as you feel your hopelessness, and as you give your support to others when they must feel the black moments of their lives.

Black willingly accepts loss as just another part of life, mourns the loss fully and deeply, and releases it all in proper time. Some blackness can be fully mourned in a day and released. Other losses take a longer time. Time is not the issue as long as you have the vision to see yourself mourning fully, and then moving on to live your life for the rest of the villagers who need you to do your purpose.

Becoming a warrior is learning to live and die a thousand deaths by doing the red-black-and white all the rest of your earth years. Ashes are part of human reality.

Boundaries in Black

Boundaries are very important in black. Since black is ashes and death, it is very hard to do alone. You must descend into it, however the village is here to support you through black. It is not here to carry you for the rest of your years because you choose to get stuck in black. They take you to the center of the village and hold your hand as you walk straight into your black heart and grieve deeply and willingly.

By the same token, I am also here to give others support as they walk through the black in their lives. I cannot do it for them. I am not here to carry them through their lives for the rest of their days. I need them to grieve loss and to get on with the life and purpose of the village which needs them so badly.

Boundaries in black respect another enough to let him feel his own sorrow while also being there as a support; knowing full well that we need to allow the grieving person time to grieve just as we know we need the grieving person to come through his grief so that he may resume his purpose as part of our community.

Respect for boundaries in black means you do not try to fix your grieving friend, even though your heart aches for him and with him. It takes deep respect for your friend and for the mysterious process of life that requires the passage through the black. It also means you must take responsibility for yourself when you are in the black. You accept the support and empathy of fellow villagers but also realize that you must grieve fully and let go so that you may reassume your responsibilities in the village.

The Pin That Can Freeze You in Black

A person stuck in black experiences a chronic, melancholy sadness that seems to spring up from some very deep fountain of sorrow. He is afraid to ever go down to the core of that fountain because he is truly afraid it would make him so depressed he might kill himself. So he stays stuck in a miserable black place with no acknowledgment of light at all. The black is the least pleasant of the colors, but it is also perhaps the one that spurs the most growth in you as a person.

Just like the red, a person stuck in black develops 'solutions'. In black, the 'pin' may take the form of avoidance or denial. Our society currently provides a massive smorgasbord of diversions, attachments, and entertainments to keep the black away. But it does not go away. It is right there under the surface. It still needs to be felt to the core. The fear of descent into black causes serious repercussions. The 'pin' of addiction is common here.

Another pin is what I call the self promise. It goes like this: "Today I am going to try to be happy all day". Anybody who has ever tried this knows it does not work long. A wound is a wound. Until it heals, it festers- whether you are trying to be happy or not.

Black can be denied through a constant, pasted on, phony white smile, or through a clinging addiction to red rage where anger is the preferred emotion.

Like anger, where we are often encouraged to 'get our anger out', so with sadness people will say, "Go ahead and cry. Get it all out". This does eliminate the avoidance and addiction, but this person finds only a perpetual fountain of sorrow every day.

What is needed is the vision, courage, and faith that if you can experience black to your core, if you can examine your wound in community, you will go through sadness. It is just a part of life.

Sadness is not an abnormal state that you need to 'get out' or 'get cured'. Doing this only keeps you stuck in its grip like an insomniac who tries to go to sleep every night. Sadness is a normal human state of being that you must descend into and ride to its completion. An individual must seek a village where he can be present and real, with an elder who has made the journey before. In this way, he can find the courage to feel the loss to the core, to examine the wound and expose it so it can begin to heal. The tears are healing in this way. It is a village grief ritual that gets done consciously with courage and faith.

The final way a person gets stuck in black is by preference. This person sticks the pin in his neck every time he gets to the transition point where black would spill over into white. Why would a person do this? This pin is the fear pin. A person would actually prefer to stay in black rather than ever take the chance to do white again. This person is afraid to be happy! After all, happiness does not last. And surely it doesn't. So this person cannot 'trust' to go through to happiness knowing it won't last.

Unfortunately, this guy lives out his life very unhappy, in anguish, with little consciousness of the fact that he is choosing black. Others proudly choose black in their dress, habits, and actions. Still others do a ping pong routine bouncing between red and black erratically in a dance defined by psychiatry as bipolar disorder. All the same all of these scenarios are simply a fear to do white and a resulting preference to remain in black.

As with red anger, most people stuck in black sorrow and depression are unaware of how they may be choosing to be stuck.

Like red, the black has a shadow side which we try to hide or deny. Denial can cause the shadow of black to overwhelm, thus, leaving you in a state where you are unable to see yourself riding the wave through to dissolution. You get consumed in the wave instead.

The Shadow in Black

The shadow side of black chooses separation as a way of life. The shadow side of black worships darkness and bestows it on the world. The shadow side of black would lead you to suicide in a world that has only darkness to offer. Black ashes are capable of self destruction or evil if you do not acknowledge their presence in your life.

Sadness comes to stay forever when loss is denied or covered up or not felt or avoided by turning to attachments or to suicidal thoughts. Therefore, you must find a way to acknowledge and to befriend the self destructive shadow parts of your being. As with red rage, shadow self destruction can only hurt you if it is not acknowledged and given light. Denial of these impulses and feelings only makes the shadow grow until it overwhelms you.

Find the courage to grieve your loss in the community of your village. The expression of grief is one of the noblest things you can do for your fellow villagers. It is also a chance for the village to demonstrate their willingness to suffer with you so you might complete the journey through the black and resume your place in the village that needs you.

Now you are flowing through sadness. Feel it. Navigate it. Accept it. Be responsible for what you do while you are in sadness. Navigate the raft through the black waters all the way to breakpoint. This is the willingness and courage of a brave warrior who loves his village very much, and who is loved by the village as well. Black felt fully dissipates in time on the shore. It may dissolve into white.

Breakpoint in Black

Birth
Coming to bloom

Yes, ashes tended to and acknowledged fully over time will eventually result in a blooming. Don't be fooled by the frozen earth outside in the middle of January. In the springtime, new life will sprout forth no matter how cold and bleak it is in January. Out of that dirt and ashes where all seemed bleak and empty comes the first little push of new life through the ground. Young warrior, so will it be for you and for me.

To do black wholly and deeply is to be a warrior capable of intense grief in the supportive arms of the village. You do this grief willingly knowing full well that the village loves you and needs you to do your purpose. It is your responsibility to do black in community and to take precious care of your own life even in the face of deep sorrow.

The consequences of your ability to do ashes as a warrior will ripple through life for years to come. New young warriors will find courage and strength to do black in their own lives.

The result of surviving your black journey is found in your character. All the best parts of the man and the woman you will become are found in the courage to survive the wounds of life. The scar that is left is a beautiful scar, a scar of character and survival.

Very often, the best traits of your character are forged through the courage to ride through the black wave. Some people even believe that we actually stumble into the right trouble that will create the grief we need to grow as a person. In any case, when you examine your story you will see that the blackest moments filled with sorrow were also the moments when the best parts of your human being were forged and solidified – if you were willing to do the black like a warrior.

As you look back on your life and the lives of others, it is your survival and your beautiful scar from healed wounds which give you your grateful heart. You take your place among all the wounded warriors of the past who suffered their blackness so that you might have a good life today. You will do the same for the future warriors now as you go courageously and willingly through to breakpoint. This is the human journey of a true warrior.

In traditional societies, the symbol of the 'beautiful' scar is an indication of healing and survival. It is a powerful symbol of your ability to live through the blackest moments of your life as a warrior fully conscious of love and duty to village.

Breakpoint is the place where one emotion, felt fully, dissolves in its own time into the next wave or emotion that comes along. Your job is to ride these waves with dignity, and respect for yourself and others.

- Acknowledge the emotion
- Accept the emotion
- Walk into the emotion in community
- Ride the emotion fully and sanely through to breakpoint
- The emotion dissolves and dissipates at breakpoint
- Repeat the process -acknowledge the new wave that rises up

In some ways, black is the noblest of the colors in that many of your most noble character traits are born in the ashes of black. You must learn to descend into black when it is time. Our culture has come to view the black as a sickness. While none of us should be consumed by the 'blues', it is important to remember that it is an ability and a willingness to experience and live through the 'blues' which will make an individual life one that approaches greatness.

Questions in Black

Black gives up and feels hopeless and isolated and alone. Black mourns the loss of a loved one and surrenders to sorrow's wave. Black is feeling as completely empty as you can possibly feel. It is despair and plunging to the depths of sorrow. Black has no cure. It is death and depression. It is real and it must be acknowledged and accepted through to breakpoint.

THE SHADOW IN BLACK: In black, the shadow must learn to be humble and to live with disappointment. It must learn to live within the limits of its own power to control things. The shadow must learn that it is not special in black. Sadness is a part of life that happens to everyone. There is no special person whose life does not come to ashes. It is part of living. The shadow gets so hopeless that thoughts of self destruction may arise. These feelings must be acknowledged with a full consciousness about how much the village needs you. In this way, the shadow is disempowered through acknowledgement that shines a light on its looming presence.

BLACK IS ASHES

1. Describe the hopeless, ashes person in yourself. What are you like in black? Talk or write about your most hopeless moments. How did you feel? What was happening?

2. What good things have you accomplished in black? Talk or write about character traits that were forged in the black ashes. How have these traits made you a better person?

3. What comfort and support have you brought to others suffering black? Talk or write about a time that you know you were there for a person who needed you.

4. How have you gone off track in black? Talk or write about times when you may have gotten stuck in the clutches of the blackness in your life. How long were you stuck? When did you break through? Are you still stuck there?

5. What are the traits of the shadow side of black that prevent you from sitting with humility in black's ashes? What scares you about the black? Talk or write about how you try to deny and avoid hopelessness when it arrives.

6. What cannot be changed that must be mourned and released? This is the key question in successful navigation through the black. Talk or write about what must be accepted or mourned and released in your life.

7. How has your ego tried to soothe itself in denial or avoidance of black? Talk or write about habits or addictions that keep you 'safe' from every having to do the black.

8. What have you thrown away while in black that should not have been thrown away? Talk or write about important relationships or life projects that were thrown away and lost because black was ruling your life.

9. Have you ever been stuck or pinned in black for years? What are the consequences? Do you know anyone stuck in black right now? What is frustrating to you in dealing with the person stuck in black. How are you sometimes like that person?

10. How have you become closer to others or closer to the truth in your own heart while navigating in black? Talk or write about close bonds that were the result of living through a hard time in your life.

11. How have you hurt yourself in black? Talk or write about self destructive acts or tendencies. Shine a light on this shadow behavior. Do you realize how much your village needs you to suffer black and to return to a productive life as part of your village?

12. How can black be good if it is about death? What does the red-black-white circle of life teach you about death? Talk or write about what you have learned about death in this course. How has your perception changed? Can you accept death as part of the earth journey?

Walk straight into the truth of black like a warrior.
Sit with it in your group. Acknowledge it and feel it fully.
You are responsible for what you do in black. Act responsibly.
You are an adult now.

BLACK ALWAYS COMES TO A NEW BLOOMING. IT IS
GOOD BECAUSE THIS IS THE WAY IT IS. WHEN IT IS TIME,
FEEL THE COURAGE TO HOPE FOR THE FIRST BLOOM OF
SPRING. PAY ATTENTION AND YOU WILL SEE THE FIRST
TINY BLOOMS. EMBRACE THIS BLOOMING LIKE A
WARRIOR.

White

Joy
Happiness

Contentment
Satisfaction
Connection
Community
Oneness
Laughter

Clinging
Holding
Capturing
Imprisoning
Suffocating

What is White?

Blooming is the symbol of white. It is a mystery. It is good because it is real and it is part of human life and the life of the universe. It is pure joy. White is the vision to see the rebirth of life out of the charred ashes of the past.

To come to bloom is to do white wholly and on purpose, consciously and passionately. Joy is best celebrated when you have someone to celebrate it with. That is what your village is here for. The village gives your life meaning and purpose and a place to celebrate your joy.

And the elder is here as well to show you how to be content with joy without trying to capture it or hold onto it or cling to it. Just enjoy it until it washes itself out on the shore and dissolves into red again.

Boundaries in White

Boundaries are very important in white. Since white is birth, it is at once anticipated for its new life and feared for its newness and the changes it brings to our lives. Learning to accept the miracle of new life is to accept changes while keeping safe all the things that matter to you in your heart: your integrity, your morals, the essence of the mystery that is you.

Boundaries get violated in white when you try to capture it or capture someone and hold them in place in white. Boundary violation in white is best understood by understanding the difference between 'love' and 'possessiveness'. Love respects and frees and allows another to blossom and grow. Possessiveness clings and suffocates and constantly violates the boundaries of another all in the supposed name of love.

Like all the colors, white passes in time and you need to willingly accept that in your life. There is no white joy that comes forever in real earth life. Sorry, young warriors. Live with it. The commercial that made you think you could be fixed forever in white was selling you a bald faced lie. Nothing is permanent at the level of earth perception. Enjoy and let go.

The Pin That Can Freeze You in White

This seems like a wonderful fate. But it is not what it seems. Just like a person can get stuck in the other colors, a person can also get stuck in white. Avoidance and denial are the pins here just like the other colors. This person surrounds herself with all the trappings of white - material things, spiritual books up the yin yang, and a pasted on smile that can't stop talking about how wonderful things are all the time. Beware of people who will only allow positive thoughts and feelings. They think they are free. But they are not. They are frozen solid in white and won't let black or red enter their lives.

A person stuck in white will deny that they ever need be in black or red again. In fact, when they see people doing red or black, they find these people to be inferior, or not quite as evolved as them. They see people doing red or black as people who need a cure or rescue. For them, red and black need never be felt again as long as you are thinking the right thoughts in the right way all the time like them.

This type of person is not really in white all the time. He wouldn't need to convince you he was in white if he really was in white. There is no need for rage or discomfort, no need for disease, no need for old age, and no need for death to be acknowledged for the person who tries to freeze white permanently in place. I believe in angels. But there probable is such a thing as too many angels for some people trying to be perpetually in the white.

A person gets stuck in white because he is too afraid to do the red or black ever again. However, manufacturing or faking white when it is not time to be in white only causes the exact opposite of the desired white feelings. It leads directly to unhappiness and to constant anxiety just under the surface of the constant programmed positive affirmations.

In warrior training, you learn that white is not a static place you want to get to and hold onto forever. It is just like all the other colors. Feel it. Make the descent into the truth of it. Enjoy it. Pass through it with your village there to celebrate it with you, then move on to the next color.

This is a hard thing to learn. Have you ever taken a course that taught you it is good to be mad or to be deeply sad? This course is teaching you just that, young warrior.

The other side of your ability to do white fully is to avoid white. Why would anyone avoid white if it is joy? Often, it is avoided because the person knows it does not last. It does not last. The shadow side of white tries to sabotage or avoid white when it comes peeking through the ashes with its tiny innocent bloom.

While some people say they want to be happy, the truth is some people are so afraid of happiness that that they won't let themselves experience true happiness ever again.

The Shadow in White

The shadow side of white also takes joy and tries to capture or imprison its essence as if it was something or someone to hunt and to conquer. Shadow white can be insecure to the point of constant clinging and the annoying love that expresses itself in constant jealousy. While it seems like love when you place another on a pedestal, it is not love. You are falling in love with a girl on a pedestal and not the real human being. After a period of constant clinging and excitement, you will eventually be disappointed because she did not live up to the girl that you placed on the pedestal. The truth is that you didn't fall in love with the real person. You fell in love with an image of who you wished the girl would be – your ticket to the everlasting white.

Thus, the need for forever white degenerates into a possessive or clingy relationship that tries to sustain an unrealistic dream. No one can bring you white forever. And you can never possess the white as an eternal state. The shadow of possession and clinginess must be acknowledged and dispelled as does the delusion that white can ever come to stay forever. Love is a very muddy thing, young warrior. Beware of the shadow angel that loves you too much. And beware of your own desire to be that very same shadow angel for another.

Love is wonderful and has many joyful aspects. But love also needs to learn how to fight fair in the red, and to grieve fully in the black.

These shadow feelings are part of us all and need to be tended within an honest acknowledgement in order to be contained properly so they do not affect the whole village. Just as white can release a village in total enjoyment, shadow white can lead a village to kill or conquer or violate all in the name of the false love of ownership, greed, and possessiveness.

Breakpoint in White

Boiling Point
Coming to Flame

The breakpoint when white spills to red can be called 'boiling point' or 'coming to flame'. Boiling point is a simple metaphor - an obvious transformation point. It occurs when you recognize and heat things up. Once the birth of white has occurred, it is felt fully and enjoyed as it washes itself out on the shore like a wave. White spills back to red when it begins to grow upward and outward until it breaks out into the flame of red fire again. To break into flame is to do red wholly, consciously, and passionately. It is the completion of the eternal red-black-white circle that must be repeated over and over in earth life.

An emotional alchemist understands that the process of life is a red and black and white process that must be acknowledged and celebrated in community at each stage. A warrior is not afraid to live through the colors because he has been given vision and faith.

He is not afraid because his village is there for encouragement. He knows he has a gift to bring and gifts to receive if he can learn to do the red, black, and white in community. He knows he has purpose, place and meaning when he lives in a village.

While the circle of Red-Black-White has been presented in that certain sequence in this book, it needs to be noted that the waves of emotion do not necessarily follow the order presented in this book.

A warrior just recognizes the next wave as it comes, walks into it, and rides it. Red does not always follow White as Black does not always follow Red. Do not try to force your will on your emotional life. Just recognize the next wave and ride it.

White is to be celebrated and enjoyed to its fullest. But it dissipates on the shore just like the other emotions. When it does, it is time to spill back over into the red or the black.

The waves just keep coming. Acknowledge them. And enjoy the ride.

Breakpoint is the place where one emotion, felt fully, dissolves in its own time into the next wave or emotion that comes along. Your job is to ride these waves with dignity, and respect for yourself and others.

- Acknowledge the emotion
- Accept the emotion
- Walk into the emotion in community
- Ride the emotion fully and sanely through to breakpoint
- The emotion dissolves and dissipates at breakpoint
- Repeat the process -acknowledge the new wave that rises up

That's it!!!! Now you've got it, young warrior!

Questions in White

White is content to just be. White is centered and balanced. White is nurturing and nurtured. White is peaceful like a return home after a long journey. White wants nothing and is satisfied just for its own existence. It is pure joy, rebirth, and renewal. White is innocent and fresh as the first blooms of the springtime. White is liberation. You are set free, yet you are still and content in your own bones and your own skin.

THE SHADOW IN WHITE: The ego must learn to accept joy without suspicion even though it knows white will not last. The shadow tries to freeze or possess white so that it can keep it in place. It cannot keep it in place. The mystery of the red-black-white circle will not be captured by the ego. Clinging, or even killing, in the name of love is the shadow's downfall in white. It tries to lock white in place. Joy will never be contained by the ego. Feel it fully and, like all the other emotions, release it on the shore at the proper time in breakpoint. In this way, you can have a healthy relationship with the shadow traits of possessiveness and the love that becomes abusive.

WHITE IS BLOOMING AND OPENING UP

1. Describe the joyful person in yourself. How healthy is your relationship to joy? Talk or write about times that you felt truly joyful or content in your life.

2. How do you know when you feel centered and balanced? Talk or write about a time when you felt completely at ease in your own skin. Have you ever let yourself feel this way?

3. What good things have you accomplished in white? How have you expressed your love and joy to others? Talk or write about the feelings and actions of unconditional love as they exist in your life.

4. Have you ever used drugs or alcohol as away to get to white, or to stay in white when you really weren't there? Talk or write

about it.

5. Does your ego distrust white? Is it hard for you to let go and enjoy? What stops you from letting go and enjoying when it is time to do so? Talk or write about it.

6. How have you tried to cling to white or to manufacture white in your life when it was not time to do white? Talk or write about it.

7. Have you ever tried to capture or hold white in place when it was time to let it go? What was the result? Talk or write about it.

8. Have you ever tried to fake white by acting like all is fine to others when all is not fine inside you? Do you think you are superior because you are in white all the time? Do you think people in the black or the red are inferior because they can't be in the white all the time? Talk or write about it.

Walk straight into the truth of white like a warrior.
Sit with it in your group. Acknowledge it and feel it fully.
You are responsible for what you do in white. Act responsibly.
You are an adult now.

WHITE ALWAYS COMES TO ITS OWN ENDING. <u>IT IS GOOD BECAUSE THIS IS THE WAY IT IS</u>. WHEN IT IS TIME, FEEL THE COURAGE TO LET CONTENTMENT AND JOY GO TO THE PASSIONATE CALL OF THE RED WAVE OF ACTION OR THE BLACK WAVE OF LOSS.

YELLOW

Fear
Caution
Courage

Alertness
Protection
Shelter
Firmness
Warrior

Anxiety
Escape
Panic
Frozen
Terror
Coward

What is Yellow?

Courage is the complement of fear. It is a mystery. Courage and fear are good because they are real and are part of human life and the life of the universe. Human life requires courage and healthy fear. Courage and fear comprise a final color which we will visualize as the yellow.

Healthy fear recognizes danger and acts accordingly. Warrior courage acknowledges fear and pays attention to its call to alertness.

I do not choose to give the fourth major emotion of human life, fear, a place on the wheel of the red-black-white. You may give it a place in the circle if you wish. Fear and its close counterpart courage are found running throughout all the colors as well as on the bridges or breakpoints between the red-black-white.

Yellow is the courage and power of the sun, the caution and alertness of an animal when a predator is nearby, and the yellow streak of the coward who fails to take a stand in his life and do what must be done.

Just like the other emotions, fear must be acknowledged and accepted. It is especially prevalent at the breakpoints where one color spills to the next color. Many times a person stuck in any of the colors is actually stuck in his inability to cross the bridge to the next color. This ability or inability to cross from color to color is rooted in the yellow poles of courage and fear.

Blind fear is tempered by firm courage. Blind courage is tempered by healthy fear. Blind courage and blind fear both comprise the shadow of yellow.

What is healthy fear? Healthy fear is acknowledged fear that does not stop you from doing your adult duties in the red-black-white circle. There are times when you are in danger. Fear is healthy when it is alert and listening to the voice of the great mystery for a proper reaction or lack of reaction. Courage respects fear and decides what must be done. Courage and fear are found wherever change is found in human life. Change is found everywhere in the realm of time.

Boundaries

Boundaries are very important to establish with regards to courage and fear. Since white is birth, it is at once anticipated for its new life and feared for its newness and the changes it brings to our lives. Black is the fertile ground where important changes build your character. These changes happen in the presence of both courage and fear. Red is moving away from your center and growing upward and outward. These red changes also find the presence of fear and courage in their path.

The trick for successful navigation of yellow is to find the proper boundaries that constitute your courage in the yellow of the sun, and your respect for fear in the yellow light of caution. Courage and caution are needed as you approach the all of the bridges that are the changes going on in your life.

Overplayed courage can be guilty of boundary violations. And overwhelming fear can lead to your own boundaries being flagrantly violated. Fear makes you too afraid to move forward. The support of your group, your village, can help you explore both your courage and your fear so that you might learn to navigate a healthy blend of the two poles of yellow.

The Pin That Can Freeze You In Yellow

Yes, anxiety can freeze you in fear and requires faith and the encouragement of the elders and your community. The yellow coward of fear must find the faith of the powerful yellow sun. The intelligent sun warrior respects the yellow light of caution and knows when to go and when to stop on the long journey of life.

There is an imaginary bridge between the red-black-white. Each time we cross from one color to the next the yellow light of caution-courage-fear appears. This yellow light is an indicator much the same as it is in driving a vehicle. The yellow means to be cautious but to proceed. If you stop, it should be a temporary stop. And if you go, it should not be just a blind acceleration forward.

The strength of courage is born in fear and the wisdom of fear is found in courage. Finding the courage to proceed with caution prevents freezing in yellow.

The Shadow in Yellow

Shadow yellow can manifest itself in attack when attack is not warranted. Fear can blind you to attack someone and then think you are defending yourself. An animal might attack a person trying to help it if it is in a state of panic or fear. Humans act this way too. Fear can cause overreaction and cruelty in the name of self defense. You must acknowledge this shadow part of yourself so that the shadow never controls you or your actions.

Shadow courage blindly plows forward without the caution that fear alerts in us. Aggressive action when the alert heart would clearly choose caution can cause yourself and others many consequences. This shadow aspect looks brave on the surface. But often, bravery requires caution and patience and even retreat. Healthy bravery does not let the ego's craving to conquer rule the scene.

The scary shadows of panic, anxiety, and the feeling of being trapped all must be acknowledged in the village of your group in order to learn to navigate the yellow. This is very difficult to do. Of all the emotions, anxiety is the most difficult to acknowledge. However, the shadow creates the panic attack, not the anxiety itself. Acknowledging anxiety takes away its shadow power if you find a way to walk in faith 'through' it. Although it is scary, it is a healthy descent "into" anxiety that allows release from its hold. Finger handcuffs are the best example of this. The more you panic and pull, the more consumed you are in the grip of the handcuffs. The more you accept and relax "into" the grip, amazingly, the closer you are to freedom.

Dealing with shadow yellow is best done in community. Dueling anxiety in isolation is very difficult. A therapist or medication may be necessary to learn to ride through anxiety.

Breakpoint in Yellow

The breakpoint in yellow allows one wave to wash out and another to begin. Courage and fear let white transform to red, let red transform to black, and let black transform to white.

EVERY HUMAN HAS THE COURAGE TO ACKNOWLEDGE FEAR AND THEN FIRMLY AND COURAGEOUSLY DO THE RED-BLACK-WHITE CIRCLE.

How do I know this? We will go one more time back to the metaphor of the birth canal. The birth canal is an excellent metaphor for the daily and life long journey we must make through the red-black-white. In the birth canal, you were first required to display fear and courage in healthy measure.

Initiations

Let me first take you through the process of your first human initiation. It was the day of your birth, your initiation to human life. **The day you were born was the first day you completed your first revolution through the red, black, and white**. In our society, we often talk about the difficulties of childbirth for the mother. We rarely talk about the difficulties of childbirth for the child on that initiatory day.

You had spent nine months in your mother's womb, suspended and floating in total security - the white. You were nourished, cared for, and totally loved as long as Mom took good care of herself.

On the day you were born, you took your very first red journey. You found yourself pushing your way through the birth canal. This journey was new. It was at once exciting and traumatic and it was beyond your control.

I am sure if your brain had the consciousness it has now, it might well have chosen not to make the trip. It would have been easy to stay there at the Hotel Mom. But, fortunately or unfortunately, you were not yet born to the 'Tribe of Choosers', to the human race. So you just did your purpose and up the birth canal you went.

This was your very first red journey. And a very long red journey it must have been for you.

As you pushed your way through the final stage of the journey, someone was there to greet you. It may have been a doctor, a nurse, or a midwife. But someone was there to greet you. You had completed your first red journey successfully. Now you were ready to come to ashes.

When the umbilical cord was cut between you and your Mom's belly, you did the black for the very first time. When that cord was cut, you died forever to the world of your mother's womb. You suffered your first loss. You left one land and were born in another.

As the mythical 'slap' on the rear occurred, your eyes popped open; you took your very first human breath; you made your very first human statement - probably "whaaaaa". You were a tiny, vulnerable human life with huge eyes of wonder and potential. You had spilled innocently into the white in a new world. And the fact of your birth proved that you are capable of riding the red, black, and white horses.

And so it is for this reason that it is proven that every adolescent alive has the ability to become a warrior. It is proven because no person alive on the planet Earth could have gotten here without doing the red, black, and white once successfully already. It was accomplished on the day of your birth. Do it once, you can do it again.

There is just one catch. Now you are human. Now you do have a choice. Now you have to learn how to do it because your age and your experience encourage you to deny or resist. It is the elder's job to watch you push your way through this new birth canal to adulthood. Otherwise, you may be trapped in the womb of adolescence forever. He will guide you through red, cut the umbilical cord that ties you to the black past, and he will slap you awake in white in the world of the adult, the warrior.

Questions in Yellow

Yellow is cautious and courageous. Yellow balances courage and fear. Yellow is afraid to go on, but goes on when it is time to go on. Yellow is driven to go on, but proceeds with caution at times. Yellow can stop the red-black-white process in fear or it can facilitate it through the courage of its wisdom.

THE SHADOW IN YELLOW: The ego must learn to balance fear and courage. The shadow can wimp out as coward, or can overplay itself through the false courage of rash behavior and aggressive action. The ego needs faith to find courage and it needs courage to proceed with caution and to know when to stop and when to move forward. This process takes adult maturity.

YELLOW SHEDS LIGHT ON THE TRUTH

1. Describe a time when you were called upon to be courageous? How did you do? Talk or write about an incident in which you were afraid but you did what had to be done in a situation.

2. How do you know when to be aggressive and when to be cautious? Talk or write about a time when you were not sure whether to be aggressive or cautious. What did you do? Would you do it differently now?

3. How can fear be healthy? How can it be paralyzing? Talk or write about fear as a friend even though you are afraid of it.

4. How can courage be healthy? How can it be dangerous? Talk or write how courage is appropriate. How can blind courage be dangerous?

5. Can you remember a time when you were fearful and you attacked someone in a situation where it was not called for? Talk or write about a time when the shadow overwhelmed you to attack the undeserving.

6. Can you remember a time when you were a coward when

courage was called for and you did not do what needed to be done? Talk o write about it.

7. Do you ever feel frozen in your tracks when you know you should act? Talk or write about this frozen state.

8. Have you ever acted rashly when you know it would have been better to be alert and not move? Talk or write about it.

9. Why should you respect fear? Isn't fear bad? Talk or write about the part panic and anxiety have played as part of the shadow of yellow in your life.

10. Have you ever faked courage? Talk or write about it.

11. Have you ever found the courage you needed even though you were shaking in your boots? Talk or write about it.

Walk straight into the truth of fear like a courageous warrior.
Sit with it in your group. Acknowledge it and feel it fully.
You are responsible for what you do in yellow. Act responsibly.
You are an adult now.

YELLOW COURAGE AND YELLOW FEAR ARE TEMPERED BY THE YELLOW CAUTION LIGHT. IT IS GOOD BECAUSE THIS IS THE WAY IT IS. FACING YELLOW IS BEING ABLE TO KNOW WHEN TO MOVE FORWARD, AND WHEN TO STAY STILL. THE COURAGE TO MOVE FORWARD AND THE CAUTION OF INFINITE PATIENCE ARE SKILLS I CAN LEARN IF I PAY ATTENTION TO MY SURROUNDINGS AND LISTEN TO MY HEART.

What Should You Do, Young Warrior?

The red-black-white is what you do, young warrior
You were born innocent
You received a wound given by time
You became cut off from your heart
You became educated on the details of information
And a pin in your neck cut you off from your story
The pin has put you to sleep.
While you sleep you need not experience the wound.
The wound does not heal
Until you find the courage
To walk straight into it
With no pin
And a willingness
To ride the waves of red-black-white experience
Through to breakpoint.
Ride the waves of the colors of your life
Tell your story.
Write the rest of your story.
Your story is in your own hands
Now you are dancing in the real life.
Now you are learning about love

This completes the red-black-white. However, if you have learned the red-black-white process, you understand that the red-black-white process is never completed. It is a daily life long commitment.

It is a journey you accomplished on the day you were born. It is a journey you will do on the day you die.

Be brave, young warrior. Do your part to help your village all the days of your life. Live in the dignity and integrity of self respect and respect for your fellow time travelers in your village.

We will end the challenge on Emotional Navigation with a poem about Einstein.

Einstein Was a Great Teacher

Energy equals matter times the speed of light squared. That's what Einstein figured. What was he saying? Have I learned it yet? Ours is an infinite universe ever expanding. Earth perception is an illusion.

Possibilities dawned on me as soon as I was willing to turn away from the glass. Our entire cosmos is a single heartbeat; A solitary pulse from a greater reality; The random lonely thought of a being that I don't perceive.

The pulse of that being may be God or it may be not God. But it is surely the great mystery that holds the strands of meaning and connection within the chaos and confusion that I observe daily.

It is this force that creates my purpose on earth. I was sent with a mission to accomplish as I travel through these veins of time. I have not been careful enough to watch out for what I am creating.

Every act of creation is a ripple on a pond of consequences good and bad. I never meant to hurt you like that. Forgive me my blind trespass as well as my selfish preoccupation.

Traveling at the speed of light is quite scary. Space frightens me with Its vast expanses of emptiness. Time grants me precious few years to ride swift horses of red and black and white.

I have a deal to close before I pass over through the misty border to certain death. Am I doing my part? On death day I will push through a narrow opening and remove my human mask. What a relief!

But I love my life under this blue sky on this brown and green earth. Other pulses of energy resonate with my life song; brothers and sisters of blood, sweat, and tears - travelers on a journey through time.

We are at once prisoners as well as shooting stars; As sorrowful as we are happy; As empty as we are fulfilled; As lost as we are found; As hopeless as we are in love.

In the end we are only as powerful as our willingness to accept our powerlessness. We are only as loved as our courage to accept deepest sorrow. We are only as blessed as the blessings we have given.

Life is as wonderful as it sucks. Someone please help me to let go again and again to do the things I need to do to be truly myself. And then, there you were - I found you after all these years - The courage to be the real me.

Inside the scar of the cruel wound that nearly killed me - I saw that life falls apart and comes together...And comes together and falls apart...And falls apart and comes together...

Mothers and fathers and children can only create love in tunnels; Dark birth canals where the dead are born into light and where the living must learn to die gracefully back into darkness.

Darkness proceeding through tunnels toward light that burns so bright only to surrender its spark back to dark. I was afraid of the dark until I saw it could be sweet and kind.

I was angry at the dark until it showed me the light that I wanted so fiercely. Where does it all come from? Where is it all going? Now there is a course in the miracle of powerlessness.

Einstein was a great teacher. He finally figured it out for me. I don't really know anything. Maybe I don't have to worry as much As I think I have to worry.

Maybe I don't have to think as much as I have to learn to burn this personal energy allotment clean and true in my own skin - Spirit moving through flesh and bones - My unique journey at the speed of light.

I could not see myself at all until I finally calmed down. It was then that I saw my reflection in your eyes. In your eyes I saw an opening to another possibility.

Today I am here. Here is a world that has waited patiently for me to arrive on time with my precious gift. I arrived on earth as an expert and I have grown into a fool. Thank God for forgiveness.

I was a prisoner behind Plexiglas until I saw you beating your own head. I touched you and reminded you to be kind to yourself. Then you gave me a wonderful Christmas when you showed me your barn.

I stopped beating my own head and I asked you to hold my hand. I am looking at a possibility now - The one I overlooked completely. It is me - A man with a mission - An expert at a trade that I never knew existed.

Time stops for an instant. Waves of life wash over me in surges of red, black, and white. I am reborn. I take another breath but it is like my first breath.

I open my eyes again and find them sparkling like diamonds wide and innocent like the first time. And I feel like I am finally starting to learn what love is.

JD 11/10

Find your center.

Live your life true one moment at a time.

Bring your gift - red

Face your sorrows- black

Be grateful for each blessing and joy - white

That's it. Now you got it, kid.

Keep dancing, young warrior!

Heroic Journey
Challenge #7

Unfold My Soul Through The Story of My Life

Message to Group Leader:
Writing and Telling of the personal story as it fits into the greater story of the universe brings together all the themes found in this book into a grand finale where the past is owned and released, the potential of the present is broken open and accessed, and the future becomes a glorious and mysterious ocean of possibility waiting for an initiated adult navigator in charge of his or her own vessel. Students examine their stories from innocence through the wound of lost innocence. They examine the new myth they created about themselves after the wound. They examine the mask they put on, the habits or addictions or behavior patterns they developed as a result of the wound and new myth, and they assess the place where they stand today. Finally, the story concludes with the option to create another new myth that is more in line with life purpose if the old myth doesn't work anymore.

- **What is a Myth?**

  o Definition
  o Fact and Fiction
  o The Power of Myth

- **The Myth that Powers Your Life**

  o Your Story as a Myth
  o Identifying Your Wounds and Your Ruts of Behavior
  o The Myth that is Authoring Your Life

- **Your Story – Transformational or Terminal?**

  o Multi-Dimensional Life View
  o A Terminal View of Life

- **Writing Your Story**

  o Choose a template and outline your story
  o Writing your story
    ▪ Utilizing a Template
    ▪ Utilizing the Flow Chart
    ▪ Following the Steps to Write Your Story
- **Telling Your Story**

  o Preparing to Tell Your Story In Group
  o Telling You story
  o Committing to a New Myth

- **Learning How to Hit the Curveball**

Introduction

We are now in the homestretch of our long train ride. This group has survived. It has floundered and flourished through a long journey. We have watched the warm sun of summer turn the earth to the golden days of autumn. We have seen the cold turn the golden days of autumn into the brown and dead, frozen leaves of winter. We have sat together through the dark and cold days of winter when it felt like no new life would ever appear again to see the King of Trees push slowly through the hard rock of winter into the innocent green of spring. As we approach the Banquet, we will witness the return of the warm summer days we had left behind us in those first days of our group. The end of this group is now in sight.

Our Banquet will be held at the close of our journey. It is the telling and the completion of a story. The story is the journey out and away from the village and the return to the village. The story is the test of your willingness to explore and experience the way of the warrior. It is the breaking open of the stone so that the wound of childhood may heal and a responsible adult warrior may be born.

This challenge completes the breaking open of the stone. Telling your story breaks open the stone and reveals the heart of who you really are. Being who you really are will bless the village with the gift of your purpose as well as bless you with the happiness you so fiercely have sought in so many different ways.

This is the warrior's path. A torch is being passed to you, young warrior. It will be bestowed to you at the Banquet. It is the torch of adulthood that will grant you your measure of happiness, sorrow, and desire in return for the gift that you will bring to the village. This group has been like a toolbox that gave you the tools you will need to perform the tasks of your new trade. Welcome to the union of adults.

The final leg of this journey is the embracing of your own story. Your story is who you are today. It is also a non visible pen you are holding in your hand that will author the rest of your life. It is your story. Write it well.

Embracing your story as it has been written so far will free your pen to write the rest of your story in any direction you choose. The best way to own and embrace your story is to tell it. If you are not quite ready for that, I will ask you to explore your story in writing for now. Telling is best because a story needs a teller and a listener to complete itself. However, writing down your story will be beneficial in that you will begin to understand that you have a story.

There are two kinds of people as we approach adulthood - people who are authoring their current story from the freedom of the present moment - and those whose stories are being authored for them by the jail keeper of the unresolved, or un-dissolved past.

Embracing and telling the story is important because it is an act of forgiveness, as well as an act of empowerment within the bounds of your limits as a human being. The telling of the story places you in the balanced and focused center of the present moment. Being balanced and focused on this spot where you are standing now gives you the power to author the rest of your life story the way it was meant to be written - from the purpose found inside your own heart.

Happiness is found the instant you free yourself from the past and you unlock the door to your own deep heart, the heart that is as alive and resilient as the King of Trees, a force within that no wound can ever destroy. Once told, the story frees you to be yourself and to keep dancing the red-black-white circle of human experience all the rest of your life. You have found the key to happiness.

What is your personal story? What is the archetypal myth that has authored your story so far? Where are you now? Who are you? What do you want? Do you need to change your myth? How would you know if you did need to change your myth? What is a myth? These are some of the questions we will answer as we unlock the telling of the stories as the final major challenge of our journey.

Let's begin!

What Is A Myth?

Myth is often defined in modern times as an 'untruth'. That is because our modern world is very much based on facts. Myth is not based on fact. Does that make it untrue? Well, if the truth were based on facts alone, then myth would be untrue. But what if the breadth of the truth extends beyond the bounds of the most prolific facts uncovered by science? Einstein seemed to understand that. A myth is a story that respects mystery. A mystery is a truth that eludes factual brain capabilities. Mystery, like myth, requires imagination. How can imagination lead us to the truth? Isn't it fictional?

Well, yes and no. In literature, there are stories and movies that are supposedly true stories because they are based on facts that really happened. But many times these 'true' stories can get twisted or exaggerated by the author in a way that makes the story quite untrue.

By the same token, there are great works of art in literature that are fictional that manage to resonate and reflect truth in the hearts of readers. The stories and characters in Greek Mythology are mostly fictional but they have endured until today because they resonate with so many mysterious truths about the human condition, spirit, and psyche.

Author, James Hillman says, "Taken straight, statistical studies stone the mind." Myth, by contrast, is fiction that is meant to break open the stone of the mind in order to find some truth that is hard to explain.

Do you have the courage to get un-stoned? To go to the core of the heart through the stone broken open is the warrior's way. It requires an exploration of myth. Myth is an exploration of mystery that is a 'realization' of some truth not easy to define or corner into a scientific formula. It is a fictional story that rings true in the deep heart. All of us have a myth that we live everyday even if that myth is that there is no myth. We live in a myth - We have a cultural myth - We have a national myth - We have a family myth - and lastly, but importantly, we have a personal myth.

Telling your story examines your myth(s) and allows you to see the ways those myths are authoring your life today. Telling your story allows you to choose a new myth if the old one seems to be hurting you or causing you to be stuck in a certain unsatisfying state of being.

MYTH IS VERY POWERFUL. If you try to change your behavior without also changing your myth, the changes are often of short duration if you can change at all. Behavior modification programs are famous for these short lived changes that are rarely sustained in time. Changes that happen as a result of a change of myth are often life altering because you are altering not only the behavior but the entire vision that the behavior is justified upon and fed from.

Telling your story is making a complete inventory of the actions you have chosen so far. It is a complete inventory of the conclusions or myths you have come to believe about yourself as a result of things you were taught and wounds you have incurred.

Telling your story puts you in the freedom of the present moment where you can choose a new myth if the old one(s) are not working for you anymore. Change your myth about yourself and you will change the personality you are and the person you will become. Telling your story examines your myth. Your story grows out of your myth. Your life is the myth you are living. As grown human beings, we are perfectly free to choose our myths. Choose your myth well.

Carl Jung has said, "The most important question anyone can ask is 'what myth am I living?" You are living out a myth in your life right now as we speak. What is your myth? Is it helping you? I am not sure. That is for you to decide. And that is why you tell your story.

Why Do You Have A Story To Tell?

If time and memory had not entered into the equation of life as consciousness, the story might be quite simple. You would be born in innocence. You would live in innocence. And you would die in innocence. Your death would be equally as innocent as your birth and no conflict would exist. Myth would probably be irrelevant.

But one of the main characteristics that set us apart as humans is that we are storytellers. We live in a consciousness of story and myth. So your story is a direct result of time and memory. In time, as the story goes, a wound happens to you that makes you think that innocence has died. Your memory keeps the wound in place while your brain gets busy creating a new myth to replace innocence lost.

It is an attempt to survive the wound. The wound happens at a time and place where you cannot make sense out of it. It does not fit into innocence. Your innocent myth was one of safety and security and wonder that became interrupted by a wound. Innocence then gets replaced by any one of a number of possible new myths. Just like innocence ruled the waters of your early years, so now the new myth comes to try to save you in the troubled waters of lost innocence. As soon as you wade into the water of human reality and experience, it is guaranteed that the waters will become troubled. That is a guarantee in human life. No matter how well we raise our youth, innocence will be shattered by time. Time is the wound giver.

The myth you choose at the time of your wound authors your life for years. Parents wonder why a child suddenly begins to fail at school, why one child turns to drugs, why one is so obsessed with getting 'A's' in school that she cannot relax and enjoy life or even enjoy school where her grades are so good.

In the days of the village, the elders would take you to the countryside at the right moment in order to expose the wound, to give it meaning, to embrace the truth of it, to show the way to heal it and admire its beautiful scar as a sign of survival. The new myth of survival led the youth to see the importance of their personal lives in the context of a bigger story, and in a context of the myth of a village that needed them so badly to bring their individual gifts.

In this way, the wound became a source of passage to adulthood. It was not diagnosed into pathology by adults as it is today. Nor was it parsed for treatment and cure. The truth is that you were not nearly as damaged by the actual wound as you were by your own chosen response or myth. Therefore, it is time to descend back into the wound and explore this myth.

What was your innocent childhood like? What is your wound? What was the myth you created after the wound? How did it change your behavior and your thoughts and the quality of your daily life? How did you drift off course and off of your life purpose? Answer these questions and you are telling your story.

What Is The Myth That Has Authored Your Story?

What myth did you choose after you were wounded? From this point on, I must warn you that as the elder, I can only lead you to the truths in your heart. Students often come to me and ask me to figure out what their wound is. I cannot do that. I have too much respect for your personal life to do any more than lead you to the doorstep of your wound.

You decide if you were wounded, when you were wounded, how you were wounded, what you did with the wound, what myth you created as a result, and finally, whether or not you should change the myth that is authoring your story and your life. It is not my business to author your life for you. I am the author of my life. You are the author of yours.

Tara Bennett-Goleman outlines several 'schemas' or ruts that a person chooses in life and then repeats over and over again. A rut is a way of behaving that is the result of a pattern of thinking. The pattern of thinking comes from the myth you have chosen to believe about yourself.

The rut thus becomes a way of living that is repetitive in that it gets reinforced consistently by a certain pattern of thinking and believing. When this scenario interferes with your daily ability to do your life purpose, you become unhappy. But you find it very hard to change by this time. The rut is deep and your wheels just naturally keep falling into the ruts and following their unsatisfying behavioral path.

The rut of your current pattern of thinking and behaving is forged into the ground by the myth you have chosen about yourself when you incurred the wound. That is the bad news. The good news is that you may change the myth anytime you want as long as you are willing to change your mind. This examination needs an elder's help.

Here are some of the ideas about wounds that Bennett-Goleman outlines in her book, "Emotional Alchemy". Along with the wounds, she sets up an exploration of ruts which lead directly to behaviors rooted in the wound. These ruts actually are spawned by the myth that you created after the wound. Thus, these ruts of behavior become very difficult to change.

As serious as the wound may be, it is the choice of thoughts about the wound that really affects our lives and determines our behavior changes. Until the spell of the myth is broken, you tend to stay stuck in the same repetitive thought process and behavior pattern – sometimes for years and years. Some people stay in this stuck position their entire lives.

At a workshop, Bennett-Goleman presented a fascinating explanation of 'ruts'. For purposes of this book, we are exploring these 'ruts' of behavior as they relate to 'wounds' that are cut very close to the heart. These wounds trigger different responses in different people. That is because the same wound can trigger different thought processes and different conclusions or myths. This is what I mean when I say that the wound was not nearly as catastrophic as the conclusions you came to believe about yourself as a result. The same wound can trigger a thought process that leads one child to jail, while it leads another to obsessively follow all rules. Although the wound is the same, the myths chosen are different. This leads to completely different behavior choices even though the two wounds are very similar.

Here are the wounds with some examples of different myths that spawn behavioral choices which arise from the individual thought process of the wounded person. This is a generalized presentation of some ideas from Bennett-Goleman. Refer to her book, *Emotional Alchemy* for her in depth study of these ruts.

- ABANDONMENT - My wound is one of abandonment. I feel that I was left alone or abandoned by someone who should have stayed and loved me. Once I adopt this myth as my new myth, it triggers any one of several ruts in my life.

  I may become a very needy person seeking love constantly and never finding it. I may choose a rut where I am alone and let no one get close to me. An abandonment wound coupled with a myth that my own unworthiness is the reason why I was abandoned can change my whole outlook on school and its importance. School can be pushed to the background as I seek attention in the wrong places. It can also be pushed to the background if I am stuck in an 'alone' state of mind where nothing matters. I can use failing in school as a way to prove I am not worthy. I can even use failing in school as a way to get back at the person who I feel has abandoned me. Is your wound one of abandonment? What is the myth you created to deal with this abandonment?

- VULNERABILITY - My wound may be one of vulnerability. Someone whom I should have been able to trust has hurt me deeply. If my wound is one of vulnerability, I might choose a myth or rut that I am invulnerable and no one can ever hurt me again. This can cause me to feel alone all the time while keeping me safe in my myth's point of view. Or I can do quite the opposite and continue to desperately make myself vulnerable in all sorts of places where I should not be making myself vulnerable. My new myth is needy and desperately seeking love in places where I should not be making myself vulnerable or available. Is your wound one of vulnerability? What is the myth you have chosen to deal with the wound you received when you were vulnerable to someone who hurt you?

- REJECTION - My wound may be one where I felt rejected and worthless in the eyes of someone who was abusive with me or did not care for me properly. If my wound is one of rejection, I may now live a life where I reject others before they have a chance to reject me. My myth tells me 'no one can be trusted' and I will reject before I get rejected.

Or, quite the opposite, I may be choosing risky behavior where I am desperately trying to be accepted by someone else. My myth leads me to believe that I must blindly accept everyone in sight to try to establish the relationship that was lost. Is your wound one of rejection? What is the myth you have chosen to live out as a result of this rejection?

- MISTRUST - Trust may have been broken in my life and this may have caused me a deep wound and hurt. If my wound is one of mistrust, I may now be unwilling to trust again even in situations where I know I should risk trust.

Again, quite the opposite can also be true if my wound is one of mistrust. I may blindly trust everyone in sight blindly hoping I can find trust somewhere. Is your wound one of mistrust? What myth did you choose after you incurred this painful wound?

- FAILURE - Is your wound one of being made to feel like you are a failure? If my wound is one of experiencing myself as a failure, I may repeat this failure in school and everywhere I go as a way to live out the myth of failure that I believe about myself.

Quite the opposite, I may deal with my wound of failure by acting like I am a know-it-all in all situations because it is a way to hide my failure wound. Is your wound one of failure? What is the myth you live out since you received this painful wound?

- SUBJUGATION - Did someone wound you by abusing you sexually or by entrapping you in some way? If my wound is one of subjugation, I may constantly allow myself to be abused by others in relationships because now that is who I think I am in my new myth. I may have concluded that I deserve to be treated this way, or worse, that it was my fault that I was treated this way.

I may feel very claustrophobic or trapped in school or in a relationship that starts to get too close. I may believe that intimacy always leads to abuse or entrapment.

Quite the opposite, I may not be able to stay in school the whole day. I may constantly be trying to go or stay away or I might keep my mind or body racing constantly to avoid the feeling of being subjugated. My new myth told me to keep moving at all times. Is your wound one of subjugation? What is the myth you are now living out because of the conclusions you came to over this wound?

- ENTITLEMENT - Some people have a wound that might be called a reverse wound. If this is my wound, I have been told so many times that I am special that I become wounded when I find out that I am quite ordinary and that I get hurt and wounded and mistreated like everyone else. This person will choose the rut of entitlement. Entitlement means that 'you think life owes you because life has been unfair to you.' The person stuck in this rut will demand special treatment and will see himself as victimized if he doesn't get treated special. He will walk around the school all day just looking for a reason to be able to say "That's not fair". He will often be found in the discipline office complaining that he is being victimized.

On the other side of the entitlement coin, a person could become quite selfish and greedy and choose to take all he can get for himself in all situations without regard to others. My myth concludes life revolves around me and my immediate needs. Is your wound one of entitlement? What is the myth you are now living out in your life as a result of the conclusions you came to over this wound.

- DEPRIVATION - Some people have a wound caused by deprivation. They were deprived of things they needed including love and nurturing. If my wound is one of deprivation, I might conclude that there is not enough to go around for everybody. I will horde things including love. I will not see love as energy capable of unlimited creation. I will see love as a limited commodity that might disappear at any second. I am the kind of person that keeps 'score' all day to make sure I am getting enough love. I will say things like, "Why did you say that to her? You never say that to me?"

On the other side of the coin, I may refuse all love altogether all the time as way to continue in my self-fulfilling viewpoint that life is lacking love. My myth has concluded that love is lacking and flawed and I want no part of it. Is your wound one of deprivation? What is the myth you are now living and acting out as a result of this wound in your life?

Do not get caught up in trying to be dramatic or original in your story. Your story must be honest. If you do not have any vivid memories of a wound in your life, do not make them up. A well told story that is honest and can recall the 'feelings' of becoming separate and alone inside is much better than a story full of facts that is detached from the heart and trying to impress others.

Your story is about your innocence followed by the path you took away from your own heart. What did you feel like? What new conclusions did you make about yourself? What were you searching so desperately for? What mistakes did you make? Who did you wrong? Who did wrong to you? What were your ruts of behavior?

Here is a list of possible 'myth' changes that may have occurred at the time of the wound. Look over the list of possible 'belief' changes. Can you identify with any of these changes in 'myth'? For now, just circle the one(s) that you think apply to you.

It is a partial list. The range of possible myth changes is very extensive. Feel free to add your own myth to the list if you do not see one that looks familiar.

I concluded I was a dummy.
I thought something was wrong with me..
I felt like I did not belong.
I can't do anything right.
I didn't think I was acceptable as I was.
I can never do enough. I am lacking as a person.
I thought I was just a doormat.
I concluded that I was not special.
I concluded that I was special.
I concluded that no one liked me.
I didn't think I was worthy of others

I thought I should be punished or that I did not deserve to be happy
I concluded that nothing matters.
I am insignificant in the eyes of the world.
No matter how I try, I always mess up.
I'm insignificant and no one cares what I have to say.
I have no good qualities. I am useless to myself and others.
My life does not make a difference.
I am just a 'nobody'.
I am a bad person
They told me I was a mistake and I believe it.
People think I am ugly and flawed.
I concluded that I am better than everyone else.
No one will ever love me.
I fail at whatever I do.
No one cares about me.
I can't trust anyone.
I am worthless without a girl or a guy in my life
I deserve to be alone

Did you identify with any of these new myths in your story? These myths, once adopted, become like self fulfilling prophecies. Once you were wounded, you needed to find a way to make sense of the wound. It knocked you off of your ground and out of your innocence. It was very harsh.

Thus, your choice of myth was your conclusion, your attempt to make sense of the wound. It led directly to behaviors that protected you and helped you at first. But now, these behaviors may be stunting your growth or hurting you.

Now to begin the rough outline of your story, sit with your mentor or counselor and make a rough outline. Choose the wound(s) that you most identify with. Begin to identify the myth or new way of thinking that was the result of your wound(s). Finally, use the list to try to identify the myth you chose as a way to survive the wound.

When you are finished, you should have a rough idea of the wound(s), of the change in your myth about yourself, and of the ruts of behavior that became part of your life.

Your Story: Transformational or Terminal

As you formulate your story, you will have to decide whether to paint your story as a one dimensional straight line that exists in time only, or, whether to make your story a multi-dimensional story that moves in the circle of the red-black-white.

Life Story Perception #1
One Dimensional

Birth - Childhood - Adolescence - Adulthood - Old Age -Death

WHITE_____RED_____BLACK

In this one dimensional viewpoint of your life story, life begins with your birth and it ends with your death. The connections or strands of your life are not seen as coming from your ancestors or extending past the day of your death. The circle of the red-black-white, if it is acknowledged, is seen as a linear story that is your personal story. It is limited in its scope and vision.

This myth fosters a fatalistic outlook. Birth is not looked at as death from the world of the womb. Death is not looked at as the birth canal to the unknown. It is easy in this one dimensional schema to feel that life is all about you. You exist as an insignificant particle of the universe and the story of your life is not the story of the ages but a story that begins, scoots through time, and quite abruptly ends.

Your life is a linear story on a time line. It starts in a diaper and it ends in a box in the ground. You are going to die. Your story is terminal.

Life Perception #2
Multi-Dimensional

A multi-dimensional story is one that acknowledges the visible, the invisible, and the non visible. You see your life in terms of the community, in terms of history, in terms of your ancestors who are still alive in your heart, and in terms of the great mystery of life. You are an insignificant particle of the universe. Your particle is filled with the spark of the energy of the knowledge of the center of the stone. You are connected to the universe like the stars at distant ends of the galaxies are connected in mysterious ways that can't be understood.

Your life is not simply a straight line in time. It is a multidimensional ripple or spiral that extends beyond the grave in the force of your character. The outer appearance of the stone will someday crumble, but not the spark at the core of the stone. Your life has a center. It acknowledges mystery and understands the red-black-white as an infinite process. Your personal story fits into the pattern of the bigger story. Your story is transformational.

In a one dimensional viewpoint of your story, your story is a straight line that begins and ends. Ashes are ashes and they never come to bloom. It is the story of your ego and your ego only. It is much harder to give your life a meaning with this viewpoint. It does not have a center except that life revolves around your own daily needs. It is not spiraling inward into the mystery of your heart nor outward into mystery of the infinity of the universe.

In a multidimensional viewpoint of your story, your story is a spiral that extends beyond your side of the box. Your life is a process that extends into the mystery of life's infinite process. This viewpoint gives your life meaning, it recognizes a center. It understands that life did not begin with the birth of your ego and it will not end with the death of your ego.

Whether you choose a one dimensional viewpoint or a multi-dimensional viewpoint is up to you. It is my job as a village elder to open your eyes to the multi-dimensions so that your adult life, with its future triumphs and heartaches, will have a center and a purpose and meaning that resonates with the mystery of the universe. If, however, you choose a one dimensional viewpoint of your life in the visible world in time, I will respect that.

As a teacher of mystery, I am basically teaching you that I don't know what I am even talking about anyway. So why would I make a demand on you about how you should view your life. I opened the door to the multi-dimensional. That's all I do. Walk into the multi-dimensional view of life if you like. It sees your life as connected in a great tapestry of life where you have a destiny to accomplish in the earth part of your journey.

However, I do wonder why someone would choose a morbid one dimensional dream of death when a nicer dream that gives life meaning and purpose is available. The shepherds on the hillside recognized the multi dimensions and they had no education. Einstein recognized the mystery too. In the end, you choose your own dream and you pay as you go.

The templates for telling your story that follow can be used in both one dimensional and multi-dimensional viewpoints. Songwriter Kevin Welch once wrote "there's gonna be two dates on your tombstone. Everybody's gonna read them. But all that's gonna matter is the little dash between them."

Your story is the story of your dash through time on this planet. It will have repercussions on those you encounter on your journey. It will have consequences and rewards for you too. Tell it well. You are the author of the dash through time.

Consider the myth you are living out. The truth is that the myth that you choose is the one that gets bigger. What you pay attention to gets bigger. So then, choose carefully. What you ignore is potential unrealized. You choose the reality you bring into being by the myth you choose and the actions you choose in living out that myth.

WHAT YOU PAY ATTENTION TO GETS BIGGER.
YOUR MYTH IS WHAT YOU ARE PAYING ATTENTION TO
IT IS HOW YOU SEE YOURSELF AND YOUR LIFE
IT GETS BIGGER
EVERYDAY YOU REINFORCE IT
BY PAYING ATTENTION TO IT
WHAT IS YOUR MYTH?
HAVE YOU FORGED A RUT THAT YOU ARE STUCK IN?
IS IT HELPING YOU OR BRINGING YOU DOWN?
WHAT ARE YOU IGNORING?
IS IT HELPING YOU?

IF YOU CHOOSE TO SEE YOURSELF AS A WARRIOR
DOING THE RED, BLACK, AND WHITE
YOU WILL BE A WARRIOR
AND THE MYTH WILL GROW
AS YOU PRACTICE IT
AND PAY ATTENTION TO IT

TELLING YOUR STORY IS EXPOSING YOUR MYTH
TO YOURSELF FIRST
AND THEN TO OTHERS.
IT ALLOWS YOU TO CHOOSE A NEW MYTH
IF THE OLD ONE IS NOT HELPING YOU
THE POINT OF ALL THIS INQUIRY
IS TO GROW INTO A PROSPEROUS, HAPPY ADULT

Telling Your Story

Three templates follow. They are meant to help you formulate your story. You may choose one of them or you may pick parts from each of them. Template 1 is more abstract. Template 2 is more concrete. Template 3 is a combination of abstract and concrete. These templates are not meant as ruts you have to follow in the telling of your story. They are presented only as aids to you in case you do not know where to begin or how to organize your story.

Let your counselor or mentor help you to further develop your outline of your story.

Choose a template and your teacher or mentor will help you examine your own story by helping you organize thoughts around each idea or marker along the journey of the template. You will use your writing skills, your imagination, and your historical knowledge about the time and place where you were born to forge your story.

Writing Your Story

It will be helpful to write your story prior to trying to tell it. Writing out your story will clarify things for you such as major turning points in your life as well as times in your life where your behavior may have changed drastically. These places are the very places where you may have made changes in the myth that informs your life. Getting to the heart of your myth is to get at the heart of all your behaviors and outcomes. It also gives you the opportunity to change your myth now if the old one no longer works.

Another reason for writing your story is because you may not feel quite ready to tell your story yet. Although it is best to 'tell' a story, writing it is still helpful both for your own self knowledge and also to prepare you for the day when you do feel ready to tell your story.

A process for writing your story is found in the flow chart in the next few pages. Your teacher will direct you and help you pick a template and then you can follow the flow chart as an aid for writing and/or telling your story

Template #1 - Abstract

First birth canal
Humanity-earth
World of Time
Innocent childhood
Connected and whole
Wound
Loss of innocence
Disconnected and separate
I am not the same
Pin puts me to sleep
Amnesia of the real me
Creation of a new myth of who I am
Fire
Power trip
Red journey away from center
Fun
Lost
Off track
Alone
Crash
Ashes
Powerless trip
Hopeless
Accept and sit in ashes
Move into my wound
Warrior test
Tell my story
Second birth canal
Remove pin-Wake up
Rebirth
New myth?
Beautiful scar-Survival
Connected yet Separate
Comfortable
Red-Black -White Warrior
Live and die a thousand times
Do life purpose as a responsible adult

Template #2 - Concrete

Guidelines For Telling Your Story In Your Group

1) Describe your early years
    What are your happiest childhood memories?
    Who were important people in your childhood life?
    Do you remember a day when you felt perfectly safe and happy?

2) How old were you when you received the 'wound'?
    What loss or betrayal happened wounded you?
    How did it change you and your conclusion about life?
    How did your personality change?
    Did you go into red first or black first?

3) How did you try to get power and deal with your problems?
    What did you do to cope?
    How did your behavior change?
    How did your choices help you or hurt you?
    What friends did you choose at this time?
    How did you go 'off track? What attachments did you find?
    What were the consequences?
    Were you in the victim stance? Describe that?
    Who did you hurt? others? Yourself? Both?

4) What was your low point? Your bottom? Have you hit bottom yet?
    What did you have to accept about life?
    When did you first realize you had to make some changes?

5) Who did you turn to for help?

6) How is it for you now? What is still left to be done? Are you working on it?

7) How do you picture the rest of your story?

Template #3 -Combination

1. Birth - Innocence - Ages 1-3
   What was your childhood like?
   What are your happiest memories?
   What stories were you told about your childhood? Ages 4-9
2. Development and Education and Socialization
   Talk about your upbringing
   Who were your role models?
   How did you see life? What myth did you hold?
3. Wound Age 9+
   Something happened and you were not the same.
   Your behavior changed. Your myth changed. What myth did you choose?
4. New You
   You leave the innocence behind and you put on the mask
   Describe the mask of your new myth about yourself
   You start out on your red journey in search of happiness?
5. Red Journey
   Where did you search for happiness?
   What did you find?
   What habits came out of your myth and your search?
   Whom did you hurt? Who hurt you? Describe your mistakes.
   What are the shadow parts of you that you don't like?
   What good came of your red journey?
6. Crash   Age?
   Can you remember when your red journey came to ashes?
   What happened? How has your illusion shattered?
   What was your Plexiglas?
   What was the emptiness you felt inside?
7. Challenge - Initiation
   Someone challenges you to sit in your emptiness
   What was it like without attachments and illusions?
   Did you successfully sit with your emptiness?
8. Rebirth
   What is the spark of life you felt in the ashes?
   What changes have you made in your life?
   Do you have a new myth?
   What is it?

9. Future

    How do you see your future?

    What do you picture as you see yourself going forward?

    What do you seek?

    How have you grown up?

    Be specific.

Before we proceed further, I want you to know how much I respect your effort and your willingness to begin to explore your journey and to become a warrior. If you would like to tell your story in group, you will have the opportunity to do so. If not, you will have a written story that can help you crystallize all the major 'turning points' in your life along with all the important 'choices' you made in your thinking and in your behavior at each of those turning points.

An Outline of the Journey of Your Story

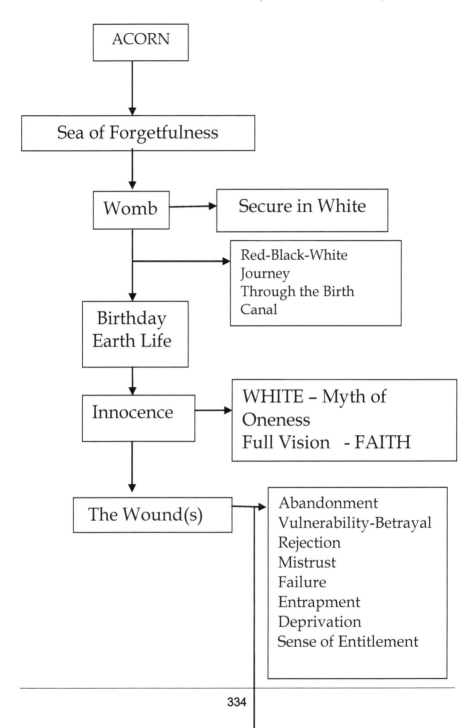

ACORN

Sea of Forgetfulness

Womb → Secure in White

Red-Black-White Journey Through the Birth Canal

Birthday Earth Life

Innocence → WHITE – Myth of Oneness Full Vision   - FAITH

The Wound(s) → Abandonment
Vulnerability-Betrayal
Rejection
Mistrust
Failure
Entrapment
Deprivation
Sense of Entitlement

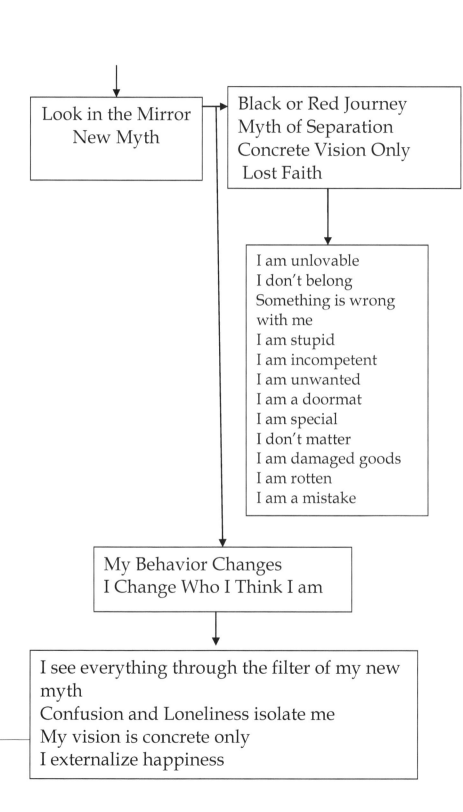

Look in the Mirror
New Myth

Black or Red Journey
Myth of Separation
Concrete Vision Only
Lost Faith

I am unlovable
I don't belong
Something is wrong
with me
I am stupid
I am incompetent
I am unwanted
I am a doormat
I am special
I don't matter
I am damaged goods
I am rotten
I am a mistake

My Behavior Changes
I Change Who I Think I am

I see everything through the filter of my new
myth
Confusion and Loneliness isolate me
My vision is concrete only
I externalize happiness

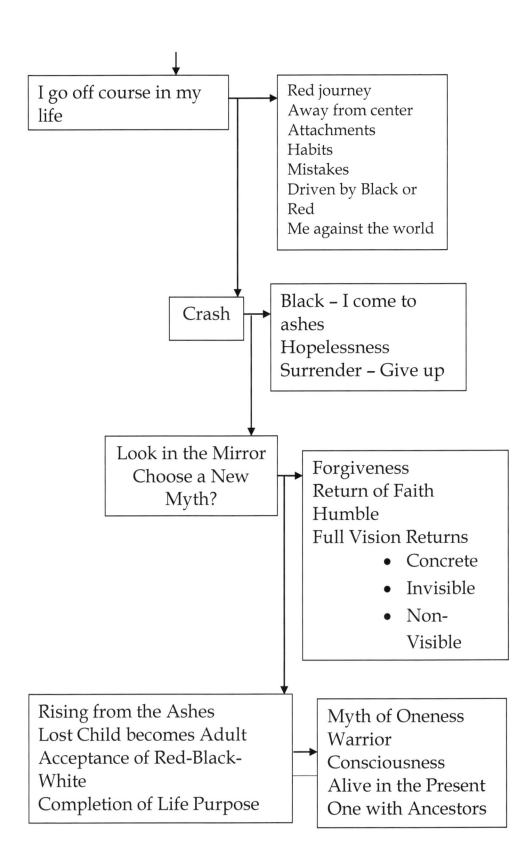

I go off course in my life

Red journey
Away from center
Attachments
Habits
Mistakes
Driven by Black or Red
Me against the world

Crash

Black – I come to ashes
Hopelessness
Surrender – Give up

Look in the Mirror Choose a New Myth?

Forgiveness
Return of Faith
Humble
Full Vision Returns
- Concrete
- Invisible
- Non-Visible

Rising from the Ashes
Lost Child becomes Adult
Acceptance of Red-Black-White
Completion of Life Purpose

Myth of Oneness
Warrior
Consciousness
Alive in the Present
One with Ancestors

Writing Your Story

Your Story is the meaning you assign to the facts, memories, and imagination of what you have been through in your life.

It is also the vision of where you are heading in your life. Without a story, your life has no meaning. A meaningless life just drifts from one accident to the next without any focus or direction. A meaningful life owns the past and revisions the myth of the person I am and the person I choose to become.

A well told story puts you on a new train – the train of your adult life and the train of your life purpose.

Without a story, you fail to board the train, or worse yet, you get hit by the train of life.

Own the truth of the past and envision the potential of the future with a myth of yourself as a warrior surviving life's hardships and thriving on purpose in a life that has meaning– and that is the myth you will actualize.

You story gives you a chance to choose a new myth and redirect the rest of your life.

Writing Your Story – Part One

INNOCENCE

Go back to your childhood. Jot down the memories you have of childhood; jot down a list of stories you were told about your childhood; jot down the ways you imagine about what your childhood was like. Look at photographs of you and recall the stories you were told about yourself. Also, use your imagination if there is not enough information or memories.

Next, formulate these notes into a written description that describes your childhood. Use the template that you have chosen to formulate your story. Or use the flow chart if you find that it is easier to follow. You should use the writing skills you have learned. Give your story flow and utilize your imagination as you describe your innocent years.

Ask your teacher for help with the flow chart or for help in matching which part of the template you should use in formulating Part One of your story.

Remember this is a story, so try to use your writing skills to connect your notes into a description that describes facts and memories, stories that you have been told by family members, pictures you have seen, and your own imaginings about your innocence into a story that describes you as the innocent child.

Writing Your Story – Part Two

THE WOUND(S)

Write down a few notes about any wound you remember that interrupted your innocence – a time when the innocence was shattered by life circumstances beyond your control. You may also jot down some notes by looking over the list of wounds that appeared earlier in this book.

Now formulate these notes into a written description that describes your shattered innocence – Who went away? And how did it feel to you? What meaning did you give to it? What fell apart that your innocence had hoped would never fall apart? What happened to you? How were you victimized by an adult or betrayed by a friend? These happenings all constitute your wound. What meaning did you give to it?

Ask your teacher for help in matching the questions of Part Two of your story to the template you have chosen, or to the flow chart.

Part Two of your story should end with a description of the child in the wounded state of being. Remember this is a story so connect it to your first paragraphs about innocence. What changed? How did life look different?

Don't just describe facts. Explore feelings and conclusions that you came to about life.

Writing Your Story – Part Three

WHAT MYTH DID YOU CREATE?

Jot down some notes as you try to think about the ways your life started to change after the wound. What was the innocent life that you wished for, and how was it shattered? How did your vision change concerning what you thought life was all about? Did you become angry? Did you become depressed? Did you become numb and just block it all out? Did you go on like all was just fine even though you felt differently inside?

Ask your teacher for help in matching the task of Part Three of your story to the questions in the template that you have chosen, or to the flow chart.

Put these notes into a written description that connects parts one and two of your story. Your writing on this part of your story should conclude with some myth that you believed about yourself or about life after the wound. It should spell out how you felt inside and how your outlook changed about life, and finally, how your behavior changed.

Use your memories, the facts you know about your life, use the reflections that family members or friends may have noticed, and use YOUR IMAGINATION of what you think it was like if you are having difficulty. You may also use the list of myths by Debbie Ford which were presented earlier in this chapter.

Writing Your Story – Part Four

JOURNEY OFF TRACK

Jot down some notes about the ways you started to go off track in your life. How did this relate to your myth about who you believed you were, and what you believed about life?

You may use your outline and the information from previous discussions to help loosen your memory as you jot down more notes. Ask your teacher for help in matching the tasks of this part of your story to the template you have chosen or to the flow chart.

Did you go into red first and start getting into trouble? Did you go into black first and start to depress about life? Did you numb yourself to the whole thing and try to act happy all the time? Did you try to regain the pleasure feelings of innocence by choosing to use drugs or another attachment? What did you reach for? How did you go off track? Or did you stay on track on the outside while feeling totally off track on the inside? Use your memories, the reflections you received from family or friends at that time, and your imagination.

Remember this is a story. Once you changed your myth about who you thought you were as a person, it was then that your feelings and/or your behavior started to change.

Was going off purpose in your life fun at first? Is it still fun? Did it help you at first? How was going off purpose destructive to you or others? Describe any attachment, addiction or habitual preoccupation that started to drive your life. Are you still on this part of your life journey? How is it working for you? How is it working against your life purpose? Are you the person you were meant to become or are you stuck in a habitual pattern?

Connect this part of your story to the previously created parts of your story. Write about your journey off purpose.

Writing Your Story – Part Five

THE CRASH

Jot down some notes about the consequences you paid for your changes in myth and behavior. Use the writings from past journal entries. Ask your teacher for help in matching this task to the section of the template that you have chosen to help you to formulate your story.

Has there ever been a low point or crisis in your life, a brush with death, a time when you realized you had to make some changes in your life? This is the next part of your story. Talk about the crisis. Was it a family crisis? Was it personal crisis? Was it a private crisis? Was it the mess you have made out of school? Or are you so obsessive about doing well that you can't relax? What made you realize that things were on a downhill slide?

This is the turning point of your story. So now formulate these notes into a written description that describes some very difficult time when you were ready to give up on life. Were you able to sit in the ashes of this mess and accept it? Can you now see yourself in this crisis as a warrior who knows how to do the red, black, and white in community?

Do you have faith now that the King of Trees will return if you stay true to yourself? If you can, write about the warrior traits that allow you to sit in the ashes of your own mess while you accept the wound, and take ownership for your own mess in the ways you went off purpose and hurt yourself or others. Are you still in this crisis? Do you need help? Do you know where to get help?

Formulate a few paragraphs that connect to the rest of your written story. This part of your story ends with some kind of new vision of yourself and who you think you are. This part of your story is about accepting your own shortcomings so you can take your place in the village and make your contribution to life.

Writing Your Story – Part Six

THE NEW MYTH

Choose a new myth about who you think you are if the old myth is not helping you. Changes of behavior will follow. If you want to be survivor who has risen from the ashes of her wound and is now living out the journey of the red-black-white as a warrior with a purpose in life, that is who you will be.

If you have already made changes, jot them down. What is your new vision of yourself? How are you able to make sense out of the parts of your story into a meaningful future for yourself? What future are you striving for? Where do you want to be in 10 years? Where do you want to be in 20 years? What are you going to contribute to humanity in the form of your life purpose?

Take your time now. Visualize the changes you need to make to become a warrior doing your life purpose. Write down the changes and commit to the changes in your group. Be specific and take this part of your journey one step at a time. Acknowledge that there may be setbacks but that you are committed to this effort in your group.

Ask group members for feedback about what they think your strengths are as a person. Do you realize you have these strengths? Write down how you might channel your strengths into a career or a way of life that contributes to your community.

Formulate this vision into a few paragraphs and you have completed your written story. Ask your teacher for help in matching this task to the template that you have chosen.

Close your story with a paragraph that connects all the parts together into the new belief that now generates who it is that you are and where your life is now going.

Finally, what is the honey that can be extracted from the sad parts of your story which can help you become a better person? What is your beautiful scar that marks your survival from the wound of lost innocence?

What must be released from your story and forgiven so that it does not interfere with your life today?

YOU HAVE COURAGEOUSLY WALKED INTO THE FIRE AND ANXIETY AND ASHES OF YOUR OWN LIFE STORY.

YOU WERE THE INNOCENT LAMB.

YOU WERE THE VICTIMIZED CHILD.

YOU WERE THE ONE THAT GOT LOST AND NEEDED TO BE SAVED.

YOU WERE THE VILLAIN TOO WHEN YOU WENT OFF PURPOSE.

AND YOU HAVE EMERGED AS THE HERO OF YOUR OWN STORY.

YOU NOW UNDERSTAND THE RED, BLACK, AND WHITE CIRCLE OF HUMAN EXPERIENCE THAT YOU MUST TRAVERSE THROUGH ALL YOUR DAYS ON EARTH. YOU ARE A WARRIOR WITH A GIFT TO BRING TO YOUR VILLAGE. BRING IT!!!!!!!!!

Telling Your Story in Group
(Message to the Teacher)

Telling of the story in group is very personal and should be left to student decision. However, if the teacher finds the courage to tell his story, and if your groups are at the 'working stage' level of group process, you will find by this time that many students will want to make an attempt to tell their stories in group.

Students may use their completed written story, but they should be encouraged to use this as a guide. A well told story flows naturally and the best story is not the one that is read, word for word from a paper. However, a read story is still better than no story.

Some students will tell a relatively chronological story that is a description. But others may tell a very emotional story of a fall from grace and an emergence as a warrior.

Signing Up to Tell Your Story

Sign up to tell your story. The story is told in the final weeks before the celebratory banquet.

When you tell your story your life will not change considerably in terms of the problems you will face. What will change are your consciousness and your myth. These in turn will change your ways of thinking. This will then change your responses to more satisfying behaviors.

Telling Your Story

Telling your story is the culmination of a long process that began on the very first week in group. As we established the rules and groundwork for our group in those first weeks, the elder was setting the table for the closure at our Banquet. The last major step in the journey toward the banquet celebration is the act of telling your story. Telling your story in the context of all we have learned in this group during this year is the act of 'breaking open the stone' of the personality on a journey back to the heart.

It is from the simple, honest and genuinely humble heart that you will be freed to live your life on purpose as a true adult warrior who is able to bring the gift of his life purpose to his fellow human travelers.

The telling of the story requires you to put into action all of the experiences and concepts you learned this year. You must have a sense that you have a life purpose. You must have a mature understanding of your relationship to power, along with an understanding of the great mystery of the universe where you reside. You must perceive the bigger story of the universe and you must see how your personal story fits into the infinite story of black holes and quasars, of quantum particles and sparks that mysteriously disappear into a non visible mist within the heart.

The telling of the story sees the red, black, and white truth of the journey of your life in the context of the red, black, and white journey of the universe. It sees the red, black, and white journey of birth as a partner to the red, black, and white journey of human death. It also sees the thousands of red, black, and white cycles that you must accomplish within the days of my human existence.

 The story remembers innocence without being maudlin or nostalgic; it remembers the pain of wounds without resorting to the victim stance; it owns all your mistakes and desperate attempts to find happiness outside the self in possessions and substances; it is willing to sit in the black ashes of your darkest hour; and it believes faithfully that the king of trees will return.

Your story will take you to the place where you are comfortable again in your own skin; where you know happiness and contentment through honesty and integrity; and where you are free to carry out the blessed purpose for which you were placed on this earth

The truth of your own heart is where your buried treasure is hidden along with the key to happiness. From the truth inside your own heart, you can live the rest of your life comfortable within your own skin. The way back into your heart is through the portal of the telling of your story.

Your story assesses your life from its innocent beginnings through the wounds that time has bestowed upon you. It explores the masks of personality that you created to protect the self from the pain of the wound. Your story looks unblinkingly at the ways you went off track in your life in the outward search for happiness in an escape from your own heart.

As you sit in the honest reality of the ashes of your mistakes, you tell your story where you walk right back through all that has happened all the way back to your wound where you re-enter the heart that was abandoned after the wound of lost innocence. It is from the center of your heart through the telling of your genuine story that you now stand poised as a full adult warrior ready to rise up out of the mud to catch the waves of red, black, and white in the fulfillment of your purpose.

Procedure for Telling Your Story

You will tell your story by following the story as you have written it. You may take notes from your written story. You may read your story as written, but the best story is told with emotion. It is not just a description of things that happened to you. It is a sinking down into the very roots of the rock of your soul so that you might break it open.

Use the following protocol:

- Go through each step of your story as you have written it. Let yourself be spontaneous and emotional.
- Connect each part of your story as you speak. Your story should flow from innocence into your wound(s) into your mask and myth etc
- Concentrate on the feelings and deep personality changes that occurred at different points in your story. This is more important than a strict telling of facts.
- As you tell your story, you might notice that some places in your story take on increased significance. They are turning points. Try to relate the 'twists of fate' that ended up defining who you are today

- As you approach the end of your story, you can tie the story together by relating any conclusions you have come to during the telling
- You may end the story by choosing a new myth to author your life. Describe how you see your life in one year, in five years, in 25 years.
- When you are finished telling your story, group members will offer their feedback about how your story impacted them. They will note which parts of your story that they identify with in their lives.

The telling of the story effectively breaks open the stone and allows you to unfold your soul in a way that frees you to live the rest of your life from within the truth of the acorn that is you.

Now that you have told your story and passed through the portal to adulthood, I grant you the right to keep living through the joys, sorrows, frustrations, and triumphs of your life as an adult. Live the story of the red, black, and white responsibly and intensely all the days of your life. I pass the torch of adulthood to you.

The final theme of this course gives you the presence you will need to do your adult life in a responsible way. You are not done getting wounds. You are not done going off track. You are not done crashing. And you are not done being reborn to each new phase of your earth life.

Learning how to hit the curveball is a baseball metaphor that helps you stay grounded, balanced, centered and focused so that you can face all the red, black, and white pitches of life.

Learning How to Hit the Curve Ball

Learning how to hit the curveball is a baseball metaphor that describes the difference between the players who make it to the Major Leagues, and those players who never do get to the Majors. The saying, "If you want to play in the Big Leagues, you have to be able to hit the curveball" applies. The same rule could apply to successfully making it to adulthood.

A baseball batter has less than one second to see the pitch coming, choose whether or not to swing, and to physically swing or not swing. Not only that, but he must also choose the right place to swing the bat. What is amazing is that it is even possible for this feat to be accomplished in less than one second. Think about it. Less than one second to see the pitch coming, to decide whether or not it is a good pitch to swing at, and to complete the act of swinging the bat exactly where the ball is at exactly the correctly timed moment. Truly amazing!!!! Could it be that we can apply this same skill that so many baseball and softball players learn to the daily handling of our emotions and our life choices? Maybe we have more ability to see and appropriately ride our anger and our depression than we thought?

Just as a baseball player has only a fraction of a second to choose whether to swing and then proceed to swing, so we can learn to handle our emotions. We must pay attention and stay honest. You need consciousness, focus, balance, and desire. Get up to the plate. Accept the emotion coming your way. Choose how to handle the pitch (emotion). Swing!

In this way we can learn to accept and ride our emotions. **You cannot control the pitch that is coming your way**. The batter does not get to tell Josh Beckett to please throw the ball slower or to please stop throwing change ups.

But you can learn to handle the emotions of life if you are paying attention, if you have the right attitude, and if you have a myth that allows you to be as focused in the batter's box of life as Derek Jeter seems to be focused in the batter's box at Yankee Stadium.

You can learn to see the pitches, learn when to swing and not to swing, and how to time the swing as well. Swinging at the pitch does not mean you are controlling the emotions. It means you have learned to recognize an emotion and ride it with perfect timing. If an emotion handcuffs you one time and you miss the pitch, you get right back in the batter's box. Even the greatest hitters only hit the ball sharply 30% of the time, but this in itself is a miracle when you think about how little time they have to see, choose, and act.

When you practice, and when you adjust to the pitches of life coming at you, you grow up. Over time, life occurrences will no longer control you. Your schemas and life ruts will disappear. Just like a Derek Jeter swing, you will stand in the batter's box still and at attention. And in that fraction of a second that it takes to recognize an incoming emotion coming in, you will handle your emotions like a major leaguer. In that fraction of a second when you are not controlled by the pitches of life, you will accept the pitch that is coming your way. You have intense present personal energy at your disposal in this 'aware' fraction of a second. I am like Babe Ruth in this focused and centered moment. SWING!!!!!!

Stepping into the Batter's Box of Emotion

- Have a consciousness that you can be focused, balanced, and centered in the batter's box of everyday life

- A life occurrence happens like a warm spring day or a sudden destructive storm in your life. You are aware and you are at attention. An emotion rises and comes at you like a speeding Nolan Ryan fastball or a deceptive Jason Verlander cutter.

- If you are balanced, focused, and centered, in that split second of awareness of the emotion coming at you, you can recognize the kind of pitch or emotion, and learn to ride it just like Derek Jeter can recognize and ride a pitch for a base hit. In that magic split second of awareness and focus, you can ride the emotion instead of allowing the emotion to overpower and own you.

- If you are unaware of the pitches of life coming at you, you will always be handcuffed by life. You will never learn to hit the curveball

- Even with awareness of the moment, sometimes you will lose focus or miss a strong emotional pitch that life throws at you. An emotion will overtake you and handcuff you.

- Forgive yourself and get right back into the batter's box. There is no time for feeling sorry for poor you in the major league of life. Get back in that batter's box and try to hit the next pitch.

The pitches of life are red, black, and white. To be a major leaguer, you must learn how to ride all three pitches. You have already learned how to do it if you have worked this curriculum. Learning how to hit the curveball is about consciousness. Consciousness grants you the choice to be balanced, grounded, and focused in the present moment. When you are aware and focused on the pitches life is throwing at you, you will become skillful at this process. You will develop the confidence to handle yourself in all situations.

You can learn to get better at it. But even the greatest hitters in baseball only manage to hit the ball for a hit about 30% of the time. Before we close the year, we will try to sharpen your ability to stay conscious so you can become an all-star hitter in daily life.

Don't get down on yourself. This is your major league career in the Emotional League. Live it full and live it well. And if you should strike out, go back to the dugout and prepare to get back up to the plate next time.

PLAY BALL!!!

My Warrior Life

My eyes have seen too much
    Or maybe too little
Inside the suffocating court room
    I stammered and begged for acquittal

But the trial itself was not where I was
    And the jury of peers who convicted me
Was only me staring at myself
    In the broken mirror of destiny

Where childhood innocence was shattered
    And terrifying wounds bled freely
Onto the floor of a secret chamber
    Where no one else could see me

I was a lost and crippled boy soldier
    Who could fight but never go home.
Until a mysterious rider scooped me
    From tangled up nightmares and ruin

I held his waist as we surfaced from depths
    Of blinding black waters of separation
Into a circle where survivors tell their stories
    Of fires and floods and desperation

A place where survivors witness beauty
    Born from the blackness of the soul
And colored waves just rise and fall
    In a greatness that they don't control

I ride these waves now like a man
    On the edge of his own hopeless teardrop
The first crack of light pushes through dawn
    Shining joy on valley and hilltop

And joy has its way and then disappears
    As new waves rise up and bend
My warrior life is born in the moments
    I ride them again and again

Let's Rock

In the traditional village, it was your parent's job to keep you safe, nourished, and full of wonder through your early years. It was their job to make sure you kept your young, wide, innocent eyes for as long as possible. In a way, you were kept safe by them in a new womb for your first nine years just like you were kept safe in your mother's womb for nine months before birth. It is important that we keep children in white innocence.

As adolescence emerged, it would now be the elder's job to take you through the tests of adulthood to warrior status. If you did not pass the tests of emotional, spiritual, and physical maturity, you did not become an adult in the eyes of the village. You would have to try again the following year. No matter what your age, you were not an adult until you passed the tests.

This march to the countryside was like a red journey up a second birth canal. It was new. It was at once exciting and traumatic.

This is where you are now, young warrior. You are in the village of this group and you have completed the test. It is now time for you to take full responsibility for your own life and your choices. It is now time to realize that everything you say and do has an effect on everyone and everything around you. It is now time to face the fact that your choices have consequences. Your choices need to be made with more than just your own self in mind. It is not just about you.

Look around you young warrior. See the people. See the things that need to get done. It is time for you to bring your gift. It is time to do your purpose. As we approach your return to the village for our Banquet, I want to be sure you understand that I am honored to have watched you grow up this year.

We are about to bring the train to its final destination. We have completed our journey. We are going to celebrate. At the banquet, we will gather around the stone, the same one we gathered around at the beginning of this group and the same stone that you have bravely broken open this year.

LETS'S ROCK!!!

1. What is a myth and what does myth have to do with your life?

2. What is the myth that you used to define yourself after you were wounded?

3. Pick a day and tell your story in group using one of the templates provided if you need help.

4. Write your story out for yourself using one of the templates. Begin to understand the turning points in your story where important choices were made.

5. A baseball player must learn to see a pitch coming, choose whether or not to swing, and to swing at the right time in the right place so that solid contact is made? How many seconds does he have to do that?

6. Can you learn to master the present moment well enough to meet the challenges of your life and your emotions head on?

7. Can you forgive yourself when you forget or you fail?

8. Will you commit to always getting back into the batter's box of life any time you strike out?

9. Can you remind yourself everyday that life is a team sport, a community endeavor, and you have an important part to play?

10. Can you finally accept now that you are nobody special?

11. Are you ready for the Banquet? What is left for you to accomplish before you get to the banquet?

Review of the Group's Journey

What is this journey that we have travelled together? The journey of the warrior is the journey through initiation into full adulthood. An initiated warrior demonstrates responsibility and discipline.

The journey is accomplished by the telling of the stories. Robert Bly states that, "Stories are a reservoir where we keep ways of responding". The wisdom that we need to hand down to youth is found in the stories we tell them. Tell the stories well.

What does it mean to be a man or a woman? What is the test you must pass? How can you reunite yourself with the one from whom you go so lost- the man or woman alive in your soul?

What happens on this journey? How is it begun? The journey begins with a break from one's parents. Although parents are charged along with the rest of the village with giving us our start, our values and morals, initiation does not occur until I am ripped away from them. So, the elders that take me through initiation are not my parents.

Initiation happens in a designated ritual space. In our group that space has been our circle. Traditional initiation would take you far out into the countryside where you no longer had your TV, your phone, your beeper, your computer, your car, your drugs, your girlfriend or boyfriend. I wish I could do that in our group but it is not possible in a public school. Our circle works. Many have passed through this place in this circle and have grown up.

In this place, you have been faced with yourself, who you are, how you feel, what you do, how it affects others. This is the place where you have examined the wound until the pain of the wound reverberated outward from a center of meaning. In this place, with this wound, you told your story as an act of forgiveness that puts the present moment with all its potential at your disposal.

Without a story, you cannot examine the wound. Your story takes you into your wound. Your story told honestly prevents you from climbing above the wound to some addiction or distraction. Your story also ensures that you will not get stuck and become the wound in a state of perpetual depression. Your story allows you to take hold of the wound, to see that the wound you thought was so personal fits into the pattern of all the wounds, of every human who has walked the earth since Adam and Eve. Oh, yes, young warrior, you also learned that you are no one special. You are not special at all. We all have the wound.

This descent into the wound heats up like a hot stove in a kitchen at first, and then turns to ashes. It is in the ashes that you will rise as a warrior and do your life purpose. In the ashes is where you will meet the King - The King of Trees.

This circle was like a garden, a safe haven, a place to come to dump the truth into the center so that you might heal and become a warrior for life. Be true to your heart. Learn to live and hold the tension of all of the opposites that appear as the reality of human life. Maintain your dignity and your integrity

You have learned to ride three horses during your initiation. They are the red horse, the black horse, and the white horse. You had to demonstrate that you could ride all three to be a complete warrior in the eyes of the village. The experience of riding these horses is very intense, and not without danger. But the transformation from child to adulthood has happened here if you learned to ride all three horses with dignity and integrity.

At birth, you brought with you the golden rings of your gift (purpose). But you cannot bring your gift until you survive the wound. The wound has prevented you from moving forward. By descending into the wound, you have been reconnected to real life.

A spirit enters through the wound. It is the spirit you brought with you at birth, the spirit you got so lost from when you were wounded. The wound caused you to lose your spirit. And now, it is time to find the courage to rise from the black ashes of the wound. Your choice returns your spirit and passion to you. Somewhere in the experience of the wound, you have been given keys to do your life purpose. But first you had to find the courage to face the wound and heal the wound. Now you are a man. Now you are a woman

Through the healed scar of your survival, you are recognized as a warrior who can ride three horses with dignity and integrity on the journey of his life purpose.

The elder is now ready to take you back to the full community of the village for the celebratory banquet. At the banquet your accomplishments will be recognized, your willingness to be real will be evident, and your honesty and gratefulness may well break open the stone of the whole village.

The Return of the Heroic Warriors

A Celebration
Of
Success and Gratefulness

Closing the Circle

A Stone Broken Open

Introduction

In the next two weeks we will bring the circle to a close. The train has completed its journey, the stone has been broken open, and another group of young warriors has passed the tests of this course.

Like the flock of birds leaving South America on a migratory flight, we have arrived at Delaware Bay. It is time for a celebration before each of us flies on to live out our adult lives.

While our group has not had common quizzes and tests that you are used to taking in a course, it has been a huge test of another kind. What is the test you passed in this group?

◆ This group has challenged you to stand and deliver at school with no excuse-no exceptions, no matter what your life circumstances may be.
◆ This group has challenged you to 'get real' and be yourself in the presence of twelve other people in your group.
◆ This group has challenged you to live and work in a village where support and confrontation exist side by side. We have not avoided conflict or tension.
◆ This group has challenged you to take the torch of your adult life from an elder who has unlocked a vista to a greater perception required for a healthy adult life.
◆ This group has given you the challenging opportunity to explore and tell your own story from the deep heart.
◆ This group has led you to the doorway of the choices of the future and has entrusted you with the keys.

This circle has required you to walk through the door everyday and to treat your time here with reverence and to treat the space here as sacred space. It is now time to close this space. There never has been another group like this one. And there will never be another group like this one again. Groups are like snowflakes or children. No two are ever exactly alike.

The Banquet will be the venue where we will close our circle. It is a ritual celebration of the return of the young warriors from the tests of their initiation to the everyday life of the greater village. It is our Delaware Bay. If you have arrived at the Banquet, I salute you with admiration and awe. You survived the challenges of this course.

There are four procedures we complete at the end of the year of which the Banquet is only one.

The four procedures that close the circle are:

1. The preparation for the Banquet includes an activity called "Finishing Business" in which all unresolved tensions in the group are exposed and left inside the burden basket so they do not affect the sacred purpose of the Banquet

2. We prepare for and carry out the Banquet including decoration of the space, formulation of the procedure, and exploration of the role of each participant

3. We carry out the banquet ritual in the presence of teachers, family, friends and townspeople.

4. Finally we end the year the morning after our Banquet with a written exercise called "Departing Messages"

It has been a long and difficult journey but everyone has grown. It is time to recognize that growth. Our celebratory banquet will mark the close of a journey that demanded much of you. It is an honor for me as the elder to take you before the community as my warrior class.

Let's begin!

Finishing Business

Before we get to the celebration of gratefulness of the Village Banquet, we do have one more task to complete. It is called "Finishing Business". It is a talking stick activity that prepares a group for the intensity of the Village Banquet. In order to create the atmosphere at the banquet where that intensity might rise up again, we must make sure that there is no unfinished business in the group.

The activity is designed to make sure that all group members are 'straight' with one another before we walk into the Banquet together. The Banquet is a night of celebration and gratefulness. All burdens and inner group tensions must be exposed and left in the center of the circle. This activity takes place a few days before the banquet. It might require more than one day to complete.

When the stick is passed, each group member answers the following questions:

◆ What was it like for me to participate in this group this year?
◆ Who is one person in the room that I would like to tell that I feel most connected to in the group? Why do I feel connected most to that person?
◆ Do I have any tension or unfinished business with anyone in this group? Go around the room and tell each group member about any unfinished business or tension that I have with them. Leave the tension and the business in the center of the circle for the great mystery to hold.
◆ What has it been like to be in a group with me? Each member of the group will take turns telling you how they experienced being in a group with you.

It is important to expose all remaining tensions in the group and to leave them in the burden basket. When this activity is complete and all tensions and differences are left in the center of the circle for the great mystery to hold, we are ready for the Banquet.

The Village Banquet

Purpose

At the Village Banquet we gather around the very same stone that we gathered around on the first day of our group. The purpose of the Banquet is to allow the larger community to sit just outside the rim of our circle and witness our return to the village as we review the year long journey, as we testify to our accomplishments and as we express our gratefulness for each other and for others in the community of the Banquet room.

The metaphorical table for the banquet was set much earlier in the year when students committed to this process. In addition, the Village Banquet is a metaphor for the journey to Delaware Bay. Thus, as you read this introduction to the Banquet, understand that this banquet is much more than an awards ceremony.

While we will acknowledge where students have grown, and while students will receive awards for accomplishments achieved in their community, the banquet is an intense ritual of returning from the long challenge of breaking open the stone of your personality to find the genuine heart of your being.

On the night of this banquet, we may break open the stone of the whole town. It is not unusual at the village banquet to look outside our circle to see teachers, parents, and friends in tears. It is not something we plan for or try to manufacture. We just arrive at the banquet and do the ritual and we see what happens. It is a night of triumph and recognition of palpable and intense accomplishment.

"Some experiences are impossible to witness. If you experience something at this deeper level of being, it remains with you forever."

This quotation was a comment from an anonymous Vietnam veteran speaking about an intense battle. It applies to our Village Banquet in that much of what we have experienced in this group cannot be explained or communicated. Our experiences in this group are in our bones now. This group will be with you and I forever.

Our Banquet is a return from a difficult journey that will affect us forever. For this reason, we strive to be real and to bring the genuine heart of our experience into our banquet space.

Preparation of the Space

We prepare the space of the Banquet by constructing a large circle of chairs in the center of the Banquet room where the young warriors will sit for the final group. The center of the circle has all the objects we have had in the center of our circle during our group sessions - the box of perception, the feather, the stone, the burden basket, the innocent child, the wounded child, the key to happiness, and the talking stick.

The guests will be seated at tables all around the outside of our circle. The room will be decorated with our mosaic colored poster that we created in September symbolizing our open hands of honesty, our mosaic colored poster of overlapping foot prints that we created in September symbolizing our grounded and focused commitment. We are celebrating the successful completion of a long journey that began back at our first group.

Process

The Village Banquet represents a crossing that you are making in your life. You are crossing over to a new mentor role if you are going to remain here for another group in the future, or you are crossing over to a new adult phase of your life where you will be expected to use what you have learned in group in the next phase of your life.

It has been a tough journey where you were challenged to break open the stone of your personality and your mask to uncover the truth of the real you. This group has been a place that challenged you to stand and deliver without making any excuses.

The night of the village banquet is your return from the tests of the year and its journey. The entire village turns out to witness our evening and to hear us testify to the crossings we have accomplished this year.

How have you changed and grown as a person this year? The Village Banquet is the place to proclaim it!

It is a night to acknowledge and to tell the whole town what you have accomplished. It is also the night to speak to the question you were asked in your first session back at the beginning of our journey, "What are you grateful for?"

Expressing your sincere gratefulness to each other and to any of the invited guests is part of the Village Banquet Ritual. It is a night to put down the war of tensions between us and to remember how much we need each other. It is a night of forgiveness when mistakes are forgiven and when each of us realizes that it is time to take the torch of adulthood, the torch of our life purpose as we cross over to the next phase of our lives.

Procedure

- When everyone has assembled, the elder will give a brief welcoming message in which he briefly explains our group and explains the purpose of the night.

- At this time, everyone in attendance eats dinner. The circle of chairs remains empty. You may sit and eat dinner with your family and friends at the tables surrounding the ritual circle.

- After dinner, the designated drummers will begin drumming the beat on the Djembe drum. This is the signal that it is time for you to take your seat in the Circle of Chairs in the center of the banquet room.

- After everyone is seated, the elder will welcome everyone. He will briefly overview the purpose of the evening. He will point out that guests have been invited to the final group of the year.

- We will sing an invocation song. An invocation is a calling of everyone in the village to come to attention. The song also spells out the purpose and intention of our ritual. The song we choose to sing in our group is a song called "Gather 'Round the Stone" by an artist named Ben Harper. We sing his melody and his chorus but we have written new verses which speak to the purpose of our ritual. Your teacher may use any song he chooses for a ritual invocation. The melody for the song which I use can be found by purchasing the song "Gather Round the Stone". Contact me through the King of Trees website for the verses that I use. However, any song that invokes the purpose of the evening may be used.

- When the song is completed, the group meeting will begin. We will conduct our group meeting like every other group meeting all year. We will begin with feet flat on the floor in a minute of silence.

- The elder will review the year by repeating four stories. They are The Squirrel Story (patience and perseverance), Delaware Bay (purpose and presence), Tree of Sorrows (acceptance and forgiveness), and The King Of Trees (red-black-white process). The final story, the King of Trees will be paused at the point where the tree has apparently been destroyed and left for dead. The story will be finished at the end of the night after awards are presented.

- It is in the sorrow of this moment when the great King of Trees has been destroyed that the elder will speak to the young warriors and ask them to give testimony to the following questions

✶ What have you accomplished this year in school?
✶ What obstacles have you overcome?
✶ Who are you grateful for?
　　You may address each other
　　You may address faculty members present
　　You may address parents or grandparents or others
　　You may address friends or others

- No student is required to speak at the banquet. It is a night to celebrate accomplishment and gratefulness. If a student wishes to speak to those issues, the student need only stand and speak at the proper time. He will hold the talking stick as he speaks. No one will be put on the spot to speak at the banquet. No one should speak who does not genuinely feel grateful. IT IS NOT A NIGHT TO MAKE A SARCASTIC REMARK, A JOKE, OR TO CONFRONT SOMEONE.

- When all students who wish to speak have spoken, the elder will present awards to all students who have completed the journey of the group journey mentioning specifically what has been accomplished by each student.

- When the presentation of awards is completed, the elder calls everyone's attention back to the story of the King of Trees. The elder finishes the story where the King of Trees is found to be alive and well. If the King of Trees on Pine Hill could not be killed, then the King of Trees in my heart could not be killed either. The night ends with a reminder to bravely continue to do the red, black, and white all the days of your lives, and to pay attention and to always look for the "King of Trees" in every hopeless moment you may face in the future. If you look for it, you will see it!!!

The circle is completed

The stone is broken open

Pour your heart and soul

Into the daily pursuit of your life purpose

I bless you and I wish you well on your journey

Post Banquet Activities

Reflection

The morning after the Village Banquet, students meet at the scheduled time of their group. It is an informal day to talk about the banquet and the completion of the group's mission. Students might want to talk about the reactions of parents or others in the audience. This is not a formal meeting. The group room has been shorn of its decorations and the center of the circle does not have the usual articles of meaning.

The final formal activity in the group's year is called "Departing Messages" and it is recorded in the student journals. Thumbnail pictures of each student may be pasted where each message will go.

This becomes a keepsake and a reminder of the work that has been accomplished. Thus, the journal and workbook become a yearbook complete with pictures and a message from each group member. It is time to end this group and go our separate ways.

Departing Messages Activity

The procedure is simple. Students pass their Journals around the room much like students pass their class yearbooks for signatures. In this case, however, student messages are centered on telling each member of your group how you valued them in the group and what you wish for them in the future. The result is that each group member leaves our village with a written message from all other group members.

With this activity, the group experience is over and students take their journals as a testimony and keepsake from their yearlong experience in our village.

You have successfully completed a long, difficult journey on a train that has descended into the valley of sadness; has risen to the mountaintop of joy; and has survived storms of rage. Debris has been cleared from the tracks and you have been given a method to keep the journey of the rest of your lives in the place where your potential is always at your disposal.

I could never express the gratitude and respect that I have for you. Your willingness to stand and to deliver in your life is breathtaking. Your vigilance for the present moment, and your unblinking perseverance in completing this journey has left the teacher standing in a place of awe and wonder.

Thank you for the breaking open the stone. Go forward and complete the purpose of your life.

A DIOS

THE KING OF TREES

Look For It
And
You Will See It

Afterword

This book has been my attempt to deliver a curriculum that might address the glaring, unmet needs of our clients and students. When the diagnostic playing field littered with spreadsheets and data is put back into its proper place, we will have a chance to raise our schools and community organizations to a position of respect again. School, after all, was a much respected place back when it was called the little red schoolhouse. Public schools now have a popularity rating as low as Congress. Why?

A monster descended over education in the early 1970's. It was not a monster at first. It was well intentioned. But the monster of the medical model of education must now be tamed and disciplined. It has been out of control for years. It encourages mediocrity and passivity in students. Diagnosis and treatment as an educational tool has failed! Teachers know this but bureaucrats, professors, and politicians do not.

A second monster descended over public education in the past 20 years. The idea that our students are 'consumers' of education and that they are our customers has hurt education badly. Students are not our customers! The fact that 'customers' are always right and that 'customers' are in school to be served reinforces mediocrity. We are not managers or facilitators of education. Our children are in desperate need of elders who are intelligent, firm, and most of all, in charge! The business model of education has failed! Teachers know this but bureaucrats, professors, and politicians do not.

The current school culture has made students dependent and weak. Kids wait for us to enable and accommodate. And we always do. No meaningful change will occur in education until the medical model and the business model of education are put to rest.

The real changes that need to happen are not forthcoming from the educational establishment. Change must come from inside the heart of each local school district through the broken open stone that unlocks the passionate soul of each child. There is another way. We must forge a new path forward. This book has been my attempt to shine a light on what went wrong and what must be accomplished.

A Crippling Separation of Soul and School

A School Reform Proposal from a School Counselor

Our public schools are in need of reform. The current reform movement is not addressing the central issues that plague our public schools. Our students are in need of a more productive educational milieu that addresses both their personal needs and the needs of society.

The school reform movement consists mostly of people who rarely step foot inside of a school. These reformers tend to disregard the input of teachers whom they tend to see as self serving and/or as incompetent to envision true change. Who are these people?

- Educational bureaucrats at the state and federal level
- Professors and schools of higher education that train teachers and influence educational laws and policies
- Politicians who make the educational laws
- Business people who sense that schools are not graduating students with essential academic proficiency and minimal career entry level skills

The main thrust of the current school reform movement revolves around:

- Making teacher delivery of lessons more precise, more technically flawless, and more responsive to gaps in student education as indicated by data from tests.
- Perfecting presentation of content so that tests scores will rise and so students will be prepared for college and work.
- Removing obstacles to productive schools by curbing unions which are seen to protect teachers from hard work and accountability

The Central Issue Facing Public Schools

The central issue facing public schools is a famine of student passion brought on by a flawed educational paradigm that has been allowed to dictate law and policy in schools for the past 50 years. Lack of passion in students is due to a sense of entitlement, a lack in level of concern and urgency about school, and an atmosphere that encourages mediocrity, and in many cases, full blown apathy in students.

The best teacher technique practiced perfectly each day, informed by the most sophisticated data showing where learning gaps exist in students, and delivered in accordance with the latest educational guru's formula is still powerless to teach children who come to school every day with no book, no pen, no homework, no sense of meaning and purpose, and most of all, no idea that they must strive tirelessly. Our students now arrive with self esteem brimming so high that an "A" is expected for just sitting in a chair. There is a law to accommodate, modify, or water down at every turn. There is an acceptance that failure is unacceptable and verboten. And there is an assumption that if a child is not learning it must be due to something the teacher has done or not done.

Until student passion and level of concern are raised in our public schools, nothing will change. We can continue to tweak and improve teacher methods and strategies of delivery unto kingdom come, public schools will continue to flounder.

How do we raise student passion? We must create a community at school, a grassroots community inside each school, where policy and practice are generated from within the heart of each local school through the broken open stone of the soul of each student. The separation of church and state has lead to an unnecessary but devastating separation of soul and school. This separation must be healed if we want impassioned students and successful schools. *Breaking Open the Stone: Unfolding the Soul of Youth* is a group counseling program designed to be embedded in the normal school day of high school students. It addresses this painfully unmet need of students, teachers, parents, and schools in a tangible and hands on way.

Dysfunctional Paradigms of Public Education

The two major paradigms that generate school law and policy must be addressed.

- The Medical Model has ruled for the past 50 years. While its major tenet to give an appropriate education to each child is sound, the actual results have been much less impressive. There is an explosion of diagnoses in schools and a thousand different treatment plans to address each individual child's diagnosed needs. Further, the philosophy that spawned the special education laws and the medical model in school has been accepted as applicable to all students in school. Thus, it is the job of each school to educate each child individually with an individual plan for each child. This has not played out as nobly as it sounds. Students are very aware that they do not have to strive, that it is the school's job to figure out how to educate them, and that if they do not learn or try to learn, that modifications, accommodations, and especially a watering down of the degree of difficulty of their course levels is coming. Students are also quite aware that they will not be allowed to fail, and that it is the school and/or the teacher who is to blame if they do not learn. The lack of level of concern, the sense of entitlement, and the resulting mediocrity in performance are proof that the Medical Model must be addressed and tamed. There is a huge state and university bureaucracy however whose very survival depends on the maintenance of this dysfunctional paradigm. The medical model will not depart willingly.

- The Business Model is not as old as the Medical Model in our schools, but it has been just as devastating. The Business Model states that students are consumers of education. The idea that students in high schools are our customers has just not panned out. First of all, students are aware that the customer is always right. Second, students are aware that it is the teachers' job to cater to their needs. Third, students are acutely aware that as customers that they are under no obligation to buy what is being sold. When they do not learn, it is the teacher that must find a way to improve the product. If education is a business and students are our customers, it is clear that education went into recession 20 years ago. It still has not rebounded. We are stuck in a recession where students attend school as if it were the mall. They drift from store to store, but they don't buy much. And they are under no obligation to strive or to sweat at school. Teachers are the ones who need to sweat. Ever since the Business Model was introduced into the classroom, the wrong school population goes home tired every day. Entitled customers demand that the product be free of pain, of responsibility, of any chance of failure. As customers, they are always right. Teachers are not managers and facilitators. Teachers are elders who must be respected, obeyed, and in charge. Until we put teachers in charge, and until we demand respect from students and adherence to rules and academic expectations that are firm and clear, school will remain a substandard place of learning based on the business model.

A New Old Paradigm for the 21St Century

The paradigm of the little red school house must be resurrected. It was a place of absolute honor that was respected by the community. It was a place where teachers were not diagnosticians, clinicians, and laser like deliverers of content. School must be a place of dignity where elders are in charge, where respect is demanded, and where rules and educational standards are adhered to even if it means that some students fail.

- State and Federal Law must be overhauled to allow parents, local boards, school administrators and teachers in local school districts to police themselves. Special Education Laws will not be rescinded but they will be reevaluated so that they can no longer encourage the level of mediocrity that now exists. Students, even Special Education students, must have reasonable expectations that they must perform to in school. If they do not meet these expectations, they need to fail.

- A daily group counseling component needs to be embedded into the school day. This group needs to create a conscious community at school that teaches students about their role as young adults. It must instill a sense of meaning and purpose into school and into life outside of school. It must seek to help students to break open the stone of personality to unfold the soul of untapped potential. These groups include a fully application-ready life skills component which leads students through a meaningful and challenging process of initiation to adulthood. Students strive in conscious community, dealing with school issues, dealing with life issues outside of school, and dealing with clear expectations of what it means to be a young adult. A curriculum that encourages the return of the little red school house successfully ends the devastating separation of soul and school.

- Thus, an atmosphere of respect, dignity, and self responsibility will be returned into the schools' bloodstream. Reform will unfold from inside the heart of each school through the stone broken open in each student. Our students need a course of studies embedded into the school day that teaches them how to be grounded, centered, balanced, self aware, and acutely conscious of the sacredness of the community to which they belong. It must adhere to a firm expectation of the need for students to strive to be a part of that community in a meaningful and purposeful way. The group counselor running the embedded counseling component is not a therapist. Nor is he a priest or minister. He is an elder that is taking students through the second birth canal that all teenagers must traverse in order to make the rite of passage into adulthood.

Paradigm Shift

21st Century School Model	Late 20th Century School Model
Little Red School House	Educational Treatment Center
Initiation to Adulthood	Medical and Business Models
Students - warriors in training	Students - labeled and treated
Whole School culture	Parse/ isolate problems
Instill passion	Inject content in homogenous way
Emptying to unfold the soul	Filling up the brain
Conscious local community	Global economy feeder
Young Warriors	Consumers
Group Counseling	Individual Counseling
Comprehensive Counseling Goal	Limited to Brief Counseling
Daily counseling-community component	Occasional counsel in classes
Embedded growth and soul curriculum	Fire fighter containment

An Atmosphere Where School Reform Can Incubate

We must create a new atmosphere where policy, law, and rules will be generated from the local districts upwards through the state and federal governments. Administering schools in a top down manner from the federal and state governments has not worked. Further, allowing university professors and other gurus and experts to have more influence over local school philosophy than parents and local teachers has got to end. Professional Development in education must free itself from the limiting and restricting parameters of data analysis as a way to inform instruction. Data has a place, but it should not be the sole method of informing instruction.

- Current data informed tendencies in public education are making teachers so self conscious of every technical detail of lesson planning that we are creating a blunted generation of cautious teachers who are being fitted into educational cookie cutter molds

- Students are not attracted to technically perfect lessons delivered in laser like surgical fashion. Teachers are not surgeons implanting higher test scores. Teachers are unique individuals and spontaneous characters who must deliver education from the soul. You have to give soul to kids if soul is what you want back.

- Even school reformers, bureaucrats, professors, and politicians know that the best teachers who influenced them the most were not the technically correct ones. They were the spontaneous, passionate, and unique teachers who were gloriously flawed at times in technique and delivery. They were engaging, quirky, and unique characters. These were the teachers that commanded the attention and respect of students. They instilled passion and they are never forgotten by students.

Healing the Separation of Soul and School

Breaking Open the Stone: Unfolding the Soul of Youth tries to give schools a tool that can reform our schools from within. The heart of each school must be allowed to breathe and live. The soul of each child must be unfolded and delivered through a birth canal to a purposeful and meaningful adulthood. This is what has been lost in decades of medical model and business model approaches to education. Let the little red school house be reborn. The education of the soul is not about religion. Soul education may lead some students to seek out a religion, but it also does not interfere with the religion of students who already have a religious affiliation. Soul education is an acknowledgement of community, connection, purpose, meaning, and most of all, expanded vision that teaches to the mysterious place where science disappears into the mist. Our students must be grounded, centered, balanced, focused, and infused with a sense of meaning purpose, and community.

You cannot engage a brain until you impassion a soul.

You cannot impassion a soul until the soul is acknowledged.

Therein is the root of the crisis of modern public education.

The Separation of Soul and School has ruled for 50 years. It has brought us to the brink of ruin in public education. It is time to recover the passion for living and learning in public schools. We must break open the stone now.

This book was written from inside the muddy trench of the public school classroom, where amazingly, the soul is still alive and well, buried under piles of paper work, treatment plans, and the ghosts of national educational gurus, past and present.

The soul of each local public school is beautiful and pregnant and just waiting for the signal from society that it is appreciated and blessed and that it is safe to unfold itself into the 21st century. Let it be reborn, kicking and screaming, into a future we can live with.

References

AA World Services	*Twelve Steps and Twelve Traditions*	1952	New York
	AA World Services		
Baldwin, Christina	*Calling The Circle*	1976	Kansas City
	Swan		
Bennet-Goleman, Tara	*Emotional Alchemy*	2001	New York
	Harmony		
Bly , Robert	*Red Black White*	1993	Boulder
	Sounds True		
Bly , Robert	*Little Book On The Human Shadow*	1975	San Francisco
	Harper		
Bly, Robert	*The Maiden King*	1998	New York
	Holt		
Bly, Robert	*The Sibling Society*	1996	New York
	Vintage		
Bly, Robert	*Iron John*	1990	New York
	Vintage		
Bullfinch, Thomas	*Bullfinch's Mythology*	1959	New York
	Dell		
Cahill and Halpern	*Ceremonial Circle*	1992	New York
	Harper/Collins		
Campbell, Joseph	*Power of Myth*	1988	New York
	Anchor		
Campbell, Joseph	*Creative Mythology, The Masks of God*	1968	New York
	Penguin		
Campbell, Joseph	*Power of Myth with Bill Moyers*	1988	New York
	Parabola		
Dyer, Wayne	*You'll See It When You Believe It*	1989	New York
	Avon		
Dyer, Wayne	*Real Magic*	1992	New York
	Harper/Collins		
Eliades, Mircea	*Rites and Symbols of Initiation*	1958	Woodstock
	Spring		
Garfield, Charles	*Wisdom Circles*	1998	New York
	Hyperion		
Goleman, Daniel	*Emotional Intelligence*	1994	New York
	Bantam		
Herrera, Suzanne	*Mango Elephants in The Sun*	1999	Boston
	Shambhala		
Hillman, James	*The Soul's Code*	1996	New York
	Warner		
Hillman, James	*The Force of Character*	1999	New York
	Ballantine		
Johnson, Robert	*Owning Your Own Shadow*	1991	S. Francisco
	Harper		
Kauth, Bill	*Circle of Men*	1992	New York
	St. Martin's		
Keen, Sam	*Your Mythic Journey*	1973	New York
	Tarcher		
Keen, Sam	*Fire In The Belly*	1991	New York
	Bantam		
Kopp, Sheldon	*If You Meet The Buddha On The Road*	1972	Toronto
	Bantam		
Kopp, Sheldon	*Back To One*	1977	Palo Alto
	Science/Behav.		
Luke, Helen	*The Way of Story*	1994	New York
	Parabola		
Luke, Helen	*Dark Wood To White Rose*	1989	New York
	Parabola		

Mahdi, Louise Carus et al.	*The Quest For Contemporary Rites of Passage* Carus	1996 Chicago
Kneen, Cynthia	*Shambhala Warrior Training* Sounds True	1996 Boulder
McLaren, Karla	*The Language of Emotions* Sounds True	2010 Boulder
Moore, Thomas	*The Soul's Religion* Harper/Collins	2002 New York
Moore, Thomas	*Care Of The Soul* Harper/Collins	1994 New York
Moore Thomas	*The Original Self* Harper/Collins	2000 New York
Moore, Robert	*King, Warrior, Magician, Lover* Harper Collins	1990 S. Francisco
Moore, Robert	*The Archetype Of Initiation* Corporation	2001 Xlibris
Paladin, Lynda	*Ceremonies For Change* Stillpoint	1991 Walpole
Pearce, Joseph Chilton	*The Biology of Transcendence* Park St. Press	2002 Rochester
Pearce, Joseph Chilton	*Spiritual Initiation* Park St. Press	2003 Rochester
Pearce, Joseph Chilton	*From Magical Child To Magical Teen* Park St. Press	2003 Rochester
Schaef, Anne Wilson	*Living In Process* Ballantine	1999 New York
Slater, Phillip	*The Pursuit of Loneliness* Beacon	1976 Boston
Smith, Huston	*Religions of the World* Sounds True	1995 Boulder
Smith, Huston	*Why Religion Matters* Harper/Collins	2001 New York
Some, Malidoma	*Creating a New Sense of Home* Grove Oral Traditions	1993 Pacific
Some, Malidoma	*Ritual, Power, Healing, and Community* Swan	1993 Portland
Some, Malidoma	*Of Water and Spirit* Tarcher	1994 New York
Some, Malidoma	*Healing Wisdom of Africa* Tarcher	1998 New York
Some, Malidoma	*Yoga Journal - July-1994* Yoga Journal	1994 New York
Some, Malidoma et al.	*Who Welcomes The Newborn Child* Nineties	1999 St. Paul
Some, Malidoma et al.	*Images of Initiation* Grove Oral Traditions	1999 Pacific
Some, Sobonfu	*The Spirit of Intimacy* Morrow	1999 New York
Some, Sobonfu	*Welcoming Spirit Home* New World Library	1999 Novato
Swimme, Brian	*Canticle To the Cosmos* Sounds True	1990 Boulder
Wolfe, Fred	*Parallel Universes* Touchstone	1988 New York
Wolfe, Fred	*Dreaming Universe* Touchstone	1994 New York
Zukav, Gary	*Dancing Wu Li Masters* Bantam	1979 New York
Zukav, Gary	*Seat of the Soul* Fireside	1989 New York